Why Lenin? ✪ *Why Stalin?*

CRITICAL PERIODS OF HISTORY

Robert D. Cross and Paul K. Conkin, GENERAL EDITORS

Why Lenin?
Why Stalin?

A REAPPRAISAL OF
THE RUSSIAN REVOLUTION, 1900–1930
Second Edition

Theodore H. Von Laue
Jacob and Frances Hiatt
Professor of History,
Clark University

CRITICAL PERIODS OF HISTORY

J. B. LIPPINCOTT COMPANY
PHILADELPHIA   NEW YORK   TORONTO

*To the students and faculty
of the University of California, Riverside,
and,
with a heavier heart,
to Boris Nikolaevich Krasovskii*

ISBN-0-397-47200-5

COPYRIGHT © 1971, 1964 BY THEODORE H. VON LAUE

PRINTED IN THE UNITED STATES OF AMERICA

LIBRARY OF CONGRESS CATALOG CARD NUMBER: 79-152063

6   8   9   7   5

Preface to the First Edition

WE EXIST AND SURVIVE by making judgments. In the big issues
that shape the fate of men and nations our judgments are
based on simplifications and generalizations, on "images." The
present world of baffling complexities therefore demands the
reduction of mazes which only experts can follow—and even
they imperfectly—to simple patterns comprehensible to ordinary
men and women. All people, particularly in a democracy, deal
with and judge these issues, one way or the other. The choice
before us then is not of simplicity or complexity but of good or
bad, penetrating or misleading simplification. Generalizations
guide public opinion, public opinion influences and sometimes
determines government policy, and government policy holds the
fatal trigger of war and peace, particularly when the subject is
Russia and communism. Let our generalizations, therefore, be
knowledgeable and just.

This essay offers a novel explanation of the rise of Lenin and
Stalin. It attempts to view the emergence of Russian communism
as an integral part of European and global history, treating it,
as it should have been from the start, as a problem of comparative studies, not as an isolated phenomenon to be explained
largely from Russian conditions alone. Its bent of argument thus
runs counter to the tendency of some cultural anthropologists
and their followers in sociology and political science to derive
the causes of modern Russian development chiefly, if not exclusively, from internal factors. Without denying the importance

of the latter this essay stresses the primacy of the external conditions, of the pressure of global power politics. Russia's leaders before and after 1917, so this story runs, tried to reshape Russian state and society—and human nature to boot—in order to make their country respected in a world where power, and power in many disguises, was trump.

This treatise, however, does not aim at a miniature likeness of modern Russian history (whatever, viewed objectively, that likeness is). It presents an image drawn in the manner of a sketch. A sketch, our experience of modern art shows, is a debatable vision of reality. Yet to the artist it accentuates just those features which are crucial. So with this essay of macrohistory: It is a summary search for the best way of looking at a chain of momentous events in twentieth-century history. It wishes, by a few strokes of analysis, to set the proper perspectives, indicate the chief characteristics, and, above all, establish a sense of proportion which must guide us if we want to judge this all-important subject responsibly. The task requires that while we sketch the Russians we also scan ourselves. Portraying them we must, in one of the profiles of the subject, draw our own likeness in the same scale.

Sketching the Russian revolution is bound to be a controversial enterprise. Russian and Soviet studies are set, in the minds of most experts, into an unexamined and hidden net of basic assumptions about the course of modern Russian history. These assumptions are apt to be charged—and surcharged—with the tensions of past and current politics. The subject is alive with subtle furies; few western students (the author included) have remained immune to their siren call. Yet whatever the risks of disputation, the hidden assumptions must be brought into the open and tested by rational analysis. We easily spot the Marxist-Leninist doctrines underlying Soviet historiography, but we are purblind to the convictions on which we mount our own individual inquiries into Russian and Soviet affairs. Let this elusive background be examined; and let it be brought up to date with

PREFACE

the help of the knowledge we have gained about the dilemmas of the underdeveloped countries!

May I express at this point my thanks to Professor Robert D. Cross of Columbia University for offering an opportunity to write an epilogue to my study of *Sergei Witte and the Industrialization of Russia, 1892-1903*. I am grateful also to the University of California, Riverside, and the John Simon Guggenheim Foundation for granting the necessary leisure and material support, to the Russian Research Center at Harvard for its hospitality, and to my wife for scrutinizing every sentence of the text and patiently suffering the absentmindedness of a writing husband. Professor Arthur P. Mendel has vigorously contested my views of the problems confronting the tsarist regime; Mr. Robert C. Williams has thoughtfully commented on a number of specific and general points in the entire manuscript. While both have left no doubt that they are not responsible for any flaws, they have done their share to clarify the text. Thanks are also due to Mrs. Joan Kibbe, who has expertly typed the bulk of the manuscript, and to the editor, Mr. Stewart Richardson, who has seen it through the press.

THEODORE H. VON LAUE

West Dover, Vermont
August, 1963

Preface to the Second Edition

★

It has been said: Everybody his own historian, by which is meant that each one of us must fashion for himself his vision of the grand concourse between past and future on which we move. By the same logic it follows that each historian rewrite his histories when his vision has changed. And how our perspectives have changed in the past ten years!

In the late fifties, when the first edition of this volume was planned, it was still possible to agree with Arthur M. Schlesinger's assessment of the American condition written after the second world war: "Only the United States still has buffers between itself and the anxieties of our age, buffers of time, of distance, of natural wealth, of natural ingenuity, and of a stubborn tradition of hope." Anxiety, he said, "is not yet part of our lives—not of enough of our lives, anyway, to inform our national decisions." In those sunset years of immunity from the world's turmoil, it was possible to speak of the United States, and of western liberal tradition in general, as an untarnished model setting the pace and the standards for the rest of the world. Nothing indeed can alter the historical fact that it was so accepted, directly or indirectly, by men of affairs as well as by the run of intellectuals, even at home. For this reason the analysis set forth in this volume still holds true: the leaders of twentieth-century Russia aspired to imitate a self-confident, forward-looking America that seemed to embody the best of the western tradition.

Now we have entered a new era. Anxiety, sometimes height-ened to panic, is creeping ever more deeply into our decisions. The model of liberal-democratic America has been blackened, especially in the eyes of American youth—under fire, it would seem, still more from within the American experience than from without. The disillusionment has been swift and rather too spiteful perhaps. Whatever the motives, the prevailing mood now among American students is one of selfdoubt, confusion, and bitterness. When the traditional American promise of freedom, happiness, and justice for all is applied to an ever larger portion of mankind (as it will be in an ever shrinking world), it reveals many glaring inconsistencies and contradictions in American and, more generally, western practice. What then is freedom, happiness, and justice? What then is truth?

Under these circumstances the job of historian has become very difficult. He no longer finds commonly acceptable guide-lines for his interpretations, no more common ground for his framework of meaningfulness. He too is left, at the end of his labors, with more questions than answers, with the now all-too-familiar shrug of the shoulder that implies: "I really don't know." To be sure, in the face of uncertainty a historian's competence does not entirely vanish; he can—and must—experiment with more suitable visions and versions of the future-bound past. All the same, he must come off his high horse of professional self-assurance and, like other men in their anxiety, humbly walk the spiked ground in his stocking feet.

The changes I have made represent an occasional amplifica-tion of the original text and, above all, a timely reconsideration of the frame of general assumptions into which we weave the facts of history.

Worcester, Massachusetts
November, 1970

In praise of Crises we might first say that passion is the mother of great things, real passion that is, bent on new and not merely the overthrow of the old. Unsuspected forces awaken in individuals and even heaven takes on a different hue. Whoever has got something to him can make himself felt because the barriers have been or are being trampled down.

—Jacob Burckhardt,
Weltgeschichtliche Betrachtungen

Contents

Introduction

MORE THAN HALF a century has passed since November, 1917, when the Bolsheviks overthrew the Provisional Government (which the previous March had supplanted the Tsar and his ministers) and declared themselves masters of a new, a soviet Russia. Their coup was hardly taken seriously by the crowd on the boulevards of Petrograd or by newspaper readers, editorialists,* and even statesmen in the metropoles of the West; they were preoccupied with the threatened collapse of the Italian front in their gruelling war against Germany and Austria-Hungary. Yet, the Bolshevik seizure of power has turned into one of the key events of the twentieth century. From a revolutionary regime desperately clinging to power, Soviet Russia has grown into a political colossus matched only by the United States. Our understanding has hardly been able to keep up with the rapidly widening impact of that revolution.

Looking at the rise of Bolshevik power as a critical period in history, one can measure its dimensions only in the largest contexts, the contexts that Lenin and the Bolsheviks themselves adopted for their justification: world revolution, a vast realign-

---

* On November 10, 1917, the *New York Times* observed editorially that the Bolsheviks were "pathetically ignorant and shallow men, political children without the slightest understanding of the vast forces they are playing with, men without a single qualification for prominence but the gift of gab, and if they could be left alone long enough their mere incompetence would destroy them, . . ."

ment in the global balance of power. The framework, therefore, must be nothing less than the entire world and an ample period of time before and after the active revolutionary eruption. This essay therefore begins with the turn of the present century, when the world was still relatively at peace. It carries the narrative to the first Five Year Plan, the Great Depression, fascism and national socialism, Hitler and Stalin. These thirty-odd years, the span of but one generation, revealed in their unprecedented violence the first corollaries of the new globalism of human affairs. Mass politics, an ever-faster tempo of technological change, and the intensive interaction between Europeans and non-Europeans, "civilized" and "underdeveloped," combined to produce a more explosive instability than had ever arisen in all the past millenia of human existence. The Bolshevik revolution is one of the blast furnaces of the terrifying transformations suddenly sprung on an unprepared West during those years.

The Revolution if one looks closely was transacted on two separate stages: Russia and the global world. Obviously the Bolshevik Revolution—or rather, the entire period from 1900 to 1930—was first of all a crisis of the peoples of Russia, above all the Great Russians and the Ukranians, but also for the many other nationalities and ethnic groups that inhabit the vast spaces of northern Asia between central Europe and the Sea of Okhotsk. They passed through a social and political cataclysm unprecedented in Russian history since the Time of Troubles early in the seventeenth century.

The ordeal of modern Russia has been in the making for many years, even before 1900. Nor did it end with the Five Year Plans of Stalin. In some ways it continues, diminished yet unresolved, to the present. For, as his essay intends to show, the internal revolution revolved around two parallel long-range necessities. On the one hand, the people of Russia and their government, and also the unprivileged and the privileged strata of society, had to be more effectively related to each other than had been customary—or possible—under the tsars. In this respect the Russian Revolution followed, however vaguely, in the wake of the French Revolution. On the other hand, both Russian society and government, privileged and unprivileged, had to undergo a drastic process of westernization, of catching up to the social, economic, and political efficiency of Russia's western neighbors especially Germany (a process enforced in the last analysis, from without, by the relentless pressure of power politics). In this sense the Russian Revolution established a new category, the revolution of the underdeveloped countries. Seen from this second point of view, the "classic" events of the Russian Revolution and civil war were but surface phenomena. Underneath the travail of revolution and counterrevolution that broke over a bewildered and driven people, of terror and counter terror, the deeper necessity took its course. Not always clearly expressed in the bloody scuffles, it aimed at the conversion of Russian state and society to modern industrialism. Both of these internal revolutions are hardly completed at present. A gulf still separates the regime from the people, and the unnatural harness of the "new Soviet man" imposed by the Communist party cruelly chafes against native spontaneity and tradition.

The shifting battles for the modernization of Russia were fought, as we have learned to our sorrow, under the ever-brighter limelights of the second stage, the global world. In many ways, the trials of Russia from 1900 to 1930 anticipated the agonies of other peoples on the fringes of Europe, in Asia, Africa, or even Latin America, who awoke to political ambition and struggled for self-assertion under the western impact. The Russian state, the weakest of the European masters, was at the same time the strongest among the underdeveloped—part imperialist, part dependent on the West. In terms of cultural preparedness and ambitions of power, it bridged the gap between the two basic categories of the global community.

During the climactic battles of the first World War, when the West—England, France, Germany, and the United States—was desperately absorbed in its own affairs and least capable of meeting the novel challenge Lenin established an emotional and political link between Russia and all the backward countries (most of them not yet in existence or aware of their condition) in the name of a superior world order. Warring against inferiority in their own country, the Bolsheviks proclaimed themselves leaders in the mounting antiwestern revolt, adopting at a shriller pitch the messianic presumption of universality so characteristic of the western elite. Yet strong as they have waxed in the process, they have hardly been able to resolve the crucial problem of how the advanced western urban-industrial civilization, which relies on the spontaneity of its citizens, can organically be fused with native pre-industrial habits and institutions.

Thus, roughly, run the contents of this essay. The argument prescribes that the story start with the global periphery before advancing to the Russian center.

I

THE SETTING: EUROPE AND THE WORLD

★

THE MOST conspicuous fact about the global world at the turn
of the century was the unquestioned supremacy of Europe, specifically western Europe and, within that select company, Great
Britain. The United States also loomed increasingly large in
what came to be considered "the West," and for the same reasons that had given Britain its head start, although it did not
yet occupy the position which it inherited after the first World
War. Whatever the order of rank in the West—and it was a matter of dispute—the chief European powers jointly were the over-
lords of the globe.

The early years of the twentieth century marked the climax of a
long process of European expansion. By 1914 all (or practically
all) parts of the non-European world had fallen under the sway of
Europe. Only the American hemisphere, westernized earlier than
the other continents, was off limits, except for the restless ambition of the United States. The rest of the non-European world
was fair game. Africa, except for Abyssinia, was carved up. Asia
was taken over through outright occupation, the allocation of
spheres of influences, or, more indirectly, through the subversion
of native authority. In China, for instance, the Manchu dynasty
was overthrown by westernized Chinese because it had not been
able to prevent the despoliation of the country by the foreigners.
Considerable portions of territory had already been severed from
the Chinese Empire, and its sovereignty over what was left was
severely limited. Southeast Asia had long been ruled more directly
by the French, Dutch, or English; the English were the masters

of India as well. In Persia, Britain and Russia vied for ascendancy. In 1907, they divided the country into three parts, Russia taking the north and England the south. In the center, left to the Persians themselves, an American expert, W. Morgan Shuster, vainly tried to reconstruct Persian finance and administration on a western basis. The Ottoman Empire, long in receivership to its European creditors, survived because its existence was a political convenience to the Great Powers, yet it could not prevent sizable losses of its territory. It lingered on the brink of collapse even after the infusion of new energy by the Young Turk Revolution of 1908. Pacific Oceania, petty spoils indeed, likewise slipped under European or American occupation. The only significant nonwestern country capable of resisting subjection was Japan. In 1899 its government succeeded in repealing most privileges of the foreigners that had been imposed earlier; in 1905 it defeated the Russian Empire; and in 1911 it regained full control over its foreign trade. Yet Japan rose to its prominence only because its ruling classes voluntarily undertook westernization and did so, it is fair to say, under exceptionally favorable circumstances, such as the great distance from Europe, insularity, smallness, and the persistence of traditional social controls despite the rapid change.*

What gave that final spurt of imperialist expansion its frantic character was the intensified competition among the European powers themselves. Their rivalry, held at bay within Europe by the balance of power, was carried into the open territories beyond; the European framework of power politics was being widened out into a global one. The new tools of technology and science and the wealth of the industrial age stimulated the political appetite and thus increased the pressure of power politics to an intensity unheard-on in human history. "The future lies with the great empires," so a British statesman proclaimed, and the fear of falling behind haunted men of affairs in even the mightiest countries. The position of the weaker members of the Great

* There is no room in this essay, unfortunately, for a discussion of the westernization of Japan or for a comparison of Russian and Japanese development (however called for by the line of argument pursued here).

Power elite—of Austria-Hungary, Italy, or Russia, for instance—suffered as their governments were threatened with bankruptcy because of their armaments or bold political ventures, or with military and political defeat because of their poverty. The lesser states, Holland, Sweden, or Spain, largely standing outside the competition under the protection of the European equilibrium, counted even less. There began, in short, the brutal recasting of the traditional power structure in Europe and the world which led, within half a century, to the emergence of the "super powers" in a category above the Great Powers. Needless to say, in this intensified rivalry the price of sovereignty soared ever higher. The demands on the resources of a country which was determined—or compelled—to compete became ever more exorbitant.

Yet more was involved in the expansion of Europe than political dominion. Having cleared the way through their superior power, the Europeans poured into the nonwestern world the very essence of their civilization. There arrived among the natives conquerors, adventurers, businessmen, missionaries, scholars, administrators, rebels, saints; every kind of character and skill. With them also came machines, money, and technical know-how. At the great crossroads, in Singapore, Hong Kong, Calcutta, Bombay, Cairo, or Johannesburg, the Europeans created their own metropoles, outposts carefully segregated yet acting as "little Europes," dispersing men, methods, and standards like so many seeds into their respective hinterlands.

This outpouring of European manpower and accomplishments was as elemental and irreversible as the force of gravity. Destiny obviously was on its side. Every white man abroad felt like a missionary civilizing the world—in terms of his own parochial values, to be sure. But even if the Europeans were only writing with chalk on granite, as Kipling put it, they were convinced, with a certitude bordering on arrogance, that they alone had the right for such inscription.

The script, however, was not the same everywhere. The British derived their justification from their past successes as a colonizing

power, from the proverbial freedoms of their form of govern·
ment and their leadership in the industrial revolution. The French
claimed the traditional perfection of *la civilisation Française*.
The Germans for their part proclaimed *am deutschen Wesen
wird die Welt genesen,* and some of their publicists added that
it was Germany's duty to liberate the victims of British colonialism. The spokesmen for the tsarist regime, on the other hand,
reserved to themselves the right to rescue Asia from the western
Europeans. These were the years when every major variety of
European nationalism became universal. The common man in
the streets of London, Paris, Berlin, or Rome was taught the
survival of the fittest in terms of national enlargement, physically
and spiritually, throughout the entire globe. Yet the differences
between these messianic nationalisms were largely lost on the
non-Europeans, who were more impressed by the common features and apt to lump these influences together under the labels
"the West" or "Europe."

In those days the white man's presumption seemed indeed impregnable. He possessed the weapons, the organization, the ingenuity necessary to make his rule stick. Even his machines
exerted authority. They ordered people's lives in a new way and
thereby undermined established custom. What excited the native
population most deeply, of course, were the technical and organizational instruments of power. It could not so easily perceive the
vastly more important but largely invisible wrappings of western
attitudes and habits in which the machines were delivered—and
which remained indispensable for their continued efficient
operation.

To the more sophisticated native leadership, however, the
ascendancy of the West was made manifest not only in the
blunt form of superior machines or economic penetration, but
in the more insidious form of a universal model. This form of
power, the least noticed among the power tools of the imperial-
ists yet the most potent of all, acted as a constant silent subversion. It hollowed out the prestige of native authority and custom
and undermined the attachment of a people to their traditions
and their government. Never in all history has there been such a

vast subversive power as that of the West.* By comparison—and invidious comparison became an instinctive reaction of minds constantly confronted with novelty—western ways stood out as superior not only because of the persuasion of guns but also because they were more "civilized" than, say, the practice of suttee, child marriage, slavery, bound feet, and a host of other nativisms. Almost anything the white man did, down to his passing whims, was imitated, sometimes merely because it was different. Certain big concepts like democracy and freedom wore such a halo of prestige that even today they serve as key slogans in countries which have perverted their meaning into its very opposite. In this vast outpouring one looks in vain among the run of the westerners for the saving grace of humility or respect for native ways. They were not devoid of kindness—their own variety of kindness—but for the most part they were oblivious to the suffering caused by their impact.

The replacement of native values by western ones was sometimes a result of close and frequently profitable association of native leaders with their European masters. An Indian nationalist, Surendranath Banerjea, writing in 1895, has well described the descent of English attitudes into native society:

> We should be unworthy of ourselves and our preceptors . . . if with our souls stirred to their inmost depths, our warm Oriental sensibilities roused to an unwanted pitch of enthusiasm by the contemplation of these great ideals of public duty, we did not seek to transplant into our country the spirit of these free institutions which have made England what she is. . . . Never in the history of the world have the inheritors of an ancient civilization been so profoundly influenced by the influx of modern ideas. . . .

There could hardly have been a better vindication of Macaulay, who had wanted to make the Indians English "in taste, in opinion, in morals, and in intellect."

More often, perhaps, such transfer of values resulted from the

---

* It is only fair to add that, as native civilization was undermined or broken up, the West contributed a measure of stability by offering its own model of the good life, a taunting model, to be sure, and not a sound base reconstructed from native conditions.

embittered realization that continued adherence to one's native ways led to humiliation by the foreigner. As a Chinese intellectual, Liang Ch'i-chao, phrased his reaction in 1902:

> If we wish to make our nation strong, we must investigate extensively the methods followed by other nations and races in becoming independent. . . . Selecting their superior points, we can appropriate them to make up our own shortcomings. . . .

In 1915, when the position of China had further deteriorated, another writer, Ch'ên Tu-hsiu, made the same point with greater urgency:

> Considered in the light of the evolution of human affairs, it is plain that those races that cling to antiquated ways are declining or disappearing day by day, and the peoples who seek progress and advancement are just beginning to ascend in power and strength. It is possible to predict which of these will survive and which will not. Now our country still has not awakened from its long dream and isolates itself by going down the old rut. . . . Revering only the history of the twenty-four dynasties and making no plans for progress and improvement, our people will be turned out of this twentieth century world and be lodged in the dark ditches fit only for slaves, cattle, and horses. . . . I would much rather see the past culture of our nation disappear than see our race die out now because of its unfitness for living in the modern world.

And so this writer turned to "Mr. Science and Mr. Democracy" to cure "the dark maladies" of Chinese life.

The reluctant conclusion among Asian intellectuals—the awakening of Africa in these terms occurred only a generation later—was that the conditions of progress and improvement were those of the West. Westernization was the price of survival.

Yet was there not a flaw in the argument? If one wanted to follow the western model, should one not strive above all to imitate the white man's pride in his own native accomplishments, his belief in himself and his traditions? The Europeans did not imitate. They stood out as paragons of cultural and spiritual independence, of an uninterrupted, autochthonous development. Should westernization then not mean the affirmation of native tradition? A Young Turk spokesman, Ahmed Riza Bey, writing from Paris in 1895, made that point very clear:

> We wish to advance in the path of civilization, but we declare resolutely that we do not wish to advance otherwise than in fortifying the Ottoman element and respecting its own conditions of existence. We are determined to guard the originality of our oriental civilization.

In India the same pride in native civilization made other men turn against the British influence:

> With the spread of English rule [Brahmabandhab Upadhyay wrote in 1899] India has lost her own ideal of civilization. Our educated classes think as they have been taught by the Firinghi [foreign] masters. Our minds have been conquered. We have become slaves. The faith in our own culture and the love for things Indian are gone. India will reach Swaraj [self-government] the day she will again have faith in herself.

In the mind of Vivekananda, one of Brahmabandhab's contemporaries and a leading figure in the Hindu revival, that faith was already burning bright:

> This is the great ideal before us and everyone must be ready for it—the conquest of the whole world by India—nothing less than that, and we must all get ready for it, strain every nerve for it. Let foreigners come and flood the land with their armies, never mind. Up, India, and conquer the world with your spirituality.

The weapon of spirituality was India's own—there were no others—and spiritual superiority, of course, was the most superior of all.

Yet obviously spirituality alone could not create a modern India. Disillusionment eventually overtook every native leader who tried to convert any aspect of his country's endowment of backwardness into a creed for the future. Gandhi was succeeded by Nehru, the struggle for independence by the responsibilities of statehood. The pressure for westernization was inexorable. This, however, did not prevent constant rearguard action on behalf of other, seemingly more tenable redoubts of native tradition in dress, art, or language. The western model of autochthonous development (and the normal human preference for it) continues to exert a powerful influence to this day.*

While the ideological defense of nativism proved difficult (if not impossible), the chances were better for plain political assertion. If the western model proved anything, it was the glory of political independence and greatness. The western states enjoyed cultural pre-eminence only because they were so powerful. Native originality likewise must be protected by power. An Indian moderate, G. K. Gokhale, writing the statutes of the newly founded *Servants of India Society* in 1905, has well expressed the force of that ambition among his countrymen:

> The idea of a united and renovated India, marching onwards to a place among the nations of the world, worthy of her past, is no longer a mere idle dream of a few imaginative minds, but is the definitely accepted creed of those who form the brain of the community. . . .

Power, Napoleon once observed, is never ridiculous. It covers up many embarrassments. As native intellectuals became more sensitive to the incessant humiliations that accompanied backwardness, they began to appreciate the uses of power. The search for self-assertion, for native strength (on whatever ideological foundation), was thus a natural corollary of European penetration, whether through admiration or resentment of the example. In short, the European model was bound to undermine itself. The dialectics of westernization implied copying western power,

---

* The ideal of *négritude* in the French-speaking parts of Africa or the search for the "African personality" elsewhere in that continent is one of the most recent manifestations of this trend.

[12]

which in turn meant limiting and rejecting it. The compliment of abject imitation inevitably led to insults and blows.

The beginnings of an antiwestern revolt throughout the world were dimly visible before 1914. They grew from the westernized native intelligentsia that had been apprenticed in Europe, the United States, or in the western schools of their own countries. Sun Yat-sen in China; Gokhale and Tilak, Ghose and Gandhi in India; or the Young Turks in the Ottoman Empire established a nucleus of native ambition. The Chinese Republic in 1911 and the Kuomintang were a first practical manifestation. In India, the Morley-Minto reforms of 1909 were designed to meet the nascent Indian nationalism by giving it a share, however minimal, in the government of the country. Four years later in Egypt —the origins of the revolt are visible in many places—the rising opposition forced the British protectorate to alter the organic law in favor of native representation. While in India the reception of the reforms was favorable for the time being, the first meeting of the new Egyptian legislative assembly resulted in an anti-British riot.

At the time, these events appeared as mere straws in the cross-draft of trends. Only an obscure Russian revolutionary, searching for allies wherever they might be found, was able to perceive the beginnings of the counter tide beneath the continuing triumphant outpouring of western influence. Writing in 1913, Lenin found "the European spirit" rising in Asia. Asia was awakening and contributing to the global revolutionary movement which heralded a new era of world history. Europe was becoming backward, he wrote, and Asia progressive. In the future, he predicted, the western proletariat and the rising masses of young Asia would combine forces. But how this might be done and how, in general, the westernized leaders might weld the European tradition to their native heritage, he did not reveal. Maybe the subversion by the western model would continue even while the antiwestern revolt ran its course.

The opportunity for native assertion, to be sure, did not necessarily arise from the strength of native power alone. It might even more successfully derive from the weakness of Europe. How strong then was the West, especially Europe, at the culmination of its historic career, how capable of coping with the novel challenge to its supremacy?

The internal progress of Europe, particularly of western Europe which set the norm, demonstrated and justified its global pre-eminence. In the years before 1914, it had created a society which gave all citizens access to the best it possessed in every field of human endeavor. Formal privilege had almost disappeared. The barriers between rich and poor, high and low, had been reduced as nowhere else in the world. Western European society, and still more that of North America, was truly an "open society" where those with ability could rise to a commensurate social and economic position. Thanks, furthermore, to an unprecedented volume of production (made possible very largely by private enterprise), even the lowliest were improving their condition. The bulk of the population indeed grew prosperous with material goods and physical comforts beyond all expectations of earlier ages. Western Europe and North America, moreover, were now practicing a system of government in which every adult male citizen could cast a vote and influence the course of politics (the women, needless to say, made their voices heard too). Whatever the imperfections—we will come to them presently—it is fair to say that never before in all human history had the relationship between the rulers and the ruled been so close and political liberty so well meshed with governmental authority as under the new institutions of political democracy then being established on both sides of the North Atlantic.

The crowning triumph, however, in England, France, the United States, and even Germany, up to a point,* was the combination of political freedom for the citizen under constitutional government with power for the state in the emerging global state system. The amazing ascendancy of these countries, both in terms of power and cultural radiation, was largely the result of the spontaneous enterprise of individuals, not of their govern-

---

* The peculiarities of the German condition in the perspective here employed can, unfortunately, not be spelled out in this essay.

[14]

ments. In the case of England, which then served as the universal model, it had come about, so one writer teased, in "a fit of absentmindedness," as a result of circumstance, not of deliberate effort. Lightly indeed, by comparison, did these countries carry their burden of global power!

Yet despite these tremendous accomplishments which set them above the rest of the world, all was not well in the major states of Europe. Before the outbreak of the first World War, each of them faced a profound crisis. The advent of "mass politics" caused by the extension of the suffrage tremendously complicated the tasks of government. On the one hand, the demands made on the state were constantly increased. The common voter wanted to better his share of the good life by political means if he could not do so by any other. On the other hand, the ability of the state to provide these services was limited, above all because its citizens could not agree among themselves what they desired most. Mass participation in politics threw into bold relief all the existing varieties of regional and social outlook within a country. It even seemed as if, under the tensions of modern life, these differences multiplied and deepened.

On the surface it would appear that parliamentary debate offered the best process of mutual accommodation. Yet parliamentary procedure could operate only under certain conditions. It presupposed a deep-seated, almost instinctive willingness to make it work in all kinds of political weather. Here exactly lay the rub. In states without a long-standing parliamentary tradition and a common past, such willingness did not exist. And while most people in Europe attained universal suffrage before 1914, obviously not all of them knew how to make the best of it.

None of the major European states remained exempt from the quandaries of mass politics. Of the dilemmas of the Russian Empire we shall speak at length in subsequent pages. In the Austro-Hungarian monarchy, the crisis took the form chiefly of a clash of nationalities. By 1914 the continued existence of this once magnificent state, so essential for the stability of central-eastern and southeastern Europe, depended almost entirely on the life of one man, the aged Emperor Francis Joseph. In Italy the authority of the government suffered from the anarchy of divergent regional as well as social loyalties. Italy had been unified in 1861, yet not enough Italians of a common mold existed to give stability to the Italian democracy that was in the making after 1900. As social discord mounted before 1914, its prospects seemed more troubled than ever. In the German Empire of William II, the political scene was darkened by strife. The universal suffrage granted for the elections to the Reichstag was incompatible with the limited class vote prevailing in Prussia, and German democracy with Prussian hegemony. After the elections of 1912, the fall of the Bismarckian constitution could not long be postponed, a fact which put the conservatives in a particularly militant mood. Yet were the Germans ready for full democracy?

In France the Third Republic, although backed by the majority of Frenchmen as the regime which divided them least, suffered from a proliferation of political factions. Both on the right and on the left the extremists had no use for parliamentary democracy. In the center it was difficult to find stable majorities for major tasks of legislation. The crisis in the French polity perhaps did not build up to a climax before 1914 as it did in some other countries, yet it was a constant depressing reality.

Even England, mother of parliaments, was faced with an unprecedented breakdown in the decorum of its political household. Not satisfied with the welfare measures introduced by the liberal government after 1906, certain key labor unions were planning in 1912 to use the general strike as an extraparliamentary method to extort concessions from their employers and the government. Social tensions, in other words, proved intractable by the traditional means, even after the reform of the House of Lords in 1911 had made the parliamentary process fully democratic. Furthermore, over the issue of Irish home rule the conservatives, already embittered by social legislation and the decline of the upper chamber, were determined to foment civil war over Northern Ireland rather than submit once more.

The most disturbing feature of European domestic politics

however, was the undercurrent of dissatisfaction with the most signal accomplishments of contemporary civilization. It was expressed, although moderately, by the socialists, who pointed to the many discrepancies between the steady progress in technology and the material well-being of the ruling class on the one hand and the continuous deprivation of the masses on the other. Poverty, unemployment, disease, denials of human dignity, militarism, inequality, and exploitation still haunted even the most civilized countries. The ideals of liberty, equality, and fraternity were being only imperfectly realized (even though the peoples of western and central Europe at least enjoyed more of them than any others). The responsibility for this, according to the socialists, lay with the entire system, with "capitalism."

Most commonly their attack stayed within the mainstream of western tradition; their socialism was a liberalism carried to its logical—or utopian—conclusion. Yet there was also an extremist, pessimist undercurrent, voiced most clearly perhaps by the French syndicalist Georges Sorel. He found fault not only with the "bourgeoisie" but with the very premises of contemporary thought and life, its trust in democracy and science and its confidence in uninterrupted progress. To him, modern life had lost its savor; it was moving toward degeneracy. The escape, for him, lay in a reaffirmation of—violence:

> Two accidents alone . . . would be able to stop this movement, a great foreign war which might renew lost energies and which, in any case, would doubtless bring into power men with the will to govern; or a great extension of proletarian violence, which would make the revolutionary reality evident to the middle class and would disgust them with their humanitarian platitudes. . . .

A more resounding repudiation of western humanitarianism, and of the patient—and pacifist—rationalism which stood at the core of the occidental tradition, could hardly have been imagined.

The revolt against the established order was not limited, however, to the socialist intellectuals. The protest cropped up from many sources. What was one to make of the young men of

Germany, the *Wandervögel*, who sought refuge from the respectable routine of their parents by roaming through hill and dale and probing the mystical excitements of campfires? And what of a poet like D'Annunzio who flouted the social discipline of middle-class society and tried to recapture the essence of life in the lusts and dangers of war? Perhaps even more revealing was the thinking of Oswald Spengler, a German high school teacher of mathematics who in 1911 began to ponder *The Decline of the West* in terms of a revolt of "blood" and "race," his primitive way of describing the deepest human instincts that somehow were left unsatisfied in the modern urban-industrial world and cried out for their birthright.

What provided a common bond between the different voices of revolt was a vague conviction that life had jumped too rapidly from a slow, loosely meshed, and heroic style of life into the tight and "artificial" social discipline of industrialism and the shallow compromises of parliamentary politics. The "inner man" had been left far behind. The revolt of the irrational was strongest, therefore, where the rate of change had been most precipitous, in the newly industrialized areas and along their peripheries in central, southern, and eastern Europe. Needless to say, the new affirmation of violence was bound to have a profound repercussion on domestic politics and on international relations as well.

International relations gave cause for alarm on grounds of its own. Europe before 1914 has often been likened to a military camp. Each of the major powers was armed to the limits of its capacity (and sometimes beyond); none trusted the others. All talked of the likelihood of war and prepared accordingly. What gave their preparations their modern, limitless character was the fact that the entire population became involved, not only in body but in mind as well; all major decisions of the government now tended to be ratified, formally or informally, by public opinion. As a result, the quality of foreign policy deteriorated. All too frequently its issues were reduced to the lowest level of popular comprehension, thrown open to the prejudices of people too hard-pressed by their daily cares to take an intelligent and

[18]

continuous interest in foreign affairs, and saturated with the mounting domestic tensions. Internal maladjustments thus spilled over into international relations, to the detriment of the common European heritage.

The period of rising democracy, it will be remembered, was also the period of rising imperialism. The new mass electorates were instructed in the fundamentals of foreign policy not by the diplomats with their limited objectives but by the demagogues who preached that the future belonged to the great empires and that only territorial sway, *Lebensraum,* guaranteed the survival of the race in history. Thus were planted the dark, irrational drives in modern international relations which threatened to rip apart the traditional order of Europe and the world at large, stopping at nothing. The age of global politics and of apocalyptic ideologies had begun.

It was a frightening paradox that the disintegration of the common European outlook inherited from the past should have occurred at a time when, in fact, the interdependence of Europe attained unprecedented proportions. It was not only to the advantage of all Europeans to stand together in their dealings with the non-European world; their very prosperity at home derived from their constant and intimate cooperation. Their exports and imports, their credit structure, their transportation and communication, their scientific discoveries—all tied them ever more closely together, so closely indeed that, if human action had been prompted by economic and material factors alone, war would have become impossible. The discrepancy between the political and psychological mobilization for war on the one hand and the deepening interdependence on the other—the discrepancy between war and industrial society in general—did not escape attention at the time. Pacifism was a lively cause, and schemes for world peace under one world government were not wanting, particularly among socialist intellectuals who, for other reasons as well, had their doubts about the validity of the existing order.*

This sketch of Europe on the eve of the first World War ad-

* The idea of a world state and one common world language was, of course, an old one; Ulysses S. Grant was among its advocates.

mittedly differs from any contemporary self-portrait. Hindsight has put the pockmarks of later torments into a face still flushed with success. Never before (or since) had Europe been so satisfied, so powerful, so self-assured. Yet it would be a mistake to assume that the war, like a *diabolus ex machina,* suddenly descended upon an innocent Europe and drained away its marrow. Violence and destruction were already in its bones; they transformed the traditional power conflict and the domestic crises into a universal catastrophe which marked the end of an epoch.

In the transformation the fate of Russia was intimately involved.

II

THE CONDITION OF RUSSIA

IN MAY, 1896, a few days after the coronation of Nicholas II in the Kremlin, a disaster occurred at the Khodynka Field on the outskirts of Moscow. As was customary at a coronation, the Tsar had set out presents for the good people of the ancient capital.* Instead of waiting for the signal, the crowd, greedy and poorly controlled, suddenly surged forward toward the trinkets and trampled to death over a thousand people, turning the joyous intention into an ominous debacle. Thus began a reign beset with deepening tragedy. As the Tsar himself observed, he was born on the day of Job.

Unlike Job, however, he was never restored to calm and glory. After a sequence of revolutions that destroyed his reign and much besides, Nicholas together with his wife and children was foully murdered. The reason why the Tsar could not reap the rewards of his righteousness and kindliness (no one who observed him in his family circle denied him these attributes) was that in statecraft these qualities are not sufficient. They must be matched by political astuteness. If autocracy was to survive, the Tsar had to lead, and lead with passion. A tsar worth his title, in short, had to master the condition of Russia.

To clear away a common misunderstanding about this condition, Russia was only in part a European country by the standard criteria of that norm. In any survey of world civilizations, to be sure, Russia (whether Tsarist or Soviet) belongs to Europe. It

* The "modern" capital, built by Peter the Great, was St. Petersburg, where the Tsar normally resided.

represents a Slavic and Eastern Orthodox variant of the common Graeco-Roman, Judaeo-Christian tradition, a variant much overlaid, in recent centuries, by constant cultural admixtures from western Europe. To a visiting foreigner the observable differences, except perhaps for the Cyrillic alphabet, would not transgress the customary European variety. Nicholas' family, the Romanovs, were closely related by family ties to the Windsors, the Hohenzollern, and a host of lesser royalty. The Tsar and his wife habitually conversed with each other in English; other educated Russians might prefer French or German. Russian readers were exceedingly well informed by their newspapers and periodicals of European events in any field of human endeavor— better, in fact, than most Europeans. In the late 1890's, moreover, a remarkable economic advance took place. As a result, Russian society more than ever judged (or misjudged) its affairs by the example set by western Europe. Russia, furthermore, was closely associated with the other Great Powers of Europe. It was a weighty member of the European concert and, after 1894, intimately tied to France by a diplomatic and military alliance; after 1907 it was linked to England as well. As a European power, too, it took its share in the division of the world, penetrating into central Asia and the Far East.

Yet while emphasizing the basic European nature of Russia, one must also consider certain peculiarities which set it apart (further than even Spain or the Balkan countries); it is these peculiarities we must keep in mind whenever we think of Russia's fate in the twentieth century. By geographic location it was a continental heartland, as much an Asian as a European power, a neighbor of China and Japan, of Persia, Afghanistan, and the Ottoman Empire, as well as of Austria-Hungary, Germany, and Sweden. It was thus far larger than any of the European states. Its hugeness was the occasion of much boasting in patriotic circles—imagine a country one sixth of the world's land surface, as vast as the face of the moon! Yet its size was also the source of many embarrassments unknown to its more compact European rivals, and much of its territory was as useless as the moon!

Its population likewise was enormous by European standards, about 127,000,000 in 1897 (Germany was edging toward 65,000,000 at the time and Britain toward 45,000,000). But it could not compare in unity and cohesion, in loyalty or skill, with any European people; it was far more divided than even Austria-Hungary. The Great Russian element which had created the Russian state (and with which this essay will be mostly concerned) constituted less than one half of the total;* it did not stand on friendly terms with other Slavic groups, such as the Ukranians or Poles. The various nationalities, Slav or non-Slav, are too numerous to survey here—they numbered well over one hundred. The ethnic quilting was further mottled by religious diversity. All major religions of the world were represented, and many minor ones as well. The followers of the Russian Orthodox faith formed the largest group among the Christians, but they too were divided among themselves.

An extraordinary variety again prevailed in the levels of civilization. Hardly a step was missing in the cultural descent from the western urbanity of St. Petersburg or Warsaw to the barbarism of some Siberian tribes. The Russian Empire thus faced among its inhabitants the deep cultural cleavages which the other European states encountered only in their contact with colonial peoples overseas.†

Anyone familiar with the tortuous evolution of the modern state in western Europe can imagine the extraordinary difficulties faced by the long succession of Russian rulers whose task it was to establish secure boundaries, weld together their inchoate territories, and make their subjects into willing and capable citizens. Because of the lack of natural shelter by mountains or oceans, state-building in eastern Europe proved an exceptionally hazardous enterprise. In the vast open plains of Eurasia stability suffi-

* It was mixed, by intermarriage, with non-Slavic peoples of Finno-Ugrian and Tartar stock.

† By 1912 almost one third of the population was legally classified as "alien," too primitive for citizenship. This category, incidentally, also included the Jews (certainly not a primitive group). The treatment of the Jews in Russia, however, is too sad a tale to be told in this brief essay.

cient for continuity in government and culture had to be bought at an inhuman price of plain physical power concentrated in the hands of a single ruler. Those who cultivated their liberties, like the Polish gentry, found their state wiped off the political map. In eastern Europe far more than among the infinitely more secure peoples of western Europe raw power was crucial, for the state as well as for the ruler. Thus did their past lay an exceptionally heavy burden on the Russian people, sharply setting them off from their favored neighbors to the west. By 1900, the task was far from completed. Whatever effective unity Nicholas II could summon was the imposed unity of the state, symbolized in the guiding slogan of Orthodoxy, Autocracy, and Nationality: the vast conglomerate of peoples and territories in the Empire was to be cemented together, after the western model, by a common church (Russian orthodoxy), a common subjection to the Tsar, and a common ethnic bond (the Great Russian nationality). Needless to say, the forcible imposition of these molds aroused resentment which again hardened the differences.

How starved of cultural resources was Russia by comparison with her more favored western neighbors! Feudalism had never flowered here, nor the Renaissance, nor the quiet industry of the middle class. The dearth was reflected in the character of the Russian state. In western Europe the state could draw freely on the wealth and skills of its subjects and allow them considerable freedom in their various pursuits: what was good for the citizen had, on the whole, proved advantageous for the state, too. In Russia, on the other hand, the government did not find the prerequisite cultural resources among its subjects. It had to organize them by command, by copying western models, drafting its subjects into compulsory service, and even trying to change their very character. As a result, autocracy had always contained more than a streak of totalitarianism.* In its endeavors to build up Russian strength, it had destroyed or crippled all autonomous

* The essence of totalitarianism, I take it, lies in the endeavor to reshape, on a mass basis, the deepest promptings of the human will for political ends.

institutions and the native common law as useless or even inimical to its purpose. No middle ground of spontaneous nongovernmental public activity was left, alas, to mediate between an extreme absolutism and anarchy.

Thus, roughly, ran the formula of tsarist power at the time of Peter the Great; and thus, despite considerable admixtures of western influences (particularly after the Great Reforms of the 1860's), it continued into the twentieth century. Wherever one looked, one could detect the presence of an omnipotent state; this was another of the abnormalities which set the country apart. While in England and France civic freedom and individual initiative had gradually been harmonized with government authority, in Russia the state had grown fat at the expense of the people. The state was the biggest landowner, employer of labor, investor of capital, promoter of industry—in short, the only effective public force in society. In the minds of the people it was *nachal'stvo*—the sole agency responsible for getting things moving.

The state was personified in the autocrat ruling from his capital at St. Petersburg. No other monarch in Europe claimed such large powers or stood so high above his subjects, and for good reason. As a writer of the early nineteenth century had put it, autocracy was the soul and life of Russia. Despite terrifying obstacles it had raised the country to the position of a Great Power, protected its inhabitants from invasion and foreign rule, and upheld the glory of Russia in the world. Inevitably, the constant strain had affected its character. Autocracy was traditionally impatient and short-tempered. Too much still had to be done, too many hurdles overcome. There was never time for public argument about ways and means, no leisure for debate to convince the people at large. The Tsar always knew best. He issued the command and all Russians obeyed (in legal theory at least). Even his most powerful ministers squirmed in the Imperial presence. They were merely "servitors," not advisors.

The autocrat wielded his power through the bureaucracy, which, on the whole, contained the ablest and most knowledgeable members of Russian society. Despite all its inherent faults, the bureaucracy was a remarkable institution, carefully graded by rank and conferring nobility on its most deserving and advanced officers; until the end it offered a career open to talent. Like the Tsar, the bureaucracy was proud of its progressive role and disdainful of criticism. It too did not trust its slow-witted and wayward subjects, equating spontaneity on their part with stupidity and mismanagement. It rarely judged its charges by their native standards, but rather applied the imported concepts of western statecraft and citizenship to their activities. Like the Tsar, the *chinovniki,* as the bureaucrats were called, stood above the people, and like him they were always in danger of being corrupted by their omnipotence; their authority was apt to degenerate into arbitrariness. Besides, the poverty of the Russian state manifested in their low salaries tended to corrupt them in a material sense as well. This was true particularly of the inferior ranks. Thus, despite its great merits, the bureaucracy could not escape from the shortcomings of the country as a whole.

Russian society, too, differed profoundly from that of western Europe. It reflected—and explained—the overbearing character of autocracy. In 1900 the bulk of the population consisted of peasants, the muzhiks, poor material indeed for citizenship. Serfs until 1861, they were still confined to a tightly knit collective mode of life within the patriarchal family and the village commune. Private property and personal initative, or the western awareness of individuality, were generally unknown among them. To be sure, a small and disliked minority, the kulaks (meaning "fists"), were rising by their ruthless energy above the level of rural lethargy. But in 1900 the government had not yet decided how to treat them. It kept all peasants—and the industrial workers who remained closely tied to the village*—legally and socially segregated from the other social groups. The distinction reflected a basic—and final—fissure in the Russian body politic. On one side stood the peasant masses, the "dark people"; on the other what we might call "privilege Russia," nobles, bureaucrats, the run of educated Russians, and even the merchants, who often had risen from the peasants. "Privilege Russia" looked

---

* Until 1917, the overwhelming majority of Russian workers were legally classified as peasants, by their own preference.

upon the village with profound contempt, and understandably so. Chekhov has aptly described the peasants in a story by that name, published in 1897:

> . . . these people lived worse than cattle, and it was terrible to be with them; they were coarse, dishonest, dirty, and drunken; they did not live at peace with one another but quarreled continually, because they feared, suspected, and despised each other. Who keeps the tavern and encourages drunkenness? The peasant. Who embezzles and drinks up the funds that belong to the community, the schools, the church? The peasant. Who steals from his neighbors, sets fire to their property, bears false witness at court for a bottle of vodka? At meetings of the Zemstvo and other local bodies, who is the first to raise his voice against the peasants? The peasant. Yes, to live with them was terrible; but yet, they were human beings, they suffered and wept like human beings, and there was nothing in their lives for which one could not find justification. Crushing labor that made the whole body ache at night, cruel winters, scanty crops, overcrowding; and no help and nowhere to look for help. Those who were stronger and better-off could give no assistance, as they were themselves coarse, dishonest, drunken, and swore just as foully. The most insignificant little clerk or official treated the peasants as though they were tramps, and addressed even the village elders and church wardens as inferiors, and as though he had a right to do so.

These people furnished the soldiers of revolution in 1917 and the bulk of Soviet citizenry thereafter.

While the upper layers of Russian society had become westernized, the peasant had remained in his traditional rut, unenlightened and sometimes given to weird and frightening superstitions. In the bottom of his heart he carried an instinctive suspicion, if not hatred, of his Europeanized betters, for, in the last analysis, the westernization of Russia since Peter the Great had been carried out at his expense. What did he care under which government he lived or what role it played in the world?*

---

* The loyalty of the peasantry is a moot point in Russian historiography. The evidence suggests that it became a political factor only under extreme provocation, such as foreign occupation.

The Russian peasant, while stubbornly conservative in his ways, was at the same time far more revolutionary than his counterparts in western Europe. Traditionally rebellious, he found his resentment increased at the end of the nineteenth century by rural overpopulation, the inroads of western capitalism, and the expectation of a better life filtered down through city and town from western Europe. The instinctive peasant response was to seize, by what was known as Black Partition, all lands not especially set aside for peasant use, i.e., those of the state, church, and above all the landed nobility; more land meant a better life. The peasant lived by the ancient truth that he who does not work, and work by the sweat of his brow—no other type of labor counted in his eyes—neither shall he eat. He had long claimed a moral right to the land which, as a sharecropper or wage laborer, he cultivated for its owners. Of the discipline of citizenship under modern government—or of the complex superstructure of modern civilization—he naturally possessed only the vaguest notion; what he knew of it, he often hated.* When his discontent exploded, as it occasionally did, he was apt to drive the landlord and officials out and run his affairs by his peasant wits until the troops restored order. By 1900, elementary education was beginning to penetrate the village, but it hardly bridged the fatal gulf between the peasant masses and "privilege Russia."

"Privilege Russia," however, did not enjoy the western European boons of free and equal citizenship either. It was divided into a number of state-supervised and mutually suspicious collective organizations *(sosloviia):* the nobility, the bureaucracy, the priesthood, the merchant community (subdivided into two guilds), and what might very inadequately be translated as the "lower middle class" *(meshchanstvo).* The only group exempted from such corporate control was the growing number of men in the free professions. Higher education conferred the status of an

* In the eighteen seventies and eighties a peasant sect called "Not Ours" repudiated family, property, schools, courts-of-law, and the government. It showed its contempt by passive resistance, unyielding disobedience, even in insignificant details.

"honorary citizen," whose position came closest to that of a western citizen (which, incidentally, showed the government's solicitude for education).

Despite the ascendancy of the "honorary citizens" and the rise of a wealthy business community, the most privileged position in Russian society still belonged to the landed nobility. This group shared a common outlook with the tsar and set the tone in the bureaucracy and the armed services. It was, furthermore, the only recognized ally of autocracy in Russian society, and much pampered for that reason. Yet by 1900 it had long passed its day of glory. Increasingly impoverished and unbusinesslike, it even opposed essential measures of economic development. Moreover, some if its best members were disloyally hankering after a constitution. The decline of the nobility reflected the growing disintegration of the entire system of corporate organization. By 1900, "privilege Russia" inched toward the open society of the West.

Ever since the Great Reforms of the 1860s, the government itself had indeed contributed toward greater social freedom and mobility. The Russian defeat in the Crimean war (1854-1856) had taught a lesson: the energies of the individual Russian must be enlisted, after the pattern of western progress, in raising the strength and welfare of the country. Thus serfdom had been abolished and new agencies of "self-administration" created: (1) the zemstvos, elected from various rural groups but nearly always dominated by the landed nobility, to take charge of rural development; and (2) the town dumas, dominated by the well-to-do urban taxpayers, to promote urban improvement.* At the same time, Russian and foreign capitalists had been given a free hand for the development of a railway system and of up-to-date industries in general.

Yet the western pattern was only imperfectly transplanted. Instead of genuine cooperation, a state of uneasy coexistence between autocracy and private initiative emerged. Autocracy

---

* The zemstvos were not introduced into the border provinces; the town dumas were founded only in select towns chosen by the government.

continued its customary leadership, suspicious as ever of the spontaneity of its subjects. While it recognized the need for autonomous private initiative, particularly in the new economic and cultural pursuits essential to keeping up with western Europe, it never granted its subjects a free hand. Zemstvos, dumas, and even business remained closely hemmed in by a thousand restrictions. What guarantees did the government have that the new opportunities would not be abused for political agitation or private gain at the expense of the commonweal? The public meanwhile complained bitterly about the unceasing bureaucratic meddlesomeness. How under such conditions could the individual acquire the experience and self-confidence necessary for constructive citizenship? Each side, no doubt, was right in its protestations, yet the result was frustration for both.

The clash between popular spontaneity and government leadership pervaded all facets of Russian life. It even reached down to the very source of human motivation, causing profound harm to Russian religion. Autocracy needed the succor of the church, both as a unifying force throughout the Empire and, in the traditional ideology of absolutism, as a conscience-saving restraint on its own unlimited secular powers. And the church—or more broadly, Orthodox Christianity—possessed deep roots in the population, which, however, was not without danger. In order to control the troubled religious stirrings among the people, the state, ever since Peter the Great, administered the church as a department of government. As a result, the church rendered more service to Caesar than was fitting for the vicar of Christ. Genuine godliness, to be sure, was not entirely sacrificed; Orthodox doctrine and ritual safeguarded spiritual vitality sufficient for survival. But the live core of religion was shut off from all outlets in social and political action. Thus crippled, it could develop no modern message. Here lay one of the deepest and most tragic flaws in the Russian tradition: social and political action remained severed from the wellsprings of charity. The live religious urge atrophied in the hands of the government: it was driven underground into persecuted sects or revolutionary atheism (where it was speedily corrupted by political expediency), or it survived as a sterile solace for personal comfort unrelated to the great issues of the day and hence useless as a lubricant for social and political change. In the West, by contrast, religion remained a far more vital force, as the rise of evangelism or of "social Christianity" at the end of the nineteenth century proved.

It was a sad fact that after the emancipation of the serfs the tsarist government signally failed to win the loyalty of its subjects. In religion, economic development, or public administration the people found their goodwill rebuffed, their initiative blunted, and their spontaneity distrusted. As a result, they responded to government authority with a mood of sullen apathy, rejoicing at times over official blunders and in extreme cases, one suspects, even provoking them.

By 1900, the silent and tragic warfare between the government and "society" (the Russian term for the educated public that took an interest in the affairs of the country) had already reached an extreme form. A strict and often stupid censorship prevented free discussion of almost any political issue. Yet had there been free speech, it is safe to say, the government would have been drowned in a flood of protest, much of it utterly irresponsible.* In order to protect itself from uninformed criticism, the government had long evolved an armory of repressive weapons, which in turn had driven all determined opposition underground. The revolutionaries were hunted down by the secret police and punished, when apprehended, by imprisonment, exile, forced labor in Siberia, and, in rare cases, even death, imposed mostly by administrative decision rather than court verdict. The continuous petty war aroused the beastly passions among the hotspurs on both sides and gradually ate away what was left of the good nature of Russian society carried over from a simpler age. The most despicable practice on the government's part was the

---

* One is tempted to blame the responsibility for this misfortune on the autocrats, who were not willing to educate the intelligentsia in the problems of Russian statecraft by drawing it into their confidence. A fairer and more comprehensive judgment would ascribe this flaw to the conditions that perpetuated autocracy. In the Russian setting, one might muse, man's control over his destiny was even more limited than elsewhere.

fomenting (or condoning) of anti-Semitic riots, called pogroms, as a means of relieving popular discontent. Where else in Europe had domestic politics reached such a cruel impasse?

Where else in the civilized world was the body politic so deeply rent by internal discord? The country's ethnic and religious diversity was aggravated by the government's policy of forced assimilation. In addition there were the other two deep gulfs: between the government and "society," and between "privilege Russia" and the peasant masses. What was going to happen then in an age of political equality and democracy in which the people were bound to assert their spontaneity? It was clear by 1900 that in Russia (as elsewhere in Europe) the advance of mass politics could not be stemmed. The population down to the lowliest peasant was slowly becoming politically conscious and eager for a voice in the affairs of the country. Furthermore, their willing cooperation in all pursuits of modern civilization was vitally necessary if the country was to prosper. The stalemate between government and public only retarded progress. How then could the people of Russia be welded into a true community, transcending all their differences, and be reconciled to their government? Creating a cohesive, cooperative, mutually responsive polity was thus the first of the overriding necessities facing twentieth-century Russia.

Yet even a greater challenge than mass politics confronted the Tsar: Russian backwardness. In Western Europe generally, but most conspicuously in imperial Germany (not to mention the United States), science and technology spectacularly enhanced the well-being of the population and the power of the state. Russia, by contrast, stood far behind in the statistics of cultural and technical progress, whether measured by per capita mileage of roads and railways, number of telephones, letters carried by mail or messages sent by telegraph, infant mortality, or distribution of the national income. Critical observers would add to these indicators certain others: dirt, slovenliness, and corruption; widespread inexactness and unpunctuality; illiteracy; flagrant abuses of authority by police or *chinovniki;* the enmity between the people and the government; and a thousand other detriments to modern efficiency. In the light of this evidence one can understand the depression or fierce indignation which overcame many patriotic Russians when they looked at the condition of their country.

Most Russians, covertly or overtly, had long assumed the existence of a cultural barrier between Russia and "Europe." They considered themselves, in fact although not potentially, inferior and backward. Maxim Gorky once ran into a police officer who, disgusted with the writer's roaming through Russia, snarled at him, "This is not Russia, this is a pigsty." Some extremists went so far as to speak of the "Asiatic" character of contemporary Russia. Even the moderates were dissatisfied. As a well-known publicist and former defender of the Russian tradition, V. Vorontsov, wrote in 1906:

> Russia belongs to the family of civilized nations, and moreover has entered the 20th century of our era. This means that its needs and the forms of their satisfaction must be commensurate not with the cultural level on which it finds itself, but with those forms which have been devised and applied by western Europe. . . . We want to eat, dress, entertain ourselves and construct our homes, streets, and urban buildings on the model of what is being done in these areas by modern Europe, not by the Europe of the middle ages.

The burden of such wishful thinking was that Russia should catch up to western Europe. Other and bolder minds even dreamed of Russia's becoming a paragon of political power and cultural leadership in its own right.

In this respect Russia's position before 1914 indeed resembled that of the non-European countries mentioned earlier which had fallen under the western sway. Russian intellectuals, like some of the Indian intellectuals mentioned earlier, urged that their country be remade after "the model of what is being done . . . by modern Europe." The Russian way of life as one encountered it thoroughout the country was insufficient by comparison and thus bad. In short, the same outpouring of western norms which undermined the various non-European civilizations also subverted the traditions and customs of Imperial Russia. The silent revolution from without hollowed out the traditional authority of tsarist Russia long before it physically collapsed.

This "defeat by comparison" transferred Imperial Russia (at the same time that it was westernizing its own colonial dependents within the Empire) from the European context into the category of the underdeveloped countries. The universal norm was derived from those peoples who cultivated their own traditions, at their own speed, and exported them, seemingly without effort, as universal models. This was the enviable condition of the pacesetters among the European powers. All others, including Russia, were inferior, too weak to resist the inundation of their native creativity, and lacking in true sovereignty. Here lay the deepest difference between Russia and "Europe."

Considering the magnitude of the inundation by western norms between 1890 and 1914, the Russian reaction was surprisingly complacent. Most Russians accepted the western standards unthinkingly and turned them against their government. What specific antiwestern resentment existed was mostly focussed on the foreign penetration of Russia's economy. After the emancipation of the serfs, western business and business methods* had indeed acquired a preponderant influence in Russia. For decades the government had borrowed extensively from abroad. It was no exaggeration to say that Russia was a Great Power on credit only. Nor could it be denied that this dependence did limit the Tsar's freedom of action; he could not, for instance, freely vent his anti-Semitism. Foreign capital and enterprise also played a leading part in the development of Russian industry. The instruments of rapid economic growth came largely from abroad. No wonder then that the foreigners and their "capitalist greed" were blamed for all the pains of precipitous cultural change. The

---

*It is customary to speak of western business methods as "capitalism." Yet, considering how that term has been stretched out of shape, its use here has been avoided. We should always remember that western business methods and practice (capitalism so-called) are part and partial of the matrix of western ways of life in general. They cannot be understood, let alone evaluated, by lifting them out of the larger context, as has been done by Marx, Max Weber and many others in their manner. From the Russian perspective, to be sure, western business methods constituted an interrelated whole, a "system." It is a mistake, however, for western scholars in their pursuit of comparative studies to look at their own institutions through the eyes of uncomprehending outsiders.

[34]

fiercest denunciations of foreign exploitation were voiced on the extreme right rather than on the left. Yet all these protests went unheeded. Neither the government nor Russian business nor Russian society could do without external aid, if any progress was to be made.

One of the glaring weaknesses of the Russian condition at the beginning of the twentieth century thus was the disparity between Russian ambition and Russian resources, between pretension and realities. In the eyes of its politically conscious subjects, including the Emperor, Russia belonged to the family of civilized nations and was a Great Power destined to be a leader in the affairs of mankind. If they looked at Russian literature or music or all that Russia had already accomplished despite superhuman difficulties, they were convinced that it had much to offer. But how could their country play that forward role while it was still poor, uncivilized, and ruled by a government repudiated by most of its subjects?

Out of this discrepancy, which was as yet barely understood even by the more perceptive contemporaries (let alone Nicholas II)*, emerged the second great overriding necessity facing the Russian people in the first half of the twentieth century. The fatal gap between ambition and resources had to be closed somehow, at whatever price. The great question which was to determine Russia's destinies for the next generation (and longer) was how the ever-rising costs of true sovereignty could be met out of the native wealth of Russia.

But the riddle remained: How could that native endowment be made to bear riches equal to those of the West when it had produced only backwardness in the past? All modern Russian development was overshadowed by that riddle. And the statesmen who could find no answer perished like the victims of the Sphinx.

* Even now many western historians, taking their clues from the evidence and insights of that generation, refuse to face up to the condition of Russia in the European balance of power or in the emerging global perspective. Standing on the inside of Russian state and society one would naturally be impressed by the force and density of native continuity. Yet this perspective hardly prepares our understanding of the Bolsheviks, who took a global and comparative view.

III

THE FIRST CRISIS, 1900–1905

✪

THE AGE of revolution in Russia began, one might argue, not in the year 1905 but in the decade preceding it. Inasmuch as great changes can be attributed to the work of individuals, one might say that the Revolution began from above rather than below, as as unsuccessful effort of a solitary member of the government to solve the riddle of backwardness. The effort was the work of Sergei Witte, when he was Minister of Finance (1892-1903.) *

Witte was the last of the great statesmen of the Imperial period, a complex man of great energy and quick mind, inspired by a sense of modern efficiency derived from railroad management; strong-willed, even headstrong, calculating and devious, blunt or charming depending on circumstances; worshipped by his subordinates, feared and hated by his enemies. Impatient to make Russia strong, he was a forerunner of Stalin rather than a contemporary of Nicholas II. His work revealed the basic problems which have haunted Russia ever since.

As Minister of Finance he was fully aware of the weakness of his country. Its economy was of the colonial type, exporting unprocessed raw materials, grain, oil, minerals, importing manufactured goods, and depending on a constant influx of foreign capital to keep the government solvent. When Witte assumed his

---

* This is not to deny the pressure of general trends, such as the spurt of industrialization in Europe (especially in Germany) toward the end of the century, the move of European capital into peripheral areas, the heightened mobility of population, the spread of literacy and the increased opportunities for invidious comparison, and the rise in political tension among the great powers of Europe, etc.

post, Russia's economic condition was particularly strained as a result of the Great Famine of 1891. In many parts of the country the peasants were starving; in the capital·the treasury was empty, the government on the verge of bankruptcy. Yet despite such poverty, the routine obligations of a government that claimed to be a major power had to be met. Russia's armed strength had to match that of Germany and Austria-Hungary. The huge country had to be tied together by a modern network of communications. Better and more schools were needed in order to lower the appalling illiteracy rate.

These and a thousand other demands stared daily at the Minister of Finance. Where was he to find the necessary revenue? The tax screw was turned as tightly as possible, too tightly to judge by the recent famine. Foreign loans were expensive; the government, already deeply in debt, could hardly afford more, nor could the country at large, for foreign loans had to be paid, in the last analysis, out of Russian exports, which were limited. As Witte's predecessor had said, Russia had to export "even though we die"—and peasants *had* died. Exports not only maintained Russian credit abroad but also purchased the necessary raw materials for Russian industry, like cotton, or machines and instruments. Such imports were urgently needed to help Russia keep up with western Europe. Yet in 1891 these imports had been curbed by a steep tariff lest they exceed Russia's capacity to pay. There was a limit, in short, to westernization by imports. The only way out of these miseries, it seemed, was to follow the western example and increase the country's native wealth through industrialization. Under Witte, Russia thus became the pioneer of all modern experiments in deliberate economic development.

In 1900, Witte, the one statesman in Russia who was wide awake to the discrepancy between Russian pretension and Russian power, wrote an impassioned memorandum to Nicholas II, underscoring the necessity of industrialization and unwittingly formulating the leitmotif of twentieth-century Russian history:

> Russia more than any other country needs a proper economic foundation for her national policy and culture. . . .

International competition does not wait. If we do not take energetic and decisive measures so that in the course of the next decades our industry will be able to satisfy the needs of Russia and of the Asiatic countries which are—or should be—under our influence, then the rapidly growing foreign industries will break through our tariff barriers and establish themselves in our fatherland and the Asiatic countries mentioned above. . . . Our economic backwardness may lead to political and cultural backwardness as well.

Economic organization, Witte further argued, was as important as spiritual valor for "the strength of the Great Powers which are called to fulfill great historical tasks in the world"—Russia, of course, being one of these key powers.

On first sight, Witte's prescription for industrialization seemed relatively simple; by itself it was hardly a revolution. He was to raise the productivity of Russia's economy by an extensive program of railroad construction (including the much-postponed Trans-Siberian line). This would result, he argued, in an expansion of Russia's heavy industries supplying the necessary equipment. The growth of these industries would in turn stimulate the supporting light industries. Through the increased demand and improved transportation, even agriculture would benefit. In the end, the new prosperity would yield more revenue to the government. There still remained the problem of funds for the initial capital investment, but Witte hoped that with the introduction of the gold standard (accomplished in 1897) foreign loans would become cheaper and more plentiful and that, eventually, the boom would feed on its own progress.

No one can deny the impressive results achieved by the "Witte system," as Witte's measures came to be called. Railroad construction and the heavy industries indeed boomed. The great Siberian railroad to the Far East was constructed on schedule, over five thousand miles long; and more mileage than that was added to the rail network of European Russia. With the help of French and Belgian capital, modern metallurgical industries arose in the Ukraine, making south Russia the chief industrial base of the Empire. Other industries also began to flourish: machine building, textiles, chemicals. In the 1890's, Russian life was quickened for the first time in recent history by a rapid industrial upsurge.

Yet the economic advance was by no means an unmixed blessing. It ushered in a period of profound strain which aggravated all the ills of Russian society. In the first place, Witte's solicitude for industry did not appreciably raise the level of popular welfare; rural Russia was not lifted from its stagnation.

Crop failures and famines persisted, if in somewhat less catastrophic form; taxes bore heavily on the peasants, whose arrears piled up alarmingly in some areas; in many sections land became ever scarcer and more expensive. In 1902 the peasantry gave warning of its distress; in two provinces it rose against the landlords and the police. This was a danger signal indicating that perhaps not Russian industry but Russian agriculture should be the chief care of the government.

The industrial workers, too, were aroused. For the most part they were peasants who had gone to the factories in order to eke out a living which the village could not supply. By any standards the sudden transition from fields to factory was a harsh one. But neither factory managers nor the government, both eager to make the most of the abundant supply of cheap labor, helped to ease the pangs of adjustment.* Thus the sullen anger of the village spilled over into the factories and mills where it was heated further, sometimes to the explosion point. But the pent-up fury was not directed alone against the "capitalists" who ran the factory. Since strikes or public demonstrations of any kind were generally illegal, any outburst against the factory became also an outrage against autocracy. The workers thus were inevitably pushed on the road toward revolution. In the summer of 1903, all of southern and southeastern Russia from Baku to Kiev witnessed a strike wave which nearly grew into a general strike. It sounded an even louder tocsin than the peasant uprisings of the previous year.

Even the business community, pampered by government

* Cheap labor was an important asset in a country where, for a variety of reasons, the costs of production were high.

favors and more tradition-bound in its outlook than the landed nobility, grew restive under the accelerated change of these years. It felt the influence of western business methods and began to appreciate the freedom which western entrepreneurs enjoyed. Particularly after the onset of depression in 1899, Russian businessmen began to find fault with their government.

Indeed, all of Russian society shared a deep-seated resentment of the all-too-sudden jump into an uncongenial way of life. The hostility of the intelligentsia toward the Witte system was typical. With the exception of the famous chemist, D. A. Mendeleev, very few writers and publicists accepted Witte's vision of Russia as a leading industrial nation. Most commonly, the influential periodicals dwelt on the appalling human costs of industrialization, on the exorbitant taxes wrenched from the peasants, on the exploitation of the workers, and on the evils of "capitalism," which they associated with the brutality of the tsarist police and the stupidity of the bureaucrats. The consequences of this agitation were soon evident. During the height of Witte's power as Minister of Finance, the revolutionary movement recruited its most fanatical leaders from the ranks of the intelligentsia. By 1900 they had established close contact with the workers of key industrial centers.

Even more disturbing, perhaps, was the opposition of the landed nobility to rapid industrialization. Russian noblemen derived their livelihood, constantly diminishing ever since the early nineteenth century, from agriculture. The current misery of rural Russia, unalleviated or even hastened by Witte's policies, further undermined their social and political significance; the smouldering peasant discontent, moreover, threatened their very life. Why under these conditions should the government lavish its energies on industry, an artificial creation in Russia and a patent luxury? Among certain landed proprietors, the hatred of Witte knew no bounds. They ranted not only against Witte but against foreign capital and its pernicious effects on Russian life as well. It undermined, they said, the deepest foundations of Russian state and society. The discontent among the landed aristocracy determined the outlook also of the zemstvos. Rural Russia, in short, had no use for the Witte system.*

Through the intimate ties between the nobility and the court, the opposition of the nobility soon spread from the countryside into the capital, where Witte from the start had made many enemies, again because of his economic policies. Fellow ministers accused him of being an inveterate administrative empire builder, whose ambition knew no bounds.

His aggressiveness, to be sure, was not entirely his fault. The very logic of industrialization spurred him forward to domination. It demanded that all obstacles to economic progress be cleared away and the entire government cooperate in the great effort. For that reason Witte did not shrink from interfering in matters of foreign policy. Concentrating on economic development left no funds or energy for risky ventures in diplomacy; it called for a strict policy of peace.† By the same token, Witte began to meddle in all aspects of domestic politics. If, for instance, illiteracy stood in the way of industrial growth, something had to be done about it, despite the widespread fear in government circles lest education intensify the subversion of popular loyalty (already so noticeable among the educated public). As Witte once addressed the Emperor:

> Maybe education would lead the people to corruption. All the same, education must move forward vigorously. . . . Our people are coarse and unenlightened in their medieval frame of mind. But an unenlightened people cannot be made more accomplished. Not going forward it therefore falls behind as compared with people that do move forward.

Thus Witte pressed for better public instruction and took all advanced technical education under his jurisdiction.

But his ambition would not stop with small ventures. If the

---

* Russian liberalism, on the whole, was anti-industrial, unlike European liberalism.

† Witte's Far Eastern policy was expansionist only while expansion seemed safe. When the risks mounted, Witte became cautious. Foreign policy, however, was not his forte.

structure of Russian society obstructed economic progress, it too had to be changed. Witte advocated no less than recasting the upper layers of Russian society, putting the business community, tiny and unpopular though it was, ahead of the landed nobility. From the viewpoint of modern trade and industry, nothing was to be expected from the landlords (as Chekhov's *Cherry Orchard* well illustrates). Still more important to Witte was the revamping of rural society. Industrialization by private enterprise—such, despite his emphasis upon government direction, was his ideal—required the dissolution of the peasant commune. Private initiative had to be introduced among the peasant masses as well. Thus he called for a huge transformation in the very depths of Russian life.

Yet he sensed that something even more basic stood in his way: the unseen motives and values that made men and women perform their daily routine. He had to replace the slow-minded, moody conservatism of an agrarian and almost medieval mode of life by the quick rationality of urbanism and the innate drive for hard work which has been called, since Max Weber, the Protestant ethic. The carelessness and nonchalance of many top officials in the government (not to mention the members of the Imperial family) were the despair of Witte, who himself lived by an inherited Teutonic self-discipline. But a similar casualness and listlessness pervaded all other ranks of society as well. How could these deepest layers of human motivation be quickened?

Rapid westernization, Witte gradually came to realize, was a comprehensive revolutionary process shaking Russian society to its depths and mobilizing all vested interests against him. (And who did not have a vested interest in gradualness and slowness of adjustment?) Hence a final question arose for Witte: Could autocracy assume leadership over this vast and unpopular metamorphosis?

To his sorrow, Witte soon realized that Nicholas II was not meant to carry this burden. The Tsar was temperamentally unfit to be autocrat in time of crisis. His weakness of will was obvious from the start, even to himself. As he observed to one of his uncles in the year of the coronation, "I always give in and in the

THE FIRST CRISIS, 1900–1905

end am made the fool, without will, without character." His uncertainty made him—and his wife Alexandra—all the more determined to uphold the dignity and power of his office. Yet how could he do this when he was never master of the situation? He winced in Witte's presence and always agreed with the person whom he had seen last.

It was not that Nicholas was devoid of goodwill or determination. Every day he dutifully applied himself, with a wistful glance at the weather outside, to reading and annotating the official reports. He meant to be a good father to his people, stern, even ruthless when necessary, but always sympathetic to their woes. The tragedy was that he could not master the harsh game of politics. Living in the splendid isolation of the Imperial palaces, he was only dimly aware of the rapid changes in the Russian polity. Perhaps just because he felt that he could not master them, he was instinctively opposed to them; he remained a partisan of rural Russia. Commerce, banking, and industry were alien influences, replete with foreigners and Jews—like so many of his subjects he particularly loathed Jews (but then, all Englishmen were Jews by definition). Significantly the figure among his ancestors whom he disliked most was Peter the Great. By contrast he inclined toward medieval Muscovy. And in time of adversity he sought solace not in a rational analysis of his mistakes, but in prayer. There could have been no more fatal opiate for an autocrat!

Yet even if Nicholas II had been endowed with a keener political instinct, his job, as defined by tradition, would have been too big for one man. The autocrat was the solitary and fragile keystone of government—head of state, policy-maker, and chief administrator all in one—at a time when the functions of government rapidly multiplied and when, furthermore, they could be performed only with the help of a disciplined bureaucracy and a loyal populace. Not possessing inexhaustible vitality, the Tsar was incapable of overseeing his vast establishment. What mockery of single-mindedness and unity of purpose was hidden behind the monolithic facade of autocracy! As the Tsar did not lead, his ministers quarreled among themselves; cliques and camarillas interfered with the conduct of government. When no agreement between rival factions could be reached, the same Imperial decree might announce two diametrically opposed policies. As for the people at large, Nicholas never deigned to take notice of public opinion, let alone invite his subjects into his confidence. His government, he was convinced, could handle its tasks as it had done in the past.

With this conclusion, Witte was inclined to agree. A single overriding will was necessary for carrying out the modernization of Russia. The people, while only too eager to consume the benefits of modernization, gave no indication of their ability—or willingness—to undertake the necessary changes on their own. Modernization and industrialization by public consent were therefore impossible. Were they then to be carried out against public opinion? This alternative Witte also denied. He hoped that under an inspiring leader the population could be aroused to the necessary pitch of enthusiasm. A friend, the journalist E. J. Dillon, summed up Witte's deepest aims:

> Witte had long the feeling that the social and political molecules of which the tsardom was composed and which were forever forming and reforming themselves into fleeting shapes, might be attracted and held permanently together by the central force of a grandiose economic transformation and by the interests which that would foster and create, seconded by educational influences properly systematized.

Solving the great national task of modernization, Witte hoped, would also impart to the body politic the tight, spontaneous cohesion required of a modern society.

It was a dynamic vision for which Witte, tragically, found no support among his contemporaries. He stood ahead of his time, attempting far more than a mere Minister of Finance could ever hope to accomplish, and far more than he himself knew. As one looks over the long list of changes which he started or at least suggested, one realizes that the essence of rapid industrialization was not establishing railroads, factories, or mills on Russian soil. The real task, of which western Europe for once offered no model, was to provide the social, economic, political, and psychological framework in which western technology could take root and flourish. What Witte had conceived as a relatively simple and innocuous economic policy tailored to the power of the Minister of Finance turned out to be an all-comprehensive scheme of industrialization. From a simple starting point it had grown into an ever more unmanageable and complex revolutionary leviathan that respected neither authority nor privilege, neither class interest nor even human dignity.

By 1902, the Witte system had become a political liability for autocracy. The peasants had shown their temper by revolting, the workers by staging ever more strikes, the students by joining the workers' demonstrations. The nobility was grumbling; even the business community was dissatisfied. There was ground then to believe that the foundations of the Russian state and society were giving way. In addition, Witte suffered a resounding defeat in foreign policy. He had been a protagonist of economic expansion (and of cautious political expansion as well) in the Far East, partly as a means of bringing business to his costliest project, the Trans-Siberian railroad, partly as proof of Russian participation in the great historical tasks of the imperialist age. By 1902 this expansion had assumed, much to his chagrin, a predominantly political and military character. As such it had run into strong opposition not only from China but also Japan, which even concluded an alliance with Great Britain, likewise an opponent of Russian expansion. In the face of such danger, Witte inevitably favored retreat, which would have amounted to a patent defeat of Russian foreign policy. But the Tsar was unwilling to aggravate the mounting domestic crisis by a humiliation in foreign affairs as well, and in August, 1903, after much soul-searching, he graciously dismissed Witte from the Ministry of Finance.

Whether a failure or not—there is much to be said in its favor on purely economic grounds—the Witte system was the first tentative rehearsal of the major problems of industrialization in Russia. One crucial problem was the tempo of economic growth. At the turn of the century, two alternatives faced the Russian government. Russia's economic growth could either develop at a natural speed, organically, utilizing purely Russian resources, or it could be hastened by recourse to foreign aid. Which was the better course? The question was answered by one of Witte's supporters, the economist Migulin:

> Of course, limiting ourselves to our own resources and working with the help of savings accumulated by our own labor we could proceed more cheaply and gain more lasting results. But time does not wait. Life goes full steam ahead. Even so we are behind all the western countries. And by walking slowly one dòes not go far, our proverb to the contrary notwithstanding. We have to live at a more rapid clip and, whether we want to or not, must resort to the services of foreigners.

The first course meant slow but sound economic growth from the rural base upward. Large-scale industries would be built only when the rural market was ready to support them. The second course called for starting at the top, with exclusive emphasis on industry, particularly heavy industry, and drawing as much as possible on foreign capital and know-how. What ruled out the first alternative, admittedly the more desirable one, was the fact that it did not help Russia catch up to a rapidly moving target. The only hope lay in the other alternative, and what a dim hope it was! (The second alternative, incidentally, suffered from a flaw not previously mentioned. Just when Russia needed foreign aid most, it might not be available because of foreign hostility, the state of world economy, or a number of other reasons.)

The main problem was, of course, the high cost of the Witte system to the Russian people. The bulk of the investment capital for industrialization, so Witte himself admitted, must come out of the living substance of the people. How could the government justify the searing austerity under a program ostensibly aimed at increasing popular prosperity? And more broadly: How could the government sustain the morale of the population (and its own) during the almost interminable hardships, while the gap between Russian poverty and western prosperity remained so

[46]

conspicuous or possibly even widened as a result of the government's effort to catch up? Witte tried a variety of tricks to cope with that question, promising quick results, creating an atmosphere of optimism by a stream of statistics proving the success of his measures, and building up a sense of Russia's world mission.* But how could a poverty-stricken country become a global model? If only he could have prevented the constant comparison with western prosperity and success which made the enforced austerity in Russia so odious to its westernized public!

But there were other insoluble problems. Where, for instance, did the final authority over the goals and methods of industrialization reside, in the government or in private enterprise? Witte's policy was "capitalist" in the sense that the drive and resources of economic modernization were to come out of the business community. He knew that the spontaneous creativity of the peoples of western Europe could only be matched (let alone surpassed) by the fullest release of the same energies in Russian society. For that reason he always deplored the red tape hampering Russian business. On the other hand, he manifested no faith whatever in the business community. Left to their own devices, obviously, Russia's entrepreneurs would never build up Russia's economic strength by the quickest means. If they had done so, there would have been no need for his efforts; Russia would be rich already. Thus Witte imposed his own regulations and pressures, guiding Russia's businessmen along an alien path dictated not by the profit motive but by a *raison d'état* they did not comprehend. His whole experiment (like Russian development in general between the Great Reforms and 1917) suffered from an ingrained paradox. It tried to combine autocracy, which by its essence was authoritarian, with the spontaneity of western society. Witte was not aware of the dichotomy; yet even had he been, what could he have done?

Finally we must touch, as any consideration of industrialization

* With Witte began the official dissemination and radiation of optimism regarding the state of the economy which has become such an essential feature of Soviet leadership under Stalin and Khrushchev.

in recent Russia history inevitably does, on the transcendent problem of political morality. Let us phrase the crucial issue in general terms: To what extent does state necessity, as pleaded by Witte, justify thwarting the will of the majority and violating the integrity of the individual by extreme demands on life, property, and human dignity? Our answer, in this global age, must be a guardedly relativist one.

We must first ask: Who has the moral right to set the standards of political morality? In the United States, and elsewhere in the West, we are apt to judge the affairs of nations from our own experience in countries that have managed, under exceptionally favorable circumstances, to combine freedom for the individual with security and global power for the state. Under these circumstances, we have been able to concentrate our sensibilities and values to an unprecedented degree on the rights of the individual. Less favored countries, on the other hand, have had to recognize the priority of the state (or the group) over the individual. In their political history, external security had to be assured before the individual could be given a free hand. The survival of the group took precedence over the survival of the individual (as is the case in our own military codes).

Each set of political conditions over the long run has created its own moral absolutes. The holiest of American (and western) political convictions center around the dignity of the individual. The equivalent among the less secure countries, one might say, is a searing, adrenalin-releasing impulse of heroism, an all-or-nothing determination to make the community prevail regardless of the life or dignity of its members. Nothing, the spokesmen of this philosophy will argue, could be more degrading than invasion or foreign rule, not even callousness, exploitation, or injustice on the part of their own government; necessity makes hardness into virtue.* Thus continental politics through the ages have preserved a harsh and basically inferior political morality. But lest we judge unfairly and assert our superiority too brazenly,

---

* This attitude, incidentally, is by no means unknown even in the western democracies, particularly in times of crisis.

let us remember that in the history of European power politics the responsibility for this adverse climate of politics in central and eastern Europe has rested rather with those western powers which did manage to combine strength with a measure of freedom for their citizens. Their success threatened their weaker neighbors (unless these were protected by geography or the balance of power—which Russia, like Prussia, was not). In trying to make Russia strong, Witte certainly did not force a new heat of rivalry on the European state system. He merely tried to undergird Russia's position in a patently ever more competitive struggle dominated by the western powers. If for that reason he imposed considerable hardship on an uncomprehending population, was he morally in the wrong? Needless to say, the opposition, guided by the imported western standards, shouted that he was.

So much for the necessity for industrialization. The second and more familiar of the necessities behind the Russian Revolution was the need for greater identity between the ruler and the ruled and between the privileged classes and the peasant masses. The foregoing pages have shown how closely the two necessities were related to each other. Industrialization, in order to be successful, called for a common pull uniting all, government and subjects, high and low. Yet we have also seen how the Witte system achieved the very opposite. By 1903, the relations between the government and the public were headed for crisis. Russian society found itself in a relentless rebellion against autocracy. The economic transformation of the country had speeded the political activation of the populace. Discontent was rife, and thanks to the new mobility the opportunities for discussing and further inciting it were greater than ever. Political programs were being evolved, organizations planned, founded, and even tested in action. All the groups destined to play a significant part in the forthcoming age of revolution had their origin in these years.

While the policy of industrialization had done its share to arouse Russian society and to accentuate its divisions, autocracy remained the chief target of the opposition. The total exclusion of the public from politics, the brutality and arbitrariness of the officials, the lack of freedom of speech or of heterodox religious worship, the constant pressure of Russification on Poles, Finns, Ukrainians, Georgians, and other nationalities—*there* was the real enemy. A broad revolutionary front clamoring for a constitution was in the making. It ran the social gamut from peasants and peasant-workers, religious and national minorities, a variety of professional groups—lawyers, physicians, agronomists, professors, and specialists of all kinds—and industrialists, to landowners active in the zemstvos and the clubs of the nobility. It even included "liberal" sympathizers in the ranks of the bureaucracy. From the start, however, an invisible flaw divided that impressive front: the traditional barrier between the educated on one side and the peasants and peasant-workers on the other. It was reflected in the emerging variety of political organization, in the split between the liberals and the socialists, and, within the latter group, between the moderates and the extremists.

After the turn of the century, the revolutionary forces redoubled their effort in a crescendo of meetings, demonstrations, and strikes, syncopated at times by the assassination of particularly hateful officials. The government replied with more drastic repression and an occasional conciliatory gesture. The combination both embittered and emboldened the opposition. What finally accelerated the disaffection into revolution was the Russo-Japanese war, into which the government had drifted in order to avoid the diplomatic retreat favored by Witte. The Minister of the Interior at the time, V. K. Plehve, at first rejoiced over the diversion: What could be better than "a small victorious war"? He was quickly disillusioned.* One defeat followed another, culminating in May, 1905, in the annihilation of Russian sea power in the Straits of Tsushima. The dreaded discrepancy between Russia's power ambition and its resources was now made manifest to all. It was fortunate that Russia, thanks partly to Witte's skillful negotiations at the Portsmouth peace conference,

* Plehve was assassinated in July, 1904.

had to pay a relatively small price affecting only a distant part of the country. Yet the damage to Russian prestige was profound.

The beginning of the Revolution is commonly dated from Bloody Sunday, January 22, 1905, a revolutionary event only because of what followed, not of what actually happened on that day.* A group of workers and their families set out, with the blessing of some officials, to present a petition to the Tsar. As they approached the Winter Palace, they were cold-bloodedly shot down by rifle fire. Such unwarranted breach of faith shattered the halo of awe still surrounding the Tsar in the minds of the peasants and workers. As the indignation spread throughout the country, the revolutionary surge became irresistible, and the government gradually lost control over the course of events.

The gravest threat to the government emerged from the countryside where the peasants rose in an elemental, anarchic rebellion. But the striking workers in key industries and centers like St. Petersburg and Moscow were hardly less menacing. It was they who prepared the climax of the Revolution in October, when a railroad strike turned into a general strike and brought the government, the economy, and all public services to a complete standstill. At the height of this strike, the workers of St. Petersburg formed a workers' council (or soviet) acting as a central strike committee and also evincing a lively appetite for taking over governmental functions. The most significant aspect of this soviet was that it represented not the broad revolutionary front but only the underprivileged element in Russian society, the peasants and peasant-workers.†

Thus, in October, 1905, in the aftermath of a resounding defeat in foreign policy, the relations between the Tsar and his subjects had come to a complete breakdown.

* All dates are given according to the western calendar.
† The leaders of the St. Petersburg Soviet, however, were revolutionary intellectuals.

IV

THE COLLAPSE OF AUTOCRACY, 1905–1917

★

COMPARED WITH the events of 1789 (or 1792), 1830, or even 1848, the Russian crisis of 1905 hardly merits the term revolution; no new ruler ascended the throne, no power was transferred from one class to another. What occurred was more like a passing squall of bad weather—this was the Tsar's view and not too far from the truth.* A tide of popular rebellion brought the regime to the verge of collapse. But at that very point the government regained the initiative by a timely concession and gradually re-established its authority; within a decade it had retrieved most of its losses. Nicholas II bent under the storm. When the emergency had passed and calm returned, he straightened out again, inwardly unchanged. The insurrections of 1905-1906, one might say in retrospect, never came to a head. They were merely a preparation for the true revolution yet to come. The nature of the tragedy was not finally established, the actors had not rehearsed their parts, and the victim was still too vigorous to be vanquished. The weaknesses of autocracy had to be revealed still more brutally.

The events that stemmed the revolutionary tide were the appointment of Witte as chairman of the newly constituted Soviet (Council) of Ministers, an institution resembling a western cabinet, and—more important—the promulgation at the same time of the October Manifesto, his last great accomplishment. The

* Only the excitement of the Russian intelligentsia transformed into a revolution the events that loosened, however slightly, the leaden rigidity of autocracy.

October Manifesto brought about two things. First, it granted basic civil liberties to all, regardless of religion or nationality; it even legalized political parties. This concession was capped by the creation of an elected legislative body, the Imperial Duma, sitting in the Tauride Palace built by Potemkin, the favorite of Catherine II. Secondly, it split the revolutionary front, reconciling the most cautious elements among the moderates, who had no heart for violence, with a government which promised to end the abuses of autocracy. For a time thereafter, the regime enjoyed a patent measure of support among the propertied classes in town and country, who formed the party called Octobrist.

The suppression of the irreconcilable majority (which included even the run of liberals) proved not so easy. Two years passed before order could be restored. From the start, Witte proceeded hesitantly and without his earlier mastery. Instinctively loyal to autocracy yet recognizing the need for public endorsement, he followed a wavering course. In mid-December he suppressed the St. Petersburg Soviet, yet soon afterwards, at the height of a bloody revolt in Moscow, granted the vote to the industrial workers. Gradually, however, he began to employ the army for quelling the continuing uprisings. It was the army which, in the last analysis, saved autocracy. Despite innumerable cases of mutiny, the discipline and loyalty of the peasant soldiers on the whole still held firm. When the powers of the Duma had been defined in a manner favoring autocracy* and a large loan granted by France made the government financially independent of the new Duma, Nicholas dismissed his first prime minister. Thereafter the government's attitude hardened still further. Under the leadership of a strong Minister of the Interior, P. A. Stolypin, summary measures were taken to put down the embittered violence that still flared up here and there and to punish the earlier misdeeds. As order was restored, the concessions granted at the

---

* It is to be noted that the Tsar laid down the basic laws governing the new constitution. Under these new laws, the Duma shared most of its powers with the State Council, a former administrative body now raised to the position of an upper chamber.

moment of weakness were severely limited. Civil liberties were again curtailed, and after two elections had produced unmanageable majorities, the suffrage of the Imperial Duma was sharply restricted.

The election of the third Duma in 1907, under rules favoring the Octobrists, reflected the equilibrium thus achieved. Now the government had created a Duma pliant enough to accept autocratic leadership. Yet remembering the overwhelming cry for a constitution, the Tsar and his minister for the time being tolerated the necessity of listening to the Duma's speeches and of justifying their actions and expenditures in public. The Duma was not a western parliament; neither was it an obedient sounding board for the government. It forced the ministers to collaborate with a small but important segment of public opinion and at the same time apprenticed the loyal opposition in the intricacies of running the country. The cooperation proved mildly beneficial to both partners. The government was spurred into greater efficiency, particularly in the armed forces, and the public was protected from the worst abuses of arbitrary power. One could almost speak of an aura of good feeling emerging from this partnership. After the revolutionary agitation was fought to a standstill, the Duma, under the leadership of the Octobrists, held the center of the political stage.

The statesman who impressed his personality upon this brief period of stability was Peter Stolypin, Minister of the Interior and soon Chairman of the Soviet of Ministers (1907-1911). He was a man of patent good sense, honest, endowed with amazing physical courage and tremendous capacity for work. He did not, however, possess Witte's insight into the depth of the Russian crisis, nor his vision. He merely thought of his country's needs in terms of agrarian reform and the consolidation of internal cohesion through further Russification. He was thus less controversial in government circles than Witte and less imperious, more capable of inspiring confidence among the various factions. He possessed, in short, the qualities necessary for carrying out the experiment of limited public participation in government. Might he not, in this manner, end the rift between the government and the public?

Stolypin's most signal step toward that goal was peasant reform.* The revision of the peasant order which Witte had vainly tried at the turn of the century was at last made possible by the Revolution. In 1905, the much-vaunted communal order had failed disastrously. Instead of buttressing autocracy it had fomented sedition. So great had been the fear of the *jacquerie* that at the height of the crisis some officials had discussed the expropriation of the nobility's lands in order to appease the peasantry (thus lightly did the sanctity of property sit on their conscience!). Eventually Stolypin adopted a more moderate scheme based largely on Witte's earlier suggestions. Its essence was the creation of a prosperous and conservative element in the countryside composed of "the strong and the sober." Through them, capitalist agriculture was to take root and act as an economic and cultural leaven. For this purpose Stolypin encouraged the change-over from the traditional (and still popular) system of periodic communal redistribution of the land to hereditary landownership. He furthermore facilitated the peasants' withdrawal from the commune, strengthening at the same time the principle of individual ownership by vesting the title to the land in the head of the peasant household (thus wiping out, at the stroke of the pen, the claims of all other members). Finally, Stolypin promoted the formation of consolidated farm plots after, say, the American pattern. Only in this manner was individual farm management with all its advantages made possible. These measures were accompanied by some improvements in the civic status of the peasantry which, however, did not abolish the barriers separating it from "privilege Russia."

The encouragement of individual farming might, in due time, have brought good results. Yet by its very nature it arrived in the countryside only in small driblets of change. Even the withdrawal of households from the commune was a protracted, complex

* In addition he undertook the extension of the zemstvos into provinces hitherto without them.

business; the creation of consolidated plots of land took decades and more to complete. Under these circumstances it was not surprising that by 1915 only slightly more than one half of all peasant households (in European Russia) held their lands in hereditary tenure, and only one tenth had succeeded in forming a consolidated plot of their own. Obviously the bulk of the peasantry was responding but slowly to Stolypin's experiment. Those peasants who managed to set up their own farms were not favored by their less energetic or less fortunate brethren. Opinion both among the peasants and democratically-minded liberals remained hostile, waiting for an opportunity to rescind Stolypin's laws.

On the whole, the years between 1907 and 1914 (and even for a little while longer) were not bad ones for the peasants. Stolypin's reforms and the government's decision to make more land available held out new opportunities. The tax burden was significantly reduced (this had been another of Witte's concessions of 1905); rural cooperatives expanded and introduced some technical improvements; elementary education advanced in the villages, and here and there a glimmer of prosperity and hope appeared.

These were not bad years, either, for the other groups in Russian society. Even under the political restrictions reimposed by Stolypin and his successors, life was somewhat freer than before 1905, the legal security greater. More spontaneity of association was permitted, the area of self-help expanded; more groups gained experience of public affairs. The renewed economic upsurge after 1906, moreover, conferred a visible prosperity on the privileged members of Russian society and some improvement on the masses as well. Industrialization proceeded apace, its tempo being among the fastest in the world. Nor was the economic advance as dependent on the state as it had been in Witte's day, nor as intimately tied to foreign capital and enterprise. Illiteracy was being rapidly eliminated. If plans proceeded on schedule, the authorities predicted there would be enough elementary schools for every youngster by 1922. At the same time the contacts with western Europe were close. Russia contributed freely to the contemporary European fashions in the arts, in literature, and in philosophy. Disregarding the pessimist undercurrent among the intelligentsia, one can agree that these were golden years deserving the nostalgia of those who fled abroad during the subsequent revolutions or of many of those who stayed behind. Seen in this superficial glow, the tsarist regime as reconstituted after 1905 did not deserve its subsequent fate.*

And yet, viewed realistically, next to nothing was accomplished in regard to the basic necessities confronting the country. The political compromise which imparted the air of good feeling had but a feeble foundation. It was never accepted by Nicholas II. At heart he always remained the autocrat, reducing the authority of the Chairman of the Soviet of Ministers, sabotaging the work of a loyal servant like Stolypin lest he himself be eclipsed, and forever urging that the scant prerogatives of the Duma be further whittled away.

Moreover, the quality of Imperial leadership, on which the future still depended, continued to deteriorate. These were the years when Rasputin established himself at court. What could have been more preposterous in the annals of modern government than the ascendancy of this incredible man? A dirty peasant with a stabbing, unforgettable glance, he was propelled into notoriety by his frightening magnetism, both spiritual and physical. Nothing in western experience can make plausible this combination, so paradoxical yet so well authenticated, of saintliness and lechery. He was, indeed, a "holy devil." His debauches were of the grossest nature. They increased as his reputation for saintliness grew at court. The Imperial couple at times worshiped him as a Christ, a Christ in the guise of a muzhik. Yet what proved to them his divinity was not only the spiritual solace he inspired but also his healing power. He was able, according to all witnesses (and there were many), to stop the bleeding of the

* If Imperial Russia had existed by itself, as on an island, its internal evolution might have taken, to be sure, a peaceful turn toward constitutional government. In the absence of the western model, however, it might have equally taken the road of seventeenth-century Poland, which ended in anarchy.

hemophiliac heir to the throne, the Tsarevitch Alexis, for whom medical science had no cure.* Because of this extraordinary gift, Rasputin ingratiated himself with the Empress, who in her Victorian prudery could never see the rot in her idol. Through her, he became a political force. Of the complexity of government and modern society in general he had, of course, no idea. Yet at moments he manifested, as is also authenticated, a simple but penetrating understanding of events bordering on prophecy.

The tale of Rasputin's depravity spread as his influence at court became known. Soon it was the talk of the Duma and the ministers. Yet by 1914 no official dared to press the matter on the Emperor's attention without risking disgrace and dismissal. Every time an honest man spoke out, the Empress prevailed on her husband to go to the limit of his prerogative in order to protect "the holy one." Needless to say, the suppressed scandal festered and helped to alienate even the well-wishers of autocracy. And as the Emperor also invoked the authority of the Orthodox church in Rasputin's behalf, it too was dragged into the mire.

There were other practices supported by the Tsar and the church that boded ill for the future—for instance, the agitation of the Union of the Russian People, or Black Hundreds. It was an organization of reactionaries stirring up, in a manner later made notorious by the Nazis, anti-Semitism and other murky instincts in order to protect an unreconstructed autocracy. Immediately after the promulgation of the October Manifesto, the Black Hundreds set off a wave of pogroms and other riots; subsequently they tried their best to discredit Stolypin. Their political value to autocracy may be doubted. They fired rather than mitigated the hatred for the Tsar among the revolutionaries. And they infused a new ugliness into Russian politics that later was to cost the country dearly.

* The recent volume by R. Massie, *Nicholas and Alexandra,* makes plausible (on good medical evidence) Rasputin's amazing healing power.

Among the revolutionary opposition, of course, the political compromise of the Stolypin era also lacked support. The mass of the population continued in its sullen hostility, even though the revolutionary ardor had cooled for the moment. The peasants had no voice in the Duma; their outlook remained anarchic; it would be decades before Stolypin's reforms would work a change. Besides, the nobility's control of the countryside continued as before. The workers likewise persisted in their enmity. Labor organizations, briefly legalized after 1905, were soon again suppressed. In certain skilled crafts, to be sure, a moderate trade union outlook emerged. But for the majority the link with the village remained intimate and kept the traditional radicalism alive. Besides, the government did not significantly expand its labor legislation. Under these conditions, the militant revolutionaries easily retained their following. As for the moderate opposition, most liberals found themselves excluded from politics and exposed to persecution as well; many of them called for a republic. If one adds to these irreconcilables among the Russian-speaking population the various non-Russian nationalities—Poles, Finns, Ukrainians, and others whom Stolypin resubjected to the odious chicanery of Russification—one can see how dubious were the prospects of the new order. No progress was made in identifying the peoples of Russia with their government.

Even during the quiet years after 1907, violence and strife were never far from the surface. Stolypin himself was assassinated by a revolutionary in the fall of 1911 (with the connivance, it seems, of the reactionaries within the government). The following year a massacre of peaceful strikers at the Lena gold fields revived the latent revolutionary energies. Before the end of July, 1914, the revolutionary agitation reached a new peak, surpassing, in the number of strikes, the turmoil of the entire year 1905. Such events did not bode well for a peaceful evolution of the constitutional experiment, even under normal circumstances.

Nor was any progress made in building up Russia's strength in the competition of the powers, as Witte had urged when he was

Minister of Finance. This competition now loomed ever larger, as Europe headed toward war, a factor often overlooked in the evaluation of this phase of Russian history. It is sometimes argued that, had it not been for Russia's participation in the war, the trend of domestic politics would have issued in a genuine constitutional monarchy and all subsequent catastrophes been avoided—as if the Russian Empire existed in a political void. Nothing could be more fallacious than this naïve assumption, which overlooks the tragic quandary of modern Russian history.

Russia was a Great Power set, as part of its harsh destiny, into the crosscurrents of European and global power politics. No Russian government, regardless of its ideology or class basis, could have abdicated from that role.* Even had it wanted to, it could never have played the part of Sweden, Switzerland, or Belgium, for in eastern Europe the balance of power has never permitted withdrawal into neutrality. Given the political ambitions of Germany and Austria-Hungary, or of Poles, Ukrainians, and other border nationalities within the Empire, the price of passivity in foreign relations was, as events were soon to prove, dissolution, foreign domination, and possible annihilation. Moreover, a power vacuum in eastern Europe and northern Eurasia was not only murderous for Russia but also highly dangerous for the political stability of the entire world. Under any circumstances, war was an inescapable contingency for the peoples of the Empire and their government.

There thus remained no alternative but to play the exhausting game like the other powers, offensively and defensively, as opportunity and Russian resources permitted. No one can accuse the tsarist government of pursuing an extravagant foreign policy before 1914. In the Far East, the disaster of 1905 prompted Russia's withdrawal from the contested area; in the future her

---

* In this respect the position of Russia was unique in modern world history. No other country among those classified as backward—neither nineteenth-century Japan, nor China nor India, not to mention the lesser ones now protected by the stalemate between the USSR and the USA—has had to bear the burden of such an extreme exposure.

policy in that area remained on the defensive. In central Asia, Russian power was stalemated by British power; there was no active contest. Persia was amicably divided into British and Russian spheres of influence; again there was no effort to push farther. A major objective of Russian foreign policy in the Near East, forever in the minds of the Tsar and his advisers, was the control of the Straits of Constantinople. But here again, active expansion was out of the question as long as the Concert of Europe was opposed; the Straits remained a diplomatic, not military, target. The only area in which Nicholas II pursued a mildly active foreign policy after 1905 was the Balkans, where Russia posed as the protector of the small Slavic states against Austria-Hungary and Germany. Still farther west the superior strength of Germany did not encourage any ambition threatening the status quo.

To be sure, like other governments the Tsar and his advisers had their maximum as well as minimum goals in foreign policy. Russia's ruling circles, too, had caught the Imperialist fever. Prince Radolin, the German ambassador, reported from St. Petersburg in 1895, "In everything which I hear they proclaim with one voice that it is Russia's mission to gain in due time the mastery of the world."

At their boldest, the hotheads talked of penetration into the Far East, into Ethiopia or South Africa, or even of unhinging the entire British Empire (a dream popular during the Boer war). Occasionally even an ideological note crept into these far-roaming ambitions. Autocracy was hailed as the spiritual rallying point for all the Asian peoples currently under western domination. In the case of Ethiopia, the Russian interests contained a religious appeal; in the Balkans they stressed the ethnic bonds. Such unlimited schemes, however, were not the sole property of the Russian ruling class. In those years, German statesmen and publicists were toying with equally overreaching plans of world power. They, too, thought of using the anticolonial and anti-western agitation in Asia as a weapon against the British Empire and of building up an African domain of their own. At their boldest they aimed at nothing less than replacing the *Pax Britannica* with German global hegemony. The British, of course—to limit the discussion to these three powers—needed no such fantastic goals. They *were* the dominant global power, the model for the political appetites of all the others. But one need only think of Cecil Rhodes, who is said to have wanted to annex the planets, to see the imperialist megalomania at work even among them.

The comparatively modest objectives of Russian foreign policy (as separate from the dreams) were voiced mostly in the inner circles of the government and shared by only a small segment of the public. The opposition generally denounced the government's foreign policy. Yet whether they admitted it or not, all politically conscious elements among the public paid close attention to the role which their country played in world affairs. In regard to the Balkans, the liberal opposition indeed shared the goals of the foreign ministry, and the Triple Entente (created in 1907) uniting England, France, and Russia as a counterweight to German power was a popular cause among the run of educated Russians.

At the center of Russian foreign policy stood, of course, Russia's relationship with Europe. What a tangle of contradictory interests and necessities it was! In the realm of economics and finance, the government had to consider the fact that central Europe—above all, Germany—was its chief market as well as its chief supplier of manufactured goods and commercial and in-dustrial know-how. The Russo-German trade agreement was for that reason a most crucial factor in Russia's economic growth. France and Belgium, on the other hand, furnished the bulk of Russia's foreign capital needed for the same purpose. Russia's economic dependence on both these partners, needless to say, carried over into diplomacy as well. Here, too, painful contradic-tions prevailed. Dynastic interest tied Russia to Germany and Austria-Hungary. The monarchs of eastern and central Europe were dimly aware that they had to stand together if they did not want to fall separately. The dictates of the European balance of power, on the other hand, tied Russia ever more firmly to the western democracies, a fact which cheered the revolutionaries but dismayed the conservatives.

In this maze of incompatible necessities the calculations of the balance of power finally prevailed. Russia could not advantageously have stayed out of the coming conflict over the emergence of German hegemony. Any advance of German power meant a threat not only to Russia's Balkan position, but, considering Germany's economic and territorial appetite, to its territorial integrity as well. Russia, therefore, had to take sides, regardless of its economic and dynastic interests.

Yet what frightful apprehensions the coming of war evoked! In February, 1914, P. N. Durnovo, a high-ranking official of unimpeachably conservative views, wrote an alarming memorandum outlining the consequences of armed conflict with Germany. He called attention to the "embryonic condition" of Russian industry, to the country's "far too great dependence on foreign industry" (mostly German), to its "technical backwardness," and its "insufficient network of strategic railroads." War, Durnovo prophesied, would bring defeat as in 1905, and defeat in turn bring revolution by the infuriated masses that would sweep all before them.

> The legislative institutions and the intellectual opposition parties, lacking real authority in the eyes of the people, will be powerless to stem the popular tide aroused by themselves, and Russia will be flung into hopeless anarchy, the issue of which cannot be foreseen.

Witte also spoke out, warning that Russia was less prepared for war than in 1904. These realists knew that, however impressive the industrial advance of the previous years had been, it had not in the least remedied the basic discrepancy between Russia's resources and its power status.

Yet one may equally wonder what the consequences would have been if, after the Austrian ultimatum to Serbia in July, 1914, the Tsar had not stood by his moral commitment to the Serbian government which the Habsburg government, with

Germany's full support, now meant to crush. Abandoning a promise of long standing—and one enjoying considerable public approval—would have produced a first-rate diplomatic defeat for Russia and its allies as well. It might very well have escalated the current domestic agitation, already at fever pitch, into another domestic explosion.* It is thus hardly an exaggeration to say that the Imperial government faced a fatal dilemma in late July, 1914. If it chose war, it would inevitably bring about a revolution as a result of the foreseeable defeats. If, on the other hand, it chose peace, the diplomatic defeat might easily provoke revolution immediately. Surely, the domestic crisis in Russia at the eve of the fighting was worse than in any other major power in Europe.†

The course of the war that broke out on August 1, 1914, bore out the forebodings of the realists. No belligerent, to be sure, was ready for the much-prepared clash of arms. The need for adjusting state and society to the exorbitant demands of the front was a grueling test for the body politic of all participants, but particularly so for a deeply divided Russia. Russia also faced an additional handicap, being cut off by the German blockade from its allies and from "Europe" in general. Thus began, at a time of supreme danger, a period of deepening isolation (and isolationism) which has lasted, in essence, to the present. The pressure of European power politics remained in its acutest form, but the uncontrolled western cultural influx which for so long had given Russia its sense of direction now ceased. Henceforth Russia became more Russian than it had been for centuries. The withdrawal from "Europe" had the immediate effect of reducing the country's ability to cope with the current emergency. In the long run, however, it forced the Russian people to solve their crises out of their own fund of ingenuity and temperament. For better or worse, the outbreak of the war ushered in a new phase of Russian history.

* The outbreak of war, indeed, suddenly ended all disorders.

† Oddly enough, the condition of Russia in the summer of 1914 and the relations between foreign and domestic policy at the outbreak of war have not yet been sufficiently clarified by historical investigation.

It was Russia's misfortune to join battle with the most powerful country of Europe (we can disregard here the minor roles of Germany's allies, Austria-Hungary and Ottoman Turkey). The German onslaught took a double form, a military and a political one. At the outset armed force stood in the foreground, as the German armies rolled back their adversaries in an almost constant advance. Within a year Russia lost Poland, in another year the Baltic coast up to Riga. By the end of 1917, the German armies were held in check only by the fact that Germany had to wage war on other fronts as well (which proved, incidentally, the benefit of Russia's alliances). The early retreats of the Russian armies also caused a disastrous breakdown of civil administration behind the front, aggravating the mounting internal difficulties.*

The second onslaught, which became more effective as the war continued, was aimed at the unity of the Russian Empire and at the home front. From the start the German government (following common practice among the belligerents) tried to fan the varied internal discontent among its enemies in order to weaken them from within. In the case of Russia, the disloyalty of Poles, Finns, Ukrainians, Georgians, Jews, Moslems, and of the extreme socialist revolutionaries furnished particularly tempting opportunities. The German war aims, as they unfolded with the victorious advance, capitalized on all centrifugal forces in the Russian Empire. The national minorities of the entire western perimeter from the Baltic to the Caucasus were to be torn from Russia and placed under German protection. What was left of Russia was to be pushed far to the east. If in the meanwhile the Russian revolutionaries could be persuaded to undermine their country's ability to fight, all the better.

The Russian defeats, incidentally, were not caused by cowardice or lack of patriotism. At the outset one found magnificent courage and contempt for death among the Russian soldiers. What was lacking were equipment, supplies, transport, medical care—in short, the industrial and scientific sinews of modern war whose insufficiency Witte had long deplored. Equally wanting

* The only successes scored by the Russian forces were victories over the Austro-Hungarian armies and, in a minor way, over the Turks.

was a sense of modern efficiency and organization in the army command. So appalling was the mismanagement in the early months of the war that the Minister of War, V. A. Sukhomlinov, was removed and eventually tried for high treason.*

The military disasters of the first year of war soon produced two major political calamities on the home front. The news of the retreat gave a spurt to public initiative. Zemstvos, town dumas, and other bodies tried to spur the war effort through the mobilization of industry and the reorganization of the medical service. True to tradition, the government frowned on such spontaneity, although it could not entirely stifle it. The public agitation also revived the opposition in the Duma, in which liberals of all shades now combined to form a coalition called the Progressive Bloc. It demanded that, at this moment of danger, the Tsar confide in his subjects and appoint a government enjoying their confidence. Some of the most capable ministers indeed welcomed such cooperation with the Duma. Yet the Imperial couple, the Empress even more than her husband, turned a deaf ear to these pleas. Thus the fragile compromise of 1907, already weakened before the outbreak of the war, was terminated—which proved, alas, that nothing had really changed.

There was no hope even that Nicholas II would exercise his autocratic prerogatives constructively. The plight of his armies persuaded him, on moral grounds, that his place was at the front. In 1915, he therefore moved to army headquarters, leaving his wife in command at the capital (now renamed Petrograd). This was the second political calamity to befall Russia, for the Empress possessed not a shred of political sense. "Do not laugh at your stupid old wifey," so she reported to him from Petrograd, "but she has on invisible trousers. . . ." She proved that she wore the pants in the Imperial family bv fighting the moderates in the government who advised conciliation with the Duma. "I assure you," she wrote her husband, "I am yearning to show these

* No treason was proved, only mismanagement (and this despite the improvements introduced earlier with the help of the Duma!). A good account of the appalling inefficiency of the Russian army may be found in B. Tuchman's book *The Guns of August.*

cowards my own immortal trousers." In the end it was Rasputin who, behind the scenes, made and unmade the top officials of the Empire, and a corrupt or inept lot they were, just when the country was asked to strain its efforts to the utmost. It was a telling paradox that the government which claimed the most extensive powers in all of Europe should prove least capable of mobilizing its country for total war. Official visitors from England and France were shocked by the contrast between the fierce exertions of their own countries and the slackness of the Russian war effort.

By 1916, the English and French had cause to worry about their Russian ally. The hopelessness of the fighting had begun to undermine the morale of the Russian soldiers; revolutionary slogans were circulating again. The dissatisfaction was greatest in the garrison towns, particularly the capital, where it was augmented by the grievances of the civilian population. The war had never been popular with the peasants. The senseless slaughter for which they furnished the cannon fodder turned them increasingly against it. Nor was it a fighting cause for strikers drafted into service as punishment.* On the home front, too, the backwardness of Russia was taking its toll. Food and fuel were growing scarce, money was losing its value, wages did not keep pace with the rising cost of living. Transportation and domestic trade were breaking down, and public order as well. Petrograd, Moscow, and the great industrial centers were among the places that suffered most. The hardships and the staggering inequalities of sacrifice before long eroded the patriotism manifest in the first months of the war. By 1916, the signs clearly pointed to another storm. In the fall, the police prefect of Petrograd reported that "the hostile feelings have attained a power among the masses which is without precedent, even in 1905-1906."

Yet, contrary to common expectation, the collapse did not come as a result of a mounting revolutionary upsurge. It began almost imperceptibly, at the center of power. By the end of 1916, the Imperial couple had become so estranged from the court and

---

* At the beginning of 1917 the number of deserters was estimated to be 1.5 million.

from the ruling circle, which for the most part had stayed clear of Rasputin, that a palace *coup* was freely advocated, even by members of the Imperial family, as the only salvation for the monarchy. "If it is a choice between the Tsar and Russia, I'll take Russia"—this was the opinion also of the generals in the field. The plans for the forcible deposition of the Imperial couple failed; it took more courage than the titled conspirators could muster. Their only victim was Rasputin, who was murdered in late December. Yet the very idea showed beyond all doubt that Nicholas had wasted every last shred of goodwill which autocracy had ever enjoyed in Russian society. Any casual gust of wind could now smash its hollow pomp.

The portents of these alarms, however, were lost on the Emperor. On January 12, 1917, the British ambassador, Sir George Buchanan, deeply perturbed over the turn of events, tried most tactfully to point out to Nicholas the need for public support. "Your Majesty, if I may be permitted to say so, has but one safe course open to you, namely to break down the barrier that separates you from your people and to regain their confidence."

Whereupon Nicholas drew himself up and, looking hard at the embarrassed diplomat, replied, "Do you mean that *I* am to regain the confidence of my people or that they are to regain *my* confidence?" And this in the age of an aroused and politically awake populace!

Within two months, history pronounced its verdict. On March 7, 1917, the grumblings of women waiting in line before the food stores of Petrograd suddenly flared into a major demonstration. When after two days of ever more rebellious rioting the authorities called on the garrison to defend the regime, the soldiers simply melted away. Late on March 12, the Tsar's orders had ceased to command in Petrograd and within a few days also throughout the Empire. On March 15, sitting in his train at Pskov, the headquarters of the northern armies, he meekly signed his abdication to the emissaries of the Duma group which now claimed power.

Autocratic government as conducted by Nicholas II in the tradition of the Romanovs had been found wanting. It had not given the Russian people the leadership which they needed in either peace or war. But more than autocracy stood condemned: the entire hybrid system, in effect since the 1860's, of autocratic leadership combined with a limited and forever suspect volume of private and nongovernmental public initiative. Neither singly nor supported by a halfhearted measure of public spontaneity had autocracy been able to provide the country with the strength and cohesion required at the moment of supreme peril. The future would decide what other system would work, whether spontaneity unhampered as in the western democracies, or a revitalized and ever more totalitarian autocracy.

V

THE TRAINING OF THE HEIRS

✪

IN ORDER to emphasize the fact that the tsarist regime collapsed under the strain of war—and collapsed, furthermore, from within rather than under revolutionary assault—this essay has said little so far of the opposition groups which in March, 1917, conjointly inherited the responsibilities of government. Yet ready they were, with programs, ambitions, and leaders, the product of a long and often raw apprenticeship dating back several generations.

The revolutionary opposition grew out of the intelligentsia, a typical by-product of the outpouring of western European civilization into Russia, a group without parallel in the West but common enough among the underdeveloped countries. It bore the brunt of the encounter between Russia and "Europe." Its mission was to transmit cultural stimuli from the West and to relate them as best it could to native conditions. In its ranks one could potentially find all educated Russians regardless of their social origin, for education in itself meant westernization, and westernization demanded that Russians see themselves in relation to "Europe." More specifically, the term intelligentsia stood for the elite that devoted itself fervently to finding answers for the manifold questions raised by the confrontation. Its members were ingrained ideologists, thinkers without self-evident native truths searching for sound foundations in comprehensive theories of historical development (all borrowed from the West). These theories were a matter of life or death to those who held them, to be defended fiercely and intolerantly against friend or foe.

As Toynbee remarked, "Intelligentsias are born to be unhappy." Forever suspended between the "ideal," derived from the philosophies of western Europe (usually the more extravagant ones), and the "real," which denoted the sordidness of Russia, the Russian intelligentsia (like its counterparts elsewhere) was a profoundly tragic group. It belonged neither to the West nor to Russia. In its isolation it sought solace in extreme visions of human happiness. Nothing less, it seemed, would satisfy its longings than utopia realized. In its misery it also felt a strong kinship with other outcasts: peasants, workers, and all suffering and alienated humanity. This theme, introduced by Belinsky in the 1840's, became one of the leitmotifs of Russian literature. None knew human misery so deeply as the Russian writers.

The intelligentsia's halfway position between Russia and "Europe" accounted for several congenital incongruities in its outlook. For instance, it displayed a double reaction to western influences. On the one hand, instinct prompted imitation of the superior norms of the West and the patterning of Russia's future after the western model (viewed most often in idealized form). Considering the continuous and all-comprehensive superiority of Western Europe, this was the dominant reaction. In Russian literature one meets a tragicomic witness of this penchant, the ardent disciple of every latest fad in European thought who never arrived at any independent views. On the other hand, an almost equally strong instinct, also mobilized by the western example, bade Russian intellectuals safeguard their native inheritance and the sovereignty of spontaneous and original creativity. They wanted a *Weltanschauung* all their own. This second tendency, called Slavophile, extolled, often in blithe disregard of fact, the Slavic genius over an inferior western one. Or, in a more reasonable mood, it favored the organic reconstruction of Russian life out of existing institutions (whatever they were at the moment) over a continual rash borrowing from abroad. Russia, the Slavophiles said, had to go its own way. The split between the occidentalists, who thought of Russia's future in terms of western development, and the Slavophiles was all pervasive. It ran crosswise through all political points of view.* Yet it was never final.

* It added a source of dissension not found in European politics. The conservatives were split among westernizers and Slavophiles; so were the liberals and socialists—as if there had not been schisms enough!

The same person might hold one or the other view at different times in his life or even both at the same time in regard to separate aspects of Russian tradition. One could hardly be Slavophile, after all, in matters of military technique, literacy, or sanitation.

The ambivalence appeared in still another form, as a love-hate relationship to the West. It was love, for the West gave the Russian intellectual his distinction in Russian society, his skills and his sense of direction. Yet there was also bitter hatred, for the West constantly humiliated him. He was a borrower, not a contributor of equal standing. Whichever emotion seemed to be on his mind's surface at the moment, its twin was never far below.

Whether viewed with love or hate, the West shook the intelligentsia's self-esteem to the depths. As compared with a Frenchman or Englishman—although perhaps not with an almost equally touchy American of the mid-nineteenth century—the Russian intellectual wore his ego on his sleeve. Yet his sensitivity also sharpened his perception. Better than those Europeans, he could see the built-in, necessary arrogance of western society. As Dostoevsky, who knew well the agonies of the Russian intelligentsia, enviously observed:

> Every great people believes and must believe if it intends to live long that in it alone resides the salvation of the world, that it lives in order to stand at the head of the nations, to affiliate and unite all of them, to lead them in a concordant choir toward the final goal preordained for them.

No Russian intellectual could rise to such magnificent self-confidence. Neither was he allowed to share vicariously in the glory of the prouder peoples. Dostoevsky's characterization of this predicament, written in 1877, a year of international crisis, is worth pondering:

> The Europeans did not want to recognize us as their own despite anything, despite any sacrifices—under any circumstances. This meant *grattez le Russe et vous verrez le Tartare* [scratch a Russian and you will find a Tartar]. And thus it

stands to the present. Among them we became proverbial. The more to please them we despised our nationality, the more they despised us. We wriggled before them, subserviently we professed our "European" opinions and convictions, and they haughtily did not listen to us, and usually added with a polite smile—as if seeking to get rid of us as quickly as possible—that "we did not properly understand them." Specifically, they were surprised at the fact that we, being such Tartars . . . utterly failed to become Russians, whereas we never were able to explain to them that we sought to be not Russians but cosmopolitans. True, of late they managed to understand something. They came to realize that we want something which they fear and which is dangerous to them. They grasped the fact that there are many of us, eighty million, and that we know and comprehend all European ideas, while they do not know our Russian ideas, and that, should they ever come to know them, they would not understand them, that we speak all languages, while they—only their own. Well, they began to surmise and suspect also many other things. It came to the point where they directly called us enemies and the future destroyers of European civilization. This is how they understood our passionate aim to become cosmopolitan.

Yet Dostoevsky did not think of conquest as the balm for injured pride. Drawing on the deep religious undercurrent in Russian thought, he wanted Russia "to become cosmopolitan." As he wrote in 1880:

The Russian destiny is incontestably all-European and universal. To become a genuine and all-round Russian means, perhaps, . . . to become brother of all men, a universal man, if you please. . . . Our destiny is universality acquired not by the sword, but by the force of brotherhood and our brotherly longing for fellowship of men. . . . To become a genuine Russian means to seek finally to reconcile all European controversies, to show the solution of European anguish in our all-humanitarian and all-unifying Russian soul, to embrace in it with brotherly love all our brethren and finally, perhaps, to utter the ultimate word of great, universal harmony, of

the brotherly accord of all nations abiding by the law of
Christ's Gospel.

In this vision Dostoevsky, however, was by no means original.
In the face of the French Revolution, German thinkers long ago
had claimed a superior spiritual role for their nation. Under
English domination, Vivekananda, as cited earlier, similarly tried
to rally the Indian intelligentsia. It was a natural reaction of
humiliated idealists to glorify the spiritual gift of their people as
the instrument of universal salvation. Yet as the German descent
from *Weltbürgertum* to *Nationalstaat,* from the lofty cosmopolitanism of a Goethe to the *realpolitik* of a Bismarck, had already
proven, pure spirituality carried little weight in modern politics.
Russian thought and practice followed the same downward
spiral, as we shall shortly see.

Most Russian intellectuals, while always keenly sensitive to
Russian prestige abroad, were not concerned with Russian might.
Power politics was part of the hated reality from which they
hoped to escape. They dreamed of transforming their country
into a paragon of social justice and human happiness, where
swords were wrought into plowshares. It was this ideal which
carried them forward into revolution.

The revolutionary impulse in Russia had a long history. It was
born, one might say, late in the eighteenth century when educated Russians began to observe the divergence of Russian conditions from the ideal norm derived from the West. When the
differences deepened, as they did in the course of the nineteenth
century, and when the tsars permitted no public discussion of
them, the revolutionary movement waxed stronger. In any comparison the Russian realities stood condemned, foremost the tsar
and his bureaucracy, but also all official Russia, including the
church. But how to change the regime?

It could never be done, so the great majority of those who
wanted a better Russia agreed, by the liberal prescription of persuasion, debate, and majority vote. Even if liberalism had fitted
the emotional needs of an alienated intelligentsia (or, in a larger
sense, the conditions of Russia), autocracy ruled it out with an

iron fist. "All constitutional change," so Count D. A. Tolstoy, the Minister of the Interior, said in 1884, "must be reconciled with the basic foundation of state order—the absolute Imperial power." To the end, the very word "constitution" remained *non grata.* What liberal tendencies survived under persecution (until easier conditions came to prevail after 1905) did so in the wide and dim border between legality and illegality, a well-meaning but ineffectual force devoted more to cultural enlightenment (for which there was always great need) than to political conquest.* Thus the good-natured rationalism and procedure-mindedness with which liberalism might have smoothed the course of social and political change just when the tempo of change was fastest possessed no roots in Russian life.

Russia could be transformed, so the futility of liberalism showed, only by illegal and revolutionary methods. This was the creed of the revolutionary intelligentsia that emerged after the Crimean war. Its revolution, however, was no longer concerned with limited political objectives. The new revolutionaries were socialists aiming at a profound social and moral regeneration in the body politic. Their extravagant visions were matched by their gigantic capacity for moral indignation expressed in terms borrowed from church Slavonic rather than western idiom. Inspired by the loftiest ideals, they constantly knocked their heads against the inhumanity of Russian life without finding legitimate remedies for their hurts.

The clash between the "ideal" and the "real" nearly always involved the powers that be. Rebellion might start at home, particularly where discipline was harsh. It always found ample opportunity at school, often amounting to a veritable war between pupils and teachers. It came to climax at the universities or technical institutes, where youthful exuberance ran strongest and the restrictions were most galling. The worst hotbeds of revolution were probably the theological seminaries, where authority was buttressed by religion. But the rebellion did not stop there.

* One need but read Saltykov-Shchedrin's brief story "The Liberal" (available in English), in order to observe the futility of liberalism in the Russian setting.

Behind a provoked father, teacher, priest, professor, or dean always loomed the policeman or the Cossack acting for the tsar. The chain of authority all too easily transformed juvenile defiance into treason. The Russian rebels were joined by others from the suppressed religious or national minorities for whom the contrast between ideality and reality was still more revolting. Considering the senseless brutality in which the authorities occasionally indulged, the boundless moral indignation of all these idealists might well soar to an immoral and nihilist intensity.

Experience showed that political action was possible only through illegal organization; the revolutionaries had to go underground. Those who chose this calling—both men and women, often of the best families—led a dismal but exciting life. Their careers followed a common pattern. They were hunted by the police. When captured they were imprisoned for long terms often without trials, interrogated until they betrayed their secrets, and sentenced to exile in Siberia where loneliness and isolation undermined body and mind. Some were executed. In order to endure in his calling, the revolutionary had to become hard.

> Promise [so a revolutionary organization addressed its members in 1878] to dedicate all your spiritual strength to the revolution, give up for its sake all family ties and personal sympathies, all loves, all friendships. If necessary give up your life without regard for anything and without sparing anything or anybody. Do not keep any private property, anything that is not at the same time the prosperity of the organization of which you are a member. Give all yourself to the secret society, give up your individual will. . . .

Besides steeling and depersonalizing himself, the idealist conspirator had to master all the dirty tricks of his craft: forgery, theft, deceit, betrayal, even murder. As Chernyshevsky, a revolutionary who left a deep impression on Lenin, wrote in 1862, "A man with an ardent love of goodness cannot be but a sombre monster." Thus the highest spiritual ends were wedded to the basest means.*

* This Russian philosopher Berdyaev has argued, with much force, that this revolutionary asceticism represents an inverted (or perverted)

The Russian revolutionaries have often been reproached for this unholy combination. Yet it was hardly of their free choice. It was the regime which drove any determined and idealist opposition underground, the policeman who apprenticed the amateur rebel in the arts of conspiracy. The secret police agent found his counterpart in the professional revolutionary. Indeed, between the two an oddly intimate relationship sprang up which made their roles almost interchangeable, as some notorious cases of men serving both causes were to prove. Of the two, the revolutionary was the more heroic, a martyr who served mankind under the most treacherous conditions; no wonder he sometimes flinched and surrendered. He had many admirers in Russian society, particularly among the youth. And he never lacked disciples.

To most Americans, of course, the fusion of idealism with criminality, of the highest ends with the most sordid means, is as repugnant as the mixture of the saint and the sinner is Rasputin.* Ends and means, to be sure, rarely interlock even in the best political system. In the Russian revolutionary tradition, however, they were eternities apart—just as in the Russian government which so often had tried to civilize the country by the knout. The professional revolutionary, the overbearing *chinovnik,* the war between ends and means—all these were but symptoms of the

form of a deep-seated Russian religious ideal, a medievalism turned modern and secular against its will.

* Since this sentence was written, a small but significant number of American youths have traversed the same gulf between ends and means, often consciously patterning themselves after the Russian revolutionaries. And a larger number of American youths apparently agree that their state and society are repressive, with but little difference remaining in their eyes between American democracy and Tsarist autocracy.

These new convictions, they argue, arise out of a novel perception of reality in the global world in which the United States and western Europe have lost their universal appeal, partly as a result of the revolution that is being traced in this book. We cannot, however, understand that revolution without sticking to the older view that stressed the difference between western liberal society and Russian society. Just ask the average educated Russian of the years before 1917 (and a few of them survive to this day), where freedom was to be found. Even Lenin in those years respected, and took advantage of, the freedom provided by liberal democracy.

same Russian disease of backwardness and of the struggle against it. They marked both autocracy and revolution.

One should not assume, however, that in the revolutionary movement (or in autocracy, for that matter) the extreme was the rule. The majority of Russian youths in the institutes of higher learning, while opposition-minded and sometimes toying with sedition, did not join the outcasts. Even among those who did, many eventually lived abroad, thinking revolution rather than carrying it into action. Or, if they remained in Russia, they preferred tilting with the censor to battling with the police. Much of Russian literature carried revolutionary overtones. And the revolutionary intelligentsia was forever haunted by the "accursed question": What is to be done? Revolution, so incessant failure taught the underground movement, required not only activists; it needed theorists as well. It could succeed only if it had a sound program and a proper underpinning of revolutionary strategy and tactics in the Russian setting. How could a small band of revolutionaries, no matter how dedicated, overthrow the autocratic leviathan and create from Russian realities a haven of justice, prosperity, and peace?

Since no industrial labor force worth mentioning existed until the 1890s, it was natural that the revolutionaries should think in terms of the peasantry. For centuries, the peasants had been an endemic revolutionary force. In their commune furthermore, so Alexander Herzen taught a whole generation of intellectuals in the 1860s and 1870s who called themselves *narodniks,** lay the seed of the future socialist society. The commune kept private property, capitalism, and all the evils of industrialism out of the village. Hence Russia could be spared the spiritual and material corruption which, according to socialist theory, they caused. Once autocracy was overthrown, the peasants would build, from the grass roots up, a new type of society embodying their deep spiritual wisdom (which most intellectuals worshipped from a distance).

The task of the professional revolutionaries, according to a

* The *narodnik* movement was the most influential revolutionary force before the advent of the Marxists in the 1890s.

school of thought led by Bakunin, was to heat the peasant dis-content to the explosion point and then to let matters take their course until autocracy, the church, and all the other trammels of established authority had been destroyed. The best society, they proclaimed, was that in which no government existed at all and the people settled their affairs by their own local arrangements. Anarchism (in this or milder form) understandably had a power-ful appeal to those who suffered from a highly centralized state. It was deeply ingrained in the revolutionary movement as well as in the peasant mind.

Unfortunately almost all who carried the revolutionary agita-tion into the village soon discovered that it was impossible to establish a working relationship with the peasants; the gulf be-tween peasant Russia and "privilege Russia" stood also in the way of the revolutionaries. How could it be bridged? The more patient revolutionaries began to devote themselves to humble cultural work among the peasants in order to mend the fatal rift. The impatient ones experimented with terror as a means of shocking the people into rebellion in order to unhinge autocracy. For over two years (1879-1880) a wave of assassination, di-rected against the most hated officials, swept the country. It culminated in the murder of Alexander II in 1881. Yet when the bomb exploded under the autocrat, autocracy as an institu-tion did not even tremble.

This failure, which chastened the revolutionary movement for years, lent support to those few theorists who had never put their faith in the people. A small elite of professional revolutionaries, they argued, should seize power in the name of the masses and hold it in trust until society had been prepared for the benefits of socialism. They did not believe, in other words, that the spon-taneous actions of the peasants held any promise for the future. What counted was organization and the ardor of the revolu-tionary elite.

Whatever the numerous experiments of revolution during the second half of the nineteenth century, none had any result except slowly to refine the infamy of political warfare between the police and the opposition. The great advance in the revolutionary movement came only after the turn of the century. The era of mass politics began, even in Russia, offering new opportunities for revolution (without, however, resolving the old problems of theory or practice). At the end of the Witte system, as we have seen, the bulk of the population had become politically activated as never before. This, for the first time, provided the revolutionary circles with a potential mass following. The relaxation of autocratic power after 1905, moreover, permitted a much larger volume of publicity and agitation. In the Imperial Duma there existed even a public forum, if only for the legal opposition. The new opportunities—and the vigorous models of liberal democracy in France, England, and the United States—prepared the way at last for an active liberal movement. A late comer, it was yet held by common consent to be the natural heir to autocracy, and it eclipsed for a time the older revolutionary tradition.

Twentieth-century Russian liberalism drew its native strength from two small but influential groups, the advanced elements of the landowning nobility which had long called, through the zemstvos, for some form of central parliament, and the growing element of a new and more substantial intelligentsia—a middle-class intelligentsia—composed of lawyers, doctors, teachers, professors, and the like who played a crucial part in the modernization of Russia. In the course of the Revolution of 1905 these two groups merged in the party of the Constitutional Democrats (Cadets). Their most forceful leader was Paul Miliukov, who had made a reputation as a historian before he ventured into politics. In the Duma or at its sidelines he became the leading parliamentary tactician steeped in English precedent. His program called for a liberal democratic regime, under either a republic or a constitutional monarchy—the party could never decide which, until the Romanovs were ousted—with a strong social orientation like that of Lloyd George or Clemenceau. The Cadets believed in the sanctity of private property and in individual enterprise, but they also favored a measure of social regulation, provided it was imposed by parliamentary procedure and hedged in by due process of law. Open-minded toward the wishes of other groups, they insisted above all on legality in public action and, by implication at least, on the leadership of the educated few. They were ready to cooperate with the revolutionary underground, realizing that the overthrow of autocracy called for a broad political front; yet they themselves eschewed violence. Many of them indeed feared the anarchism of the Russian masses. Their ends and means were to be cut from the same cloth. Their most congenial stage was therefore the Duma (despite its restricted suffrage), not the street.

Although opposed to autocracy, the Cadets were still nationalists in moderation. They thought of Russia as a Great Power carrying out its historic mission as protector of the Slavic peoples and playing a proud role in Europe and the World. A liberal regime, they expected, could do this much better than the benighted autocracy. In politics admittedly they were content to let their country be a follower of western development rather than a leader in its own right. But in science, art, and above all in literature, they were proud of what Russia had already accomplished.

These complacent perspectives made optimists of the Cadets. The natural course of political evolution, as demonstrated by western Europe, would inevitably prepare their ascent to power, an assumption which called for neither extensive inquiry into the suitability of democratic government for Russian conditions* nor elaborate organizational preparation.

Looking back in March, 1917, the Cadets might indeed conclude that history was going their way. Despite setbacks, the liberal current had run strong since 1905. Russia was allied with a democratic England and France against German militarism and reaction. In the Progressive Bloc of 1915, Miliukov and his party had assumed the leadership over the entire opposition in the Duma, including the bulk of the Octobrists. Miliukov's Duma speeches of 1916 had helped more than anything else to undermine what public confidence the government still enjoyed. Now

* Only after the failure of Russian liberalism did Miliukov, the historian, analyze its weaknesses. He found them in the fatal gulf between the educated minority and the peasant masses (as does its essay).

that autocracy was dead, who but the liberals had the necessary experience in public affairs to take over the government? Would they also have the necessary mass support? When they began to think about ways and means, they became sadly frustrated and divided. This was most obvious during the war. Could autocracy mobilize Russia for victory? No. Were the liberals then to do away with autocracy? No, for revolution in time of war would bring out the worst instincts of the rabble. When it came to the prospect of government by the Russian people, Miliukov essentially thought like Durnovo or Witte. He was condemned to stand by passively.

As the Duma liberals and their allies in the Progressive Bloc gathered on March 12 when the rebellion in Petrograd was at its height, their offices in the right wing of the Tauride Palace remained ominously silent and empty. The din of insurrection centered in the left wing of the building, where soldiers and workers were forming the Soviet of Workers' and Soldiers' Deputies. Frightened by their isolation, the liberals hurriedly proclaimed a Provisional Government to hold power until the meeting of a democratically elected Constituent Assembly, lest power slip into less competent hands.* Thus, at the moment of its triumph, liberalism was challenged by the older and more radical revolutionary groups, the Social Revolutionaries (SR) and the Social Democrats (SD), each considering itself a more appropriate spokesman for the will of the people which now had become tsar.

The Social Revolutionaries were the heirs of the *narodnik* movement and of the revolutionary organizations of the previous century. Constituted as a political party shortly after 1900, the SR possessed a core of professional revolutionaries—for a time it even boasted a "maximalist" terrorist faction—yet it suffered by constant persecution and lost its best leaders. The relative freedom of agitation after 1905 diversified the membership. It was not easy for Victor Chernov, the surviving leader of stature (who by nature was no leader), to hold together the moderates,

---

* Miliukov at this point vainly tried to create a constitutional monarchy under the Romanov dynasty.

who differed little from the liberals, and the impatient radicals who pressed for Black Partition.

By its principles, the party was pledged to obey the will of the toiling people, i.e., of the peasants. No one could deny that the Social Revolutionaries knew their rural Russia. After 1905, peasants and intelligentsia were no longer so far apart as in the previous century. The SR program voiced their common aims. Once autocracy was overthrown, it stated, the reconstruction of Russian society was to proceed spontaneously, rising from the village to higher organs of government and culminating in a federal center. The same preference for decentralization, incidentally, also applied to their party organization, which, as a result, always remained loosely knit and ineffectual.

The democratic principle was carried over into economic life. If the peasants wanted the land, so the Social Revolutionary program said, all land was to be theirs, without compensation to former nonpeasant owners. Yet the title to the land was to be held "socially" (whatever that meant in terms of law—the concept of private property was to be kept out of Russia). Each peasant household was to cultivate with its own resources as much land as it could, aided by whatever cooperative ventures it might wish to join. Nothing, however, was to violate the basic rule of equality in peasant society.

The Social Revolutionary party, it has been said, represented a state of mind rather than a program. It suffered from the vagueness typical of all efforts to rebuild Russia from the peasant base upward. How, for instance, could the regional differences of income caused by different climate and soils be equalized without the intervention of a strong central authority? What, furthermore, of the peasant commune condemned by Stolypin—should it be resurrected or allowed to disappear? And what of industry? Most Social Revolutionaries were willing to let private enterprise in that branch of the economy continue for an indefinite period. They subordinated industry to agriculture, presuming that it would develop only as the countryside prospered.

Nor could the Social Revolutionaries explain how peasant Russia might preserve its sovereignty in the power competition of an imperialist age. One writer in the *narodnik tradition,* S.N. Iuzhakov, had touched on this issue in the 1890s. In a discussion of the contemporary division of the world by the capitalist powers, he suggested that by nature Russia was predestined to lead the world-wide revolt of the pre-industrial societies against their capitalist exploiters. But nothing had come of this thought. Preoccupied with peasant Russia, the Social Revolutionaries did not think in terms of power politics. They complacently followed the common socialist belief in the international solidarity of the toilers which, after the revolution, would permanently end all power conflicts. During the war they remained on the sidelines, neither wholeheartedly supporting the war nor condemning it.

When their opportunity came in March, 1917, the Social Revolutionaries reaped the benefits of their long agitation among the peasants. The Petrograd Soviet, composed largely of soldiers who were but peasants in uniform, gave them a clear majority. If numbers were to decide the succession to autocracy, the party of the peasants would certainly be the chief heir.

In everything but numbers, however, the Social Democrats had a clear advantage over the Social Revolutionaries, chiefly because they drew on the infinitely greater intellectual vigor of Marxism.* Marxism had much to offer to Russian revolutionaries. Perhaps its greatest attraction was the imposing scope, the magnificent presumption of a philosophical system based on a knowledge of the "scientific" laws of history. Here at last the Russian intelligentsia found the comprehensive ideology for which it had been yearning, and one, moreover, which lifted it, as on the wings of religion, from despondency to the gates of omnipotence and fulfillment. What spoke especially to their condition as revolutionaries was the fact that Marxism made the industrial proletariat the preordained vehicle of social and human regeneration. Throughout the nineteenth century, the Russian peasantry had failed to heed the revolutionaries' call. Marx taught his Russian followers to take the workers as their com-

* This is not to deny that the Social Revolutionaries had also read Marx. Yet they had not absorbed the analytic rigor and the deliberate modernism of the Marxists.

rades in arms. The Marxist appeal to the Russian intelligentsia was greatest of all in the 1890s, when the growing volume of strikes first called attention to the workers' political potential.

The revolutionary comradeship with the proletariat suited, moreover, the intellectuals' spiritual need for identification with suffering humanity. They were carried away by the expectation of a socialist (or communist) society in which, for the first time in all history, man would be truly man and master of his destinies. At the same time Marx' emphasis on the strife and ruthlessness of the class struggle responded to the fighting mood of men and women harassed by daily persecution. It cheered them, too, for through Marxism they saw themselves glorified in a great historical tradition running from the French Revolution to the deliverance of mankind from evil.

When it first became a force among the Russian intelligentsia, Marxism expressed the temper of the times. Industrialization was making rapid strides in Russia; it was the wave of the future. Unlike the *narodniks* and their Social Revolutionary successors, the Marxists were modernists, at least in part. They welcomed the cultural advance that came with the rise of large-scale industry. Yet at the same time they continued the *narodniks'* moral aversion to the evils of industrialism, saying that those flaws were merely the result of "capitalism."* They would disappear after the socialist revolution, when large-scale production and the perfection of society would combine to produce an earthly paradise. In short, the Marxists could have their cake and eat it too (or so they thought).†

* Since the term "capitalism" and "capitalist" have all but lost their meaning, I have put them into quotation marks to indicate that they are employed in the Marxist sense.
Western society has long ceased to be "capitalist," if it ever was (even in Marx' day the term was but a caricature of reality, like "the economic man"). What Russian Marxists understand by this term owes its ascendancy not to the profit motive but to a complex mixture of individual, collective, and governmental initiative in which personal and public profit is curiously interlaced and egotism and altruism overlap or even coincide with each other.
† It should be noted that the anticapitalist bias in Russian Marxism catered to the same hostility to urban-industrial society which had also cropped up in Germany, Austria, and other more highly developed

As the Russian intellectuals steeped themselves in Marxism, however, it became clear that their creed, so largely based on western European precedent, did not readily fit Russian realities. The exact location of their Russia in the Marxist chart of history was—and still is, to Soviet historians—a tough theoretical problem. Autocracy, Marxists would agree, was a feudal rather than a bourgeois institution. Russian capitalism was still weak. Marxism thus might seem to require that its followers first strive for a capitalist Russia—a preposterous suggestion; to a Russian Marxist the rise of "capitalism" in Russia always signified the rise of the proletariat as a revolutionary force and a step toward socialism. They were always one step ahead of history.

Russian Marxists thus could not, as this shift in emphasis implied, strictly subscribe to the laws of dialectics as laid down by Marx. This was made clear—unwittingly, no doubt—from the outset. As Plekhanov, the father of Russian Marxism, wrote in one of his early tracts (1883) concerning the role of the individual in Marxist philosophy:

> For us the freedom of the individual consists in the knowledge of the laws of nature, and in an ability to submit to these laws, that is, among other things, to combine them in the most advantageous way.

The freedom to submit and not to submit to the laws of nature (or of history) attracted most strongly the revolutionary activists over the protest of the orthodox Marxists. But, after all, had this not been one of the freedoms of Marx himself?

And was the proletariat to be tool or master of the revolutionary intelligentsia? Seasoned Marxists answered that naturally the proletariat fashioned its own mentality (or "consciousness," according to their lingo) and thus shaped its destiny. The revo-

---

countries. But by contrast with the Sorels and Spenglers (who took industrial production for granted), the Russian Marxists regarded industrialism with awe and envy. The combination contained *in nuce* what later in this essay is called the paradox of the Bolshevik Revolution, which promised greater fulfillment to man yet imposed far more drastic controls than had prevailed in the past.

lutionary intelligentsia merely acted as a vanguard which took its orders and its very outlook from the main force. Yet would the revolutionary hotspurs be willing to mark time if the "consciousness" of the proletariat was not ready for either revolution or socialism? And was its "consciousness" ever to be trusted? These doubts led to a spate of further questions regarding the relationship between the vanguard and the main host, the character of leadership, the timetable for revolution, and innumerable details of strategy and tactics.

In the bitter disputes that arose over these issues, two distinct points of view emerged, the "soft" and the "hard." Both were advanced by revolutionaries familiar with the vicissitudes of their calling. For years the difference was one of emphasis and inclination, not of fundamentals. Only gradually did the rift ripen into schism. By 1912 the breach was complete, by 1917 it was irrevocable.*

The "softs" inclined toward the liberal-humanitarian strains in Marxism. They were willing to listen to the views of the industrial workers (but never of the peasants!) and to adjust themselves to their spontaneous activities. They cheered when the workers formed the St. Petersburg Soviet in 1905. For the same reason they preferred a party structure allowing a maximum of mass participation, after the model of the German Social Democratic party. They looked forward to the day when all their work could be legal. Necessity drove them underground, but they never felt comfortable with the conflict of ends and means which ensued; they shrunk from fanaticism. Since in their estimate Russia was not ready for socialism—it would come to Russia only after it had been achieved in the West—they leaned toward patience and tolerance. Their goal was the overthrow of autocracy and the establishment of a liberal-democratic regime with a strong labor party and a powerful trade union movement. This called for an alliance with liberalism and for continued close ties with

---

* Among the rank and file, however, the split was not final until May–June, 1917. Many simple workers indeed never understood its reasons; they often resented it.

western Europe, to which the spokesmen of this faction looked with genuine admiration and where some of them, like Plekhanov, felt rather at home. Under special conditions there might even be need to support the existing autocratic government. This was Plekhanov's attitude after the outbreak of war.

The "soft" position was generally adopted by the faction called Menshevik (the minority), so named after an entirely unrepresentative ballot at a party congress in 1903, when it had lost out to the "hards." With a quick eye for the propaganda advantage, the latter forever thereafter hailed themselves as Bolsheviks (the majority), although in fact the Mensheviks always had a larger following right down to March, 1917, when they formed the second largest faction in the Petrograd Soviet.

The "hard" position was the creation of Vladimir Ilich Ulianov (1870-1924), better known as Lenin, one of the great political figures of the twentieth century. From western and native sources he fashioned the first great western antiwestern movement, with a style suited to the temper of the outer marches of the urban-industrial West.

Historical evidence has as yet found no trait in the Ulianov family that need have pushed their two eldest sons into the revolutionary movement. As a supervisor of schools in the chief towns of the lower Volga region, Lenin's father had risen high in the ranks of the Imperial bureaucracy, advancing even into the hereditary nobility. If his sons turned rebels after his death it was, presumably, because of the discrepancy between their humanitarian ideals, innocuously—and perhaps too ardently—cultivated in their home, and the harsh reality of the autocratic regime. For his protest, Lenin's older brother soon paid with his life. While a student at the University of St. Petersburg he took part in a plot against the Tsar's life and was executed in 1887. His fate committed the younger boy to the same cause.

In constant trouble with the authorities from the start of his university studies, Lenin was trained as a lawyer. In 1893 he moved to the capital and at once immersed himself in the revolutionary agitation among the factory workers, who welcomed the solicitude of the intelligentsia (although not necessarily their revolutionary extremism).* In a short time he assumed a position of respect in the Marxist circles. Inevitably the police began to take notice, and in December, 1895, he found himself arrested. Sentenced after some delay, he was exiled to a village in the depths of Siberia, whence he called himself Lenin, presumably after the river Lena (although he had been sent no further than the Yenissei). Neither jail nor exile diminished his prodigious capacity for work. Barred from all revolutionary action, he wrote an impressive scholarly tome on *The Development of Capitalism in Russia* and translated Sidney and Beatrice Webb's volume on trade unionism, not to mention many pamphlets, articles, and letters. In Siberia he married a fellow revolutionary from St. Petersburg, likewise under sentence of exile, named Krupskaia—she continued to be called by her maiden name—who served him as a devoted and selfless companion to the end of his days. She bore him no offspring—how could they have fitted children into a revolutionary career?

After his release in 1900, Lenin went to western Europe, soon to be followed by his wife. There they stayed until 1917, with the exception of a brief Russian interlude during the Revolution of 1905, rootless aliens, unwanted and unassimilated. When Trotsky after his first escape from Siberia visited Lenin in London, Lenin showed him the sights. "This is *their* famous Westminster," he said, pointing at the Houses of Parliament. Alas, to Lenin the good things of Europe were all *theirs,* the capitalists' and exploiters'. Ill at ease amidst their comforts, Lenin never acquired an inside view of western democracy or of "capitalism." He remained close to his Russian heritage, a secret Slavophile in the Marxist ranks. With the single-mindedness of genius he pined for Russia, for revolution, and for getting the better of the "capitalists' " easy superiority.

* The most advanced elements in the Russian working class were not eager to risk their hard-won pittance of prosperity in constant revolutionary warfare. The revolutionary surge originated more commonly with those working class elements that remained close to the village.

By 1902, the revolution seemed as distant as ever. Two generations of revolutionaries had passed and accomplished nothing. Their accumulated failures now taught a still more impatient third generation, of which Lenin made himself the spokesman, to become yet hardier and craftier professional revolutionaries.* More intensively than even Chernyshevsky's "monster," Lenin armed himself to the depths of his personality for this task. Softness in any form was the supreme sin. As he once observed to Maxim Gorky:

> I can't listen to music too often. It affects your nerves, makes you want to say stupid nice things and stroke the heads of people who could create such beauty while living in this vile hell. And now you must not stroke anyone's head—you might get your hands bitten off.

The previous generations of revolutionaries had had their hands bitten off by being too emotional, too kind, too careless of their impulses. By contrast Lenin permitted himself only the most rational and cold-blooded calculations of revolutionary opportunity. In case of failure he allowed no despair, but counseled self-criticism, analysis of the mistakes, and a new and still more earnest beginning. In case of success he shunned exultation—that too was a form of weakness and courted disaster.

What counted "in this vile hell" was discipline, method, accuracy, precision, and infinite patience with detail in all the black arts of revolution. A revolutionary had to be *toujours en védette,* ready to advance when possible and to retreat when necessary, to endure above all and to preserve intact the vital revolutionary resolve. Throughout his life, Lenin retained an almost masochist fierceness toward the gentle voices that might weaken this hard-won determination, whether generosity, sentimentality, or any form of what he called "petty-bourgeois" morality. The only moral guide which a revolutionary recognized, he preached, was success in his calling. Considering the emo-

* The extraordinary length and depth of the revolutionary tradition was another peculiarity of the Russian setting, distinguishing it from any other.

tional and undisciplined ways of the Russian intelligentsia in which it had its origin, Lenin's code was a remarkable monument to the human will. Yet it still remained a product of human flesh and blood. It could be upheld—and the doubts suppressed—only by the utmost exertions of fanaticism. Thus rationality of purpose was carried to the point of a rigid irrational compulsion.* And human nature demanded a price for such outrage. All too often Lenin, who in his heart remained tuned to the music of kindliness, complained that his nerves played him tricks which kept him from working. Revolutionaries with coarser temperaments, of course, would have better nerves. And the fourth generation—the commissars—would laugh at such weakness; the trend favored the primitives like Stalin. The natural pull of Russian life, however, continued to run in the opposite direction (which, by way of compensation, perpetuated the need for Lenin's inhuman discipline).

The code of thought and feeling which Lenin prescribed for himself and other revolutionaries was accomplished by a set of rules for the organization through which they must work. These rules again can best be understood as a response to past failures. The revolutionaries had had their hands bitten off, Lenin charged, because they had been amateur organizers. Their desire to imitate the mass organizations of the German Social Democratic party had allowed the police to penetrate their ranks. What had been created with heroic effort was thus wiped out in short order; the best revolutionaries were sacrificed for nothing. His plea therefore was for a revolutionary organization capable of outsmarting the police (which at this time, under the direction of an ex-revolutionary, Colonel Zubatov, was beginning to apply the methods of modern crime detection to the revolutionary movement).

Survival—not to mention success—under these conditions was

---

* The closest European parallel can be found in the traditions of Prussian militarism, as established in the eighteenth century (with very different connotations, to be sure). Both *Junkers* and Communists refused to recognize the term "impossible."

impossible, Lenin argued, so long the the Russian Marxists believed that the revolution must proceed from the workers themselves. He angrily proclaimed the contrary view. "The history of all countries shows that the working class, exclusively by its own efforts, is able to develop only trade union consciousness."

Revolutionary consciousness, Lenin proceeded, could be carried to the workers only from without, by the revolutionary intelligentsia, an altogether different category. Whether this was universally true may be questioned. But who could deny that the Russian workers were singularly unsuited to cope effectively with the complex tasks of bringing socialism to Russia? The antinomy between the vanguard and the proletarian host remained a crucial ingredient in Lenin's political theory. It betrayed his ineradicable suspicion of all spontaneous, unorganized humanity, even of genuinely proletarian organizations like the St. Petersburg Soviet of 1905. This secret contempt of spontaneity sheltered him from the influences of the western democratic model, yet it also perpetuated the old cleavage between the educated classes and the Russian masses. (Could there have been a more disdainful approach to the man in the street than this heartless collective term, "the masses"?) Physically and spiritually, Lenin (like Marx) always kept aloof from the workers. There is no evidence, for instance, that he ever set foot inside a factory.

Revolution, then, was the concern first and last of the revolutionary leaders, the heirs of both the Russian and European revolutionary tradition and the masters of the scientific laws of historical development. They alone possessed the proper "consciousness." They devised the appropriate policy for every new set of circumstances and formulated what eventually became known as "the party line." It had to be defined precisely so as to avoid misunderstanding and to enable the members of the party to carry it out to the letter. The elite, Lenin further insisted, must be organized like a miniature army, a human machine expressly designed for revolution, disciplined and loyal to the commander. He therefore demanded that the party's Central Committee have plenary power over the entire organization, like a commanding general over all officers and troops in the field. And like a general in time of war—war and revolution were much akin—the revolutionary leader could not afford to be choosy in his methods.

> Revolution is a difficult matter [Lenin wrote in 1907]. It cannot be made with gloves and manicured fingernails. . . . A party is no girls' dormitory. Party members should not be measured by the narrow standard of petty-bourgeois morality. Sometimes a scoundrel is useful to our party precisely because he is a scoundrel.

During the low years after the failure of the Revolution of 1905, Lenin even approved of bank robbery, euphemistically called "expropriation," as a means of financing the Russian Social Democratic party. The most spectacular of these "ex's" was carried out in Tiflis under the supervision of Stalin. Later, during the war, he had no scruples about taking German money for his faction. All means were fair so long as they promoted the revolution. Needless to say, Lenin's conception of what a Russian Social Democratic party should be, so contrary to the liberal-humanitarian tradition of Marxism, did not go unchallenged. As early as 1903, Trotsky predicted what would happen if Lenin's views prevailed:

> The organization of the party takes the place of the party itself; the central committee takes the place of the organization, and finally the dictator takes the place of the central committee.

This, precisely, was the way in which the Bolshevik party evolved (and after the summer of 1917 even with Trotsky's active support).

Lenin, however, would never see the danger. He believed that in the comradeship of the common struggle no conflict could arise within the party. The flow of commands from above would be modulated by the flow of information and suggestion from below; no constitutional safeguards were needed.* At all events,

* Here again Lenin carried a *narodnik* argument into Russian Marxism.

his chief reply to his critics was unanswerable. Under autocracy —and he never believed that the October Manifesto made any difference—only a secret and highly trained organization of militant revolutionaries could prevail. It was either that or catastrophe again. Under Russian conditions, he further contended, the masses could be properly won to the party and made conscious of their role only if the party attained the quality of a tight-knit revolutionary elite. Striking workers, he wrote, would hardly risk their lives for an unwieldy, spy-ridden mass organization. They needed efficiency and the leadership of reliable underground agents to guide their work in street and factory. Successful mass action indeed depended on the expert core.

This was the way, then, in which Lenin proposed to combine the highly centralized leadership of the revolutionary elite—of himself, had he been frank—with large-scale action in an age of mass politics. The secret of success in this squaring of the circle lay in constant agitation by the elite among the masses. By propaganda and a thousand other forms of directing revolutionary discontent, including irrational means of mass manipulation, the revolutionaries were to shape the "consciousness" of the masses. Lenin early recognized the benefit of slogans and other simplified appeals geared more to the emotions than to the understanding of the man in the street. Thus the Bolsheviks learned the techniques of modern mass politics under the frontier conditions of revolutionary warfare. Never, so Lenin preached, could they afford to lose touch with the masses. In this lay their strength.

Yet, in the last analysis, the identification was never quite complete. With all their skills of manipulation, the Bolsheviks could never lure the masses into the proper consciousness. The gap between spontaneity and revolutionary consciousness remained unbridged—the circle, after all, could not be squared. The Bolsheviks thus shared the predicament of the tsars. Unlike the other opposition parties which bowed, in theory as well as practice, to the will of the people, they could not admit the population into the political decision-making process, which is the essence of democracy. By his own theory Lenin was cast into the role of a counter tsar, and the Bolshevik faction into that of a counter autocracy. Thus did the tsarist regime perpetuate itself, illegitimately, yet with improved skill; for despite the innate flaw, Bolshevik political practice was vastly superior to that of the tsars, who had never learned to work with an aroused populace.

One other strand tied Lenin, however obliquely, to the tsars —his nationalism. As one reads his famous pamphlet of 1902, *What Is To Be Done?* which sets forth the basic concepts of Leninism, one is struck by his allusions to the superiority of the Russian revolutionary movement. Fighting the most reactionary government in Europe, it was the vanguard of the international revolutionary proletariat.

> The role of the vanguard fighter can be fulfilled only by a party that is guided by the most advanced theory. To have a concrete understanding of what this means, let the reader recall such predecessors of Russian Social Democracy as Herzen, Belinsky, Chernyshevsky, and the brilliant galaxy of revolutionaries in the 1870s, let him ponder over the world significance which Russian literature is now acquiring; let him . . . but be that enough.*

The incomplete "let him" speaks volumes for the soaring national pride in Lenin, who yearned for world recognition, not on behalf of the Empire—that was moribund—but for revolutionary Russia. His thought leaped far ahead into the future. Lenin undoubtedly was guilty of what Trotsky once called "that national revolutionary messianic mood which prompts one to see one's own nation state as destined to lead mankind to socialism." And he forcefully expressed the burning hope for an escape from backwardness which we have noted earlier among Russian intellectuals. In Lenin, nationalism and the Marxist foreknowledge

---

* Russian literature, incidentally, was not revolutionary in its greatest representatives. Lenin was running out of proofs of superiority—which obviously did not thwart his ambition. In part, this ambition, incidentally, was a hand-me-down of German origin. Kautsky, the German Marxist, had just encouraged the Russian revolutionaries to think of themselves as the vanguard of the international proletarian revolution.

of history combined in a powerful stimulant to the Russian ego. Let "cápitalist" Europe beware!

Proper revolutionary organization was one leg of success, proper theory the other. In the realm of theory, one can again see Lenin's impatience at work, combining the laws of history in a way most advantageous to those who wanted revolution at once and at any price. In none of his speculation was he concerned merely with the replacement of autocracy by a bourgeois democratic regime—bourgeois democracy was for the rich only. He aimed at the next revolution thereafter, the socialist revolution. The obvious objection to such far-reaching plans, according to Marxist theory (as well as to common sense), lay in the fact of Russian backwardness. Russian "capitalism" would not have run its appointed course for a long time. But for a third-generation revolutionary such perspectives were intolerable and, fortunately for him, not entirely supported by the evidence. As the events of 1905 showed, Russia possessed a revolutionary thrust that might well carry it quickly beyond a purely bourgeois phase.

Marx already had advised the revolutionary vanguard to take any available revolutionary force as its ally. Lenin expected no help from the Russian *bourgeoisie,* a class far weaker than its western counterpart. At least one stratum of that class had been bought off by the October Manifesto; the others had not acted vigorously enough (and never could, by their very nature). It was rather the peasantry—to omit here the revolutionary potential of national and religious dissent—which had accounted for the revolutionary ground swell. And to the peasants Lenin turned in 1905, despite the fact that Marxist theory rated them as hopeless, Marx himself having spoken of the "idiocy of the countryside." Whatever the economic convictions of the peasants—Lenin always remained suspicious of their "petty-bourgeois" bent of mind—the explosive impact of Black Partition was invaluable revolutionary capital, too important to be spurned. Thus he began to speak, over the protest of the "softs," of a revolutionary democratic dictatorship of the proletariat and the peasants (the poorer peasants particularly), which was to emerge from the overthrow of autocracy.

The new perspectives also implied an adjustment of the normal Marxist pattern of social progress to Russian conditions. The peculiarities of Russia prevented a clear-cut succession from feudalism to capitalism and from capitalism to socialism. In Russia, as in other backward countries, a combined development was apt to be the rule. Feudal elements mingled with capitalist and socialist ones; a weak *bourgeoisie* and a powerful proletariat existed side by side even under autocracy. Thus, Lenin foresaw that after the overthrow of autocracy, the toiling masses would already have the upper hand, giving the new government the character of a powerful revolutionary democratic dictatorship rather than of a bourgeois democracy in the western style. Such a regime, he thought, might also have a startling effect outside Russia. It might act as a spark, setting off the proletarian revolution in the advanced "capitalist" West, riper for socialism than Russia. Having created a socialist society of its own, the West would then rush, with socialist zeal, to introduce socialism into Russia, well in advance of the natural course of its development. Trotsky, who was gradually drifting closer to the Bolshevik position, formulated an even more articulate theory—the theory of "the permanent revolution"—for those who wanted to leap forward into socialism regardless of whether Russia was ready or not. Such implacable revolutionary determination in theory and practice, incidentally, ranged the Bolsheviks on the side of the irrationalists in European politics, despite their guise of Marxist rationalism.

When war broke out in 1914, Lenin watched with choking rage the collapse of international socialist solidarity. Workers now fought workers for the defense of their national interest, for their *bourgeoisie*. During these bitter months, after settling down in cheap lodgings in Zurich, he set the basic concepts of Bolshevism into the largest possible context of global politics. Russian revolutionary theory had traditionally suffered from its ignorance of the realities of power politics. Lenin, in his famous pamphlet

Imperialism the Last Stage of Capitalism (1916), now remedied this deficiency. In that last stage, he argued, giant capitalist monopolies competed all over the world for new markets. In their rivalry they set nation against nation, people against people. Thus they had caused the first World War. Yet the very violence of the imperialist competition advanced the revolution in a double movement. The war, Lenin predicted, would make the European proletariat rise against its masters. Ever since the outbreak of hostilities, he himself had urged the European socialists to convert the international war into a civil war. Yet—and this was a new feature—it would also drive the colonial peoples, who in the period of imperialism had been enslaved by "'capitalist" rule, to rise against their exploiters (among whom Lenin included Imperial Russia). This grand conception of imperialism provided a ridiculously distorted account of both "capitalism" and the origins of the war. Yet it contained a prophetic insight. In it Lenin fused the traditional socialist revolutionary movement in Europe with the incipient antiwestern global revolt, which he had keenly eyed for several years. The "internal" and the "external" proletariat, the industrial workers of Europe and the backward peoples, were joining forces against the western ruling classes then locked in mortal combat. Posing the question of what he would do if the party of the proletariat came to power during the current war, Lenin confidently replied (1915):

> We should have to prepare and undertake revolutionary war, that is, not only should we fully carry through in the most decisive ways our entire minimum program but we should systematically begin to draw into revolt all peoples now oppressed by the Great Russians, [and in addition] all colonies and dependent countries of Asia (India, China, Persia, and so on), and also—and primarily—the socialist proletariat of Europe.

It was a sweeping vision of a counter power to the great outpouring of western civilization, a counter power centered around the revolutionary potential of the European proletariat. Thus Leninism helped to carry the seed of the French Revolution into the non-European world. Liberty, equality, and fraternity—the revolutionary quintessence of European civilization—now were set to work against the western domination of the global community.

Before March, 1917, however, all of Lenin's plans for effective revolutionary action in the imperialist age remained a matter of theory. They merely reflected his effort to keep Marxist analysis —the correct version—abreast of the rapidly unfolding events. However crucial for the political education of the "hards," they did not advance the cause. Representing the extreme left of the Russian Social Democratic Party and counting few adherents, the Bolsheviks were even more unsuccessful and divided than the other opposition groups. Despite Lenin's talk of the superior efficiency of his revolutionary elite, the secret police had succeeded in planting an agent, Roman Malinovsky, in its inner circles; he enjoyed Lenin's confidence. Paradoxically, the Bolsheviks became an effective political force only after the collapse of autocracy.

At the time of the March Revolution, the Bolsheviks were still a negligible group. Their leaders were scattered: Lenin in Switzerland, Stalin in Siberia, Trotsky (whom we may henceforth include among the "hards") in New York. They possessed but a handful of delegates in the Petrograd Soviet. Yet when Lenin heard of the fall of autocracy, his mind was made up. A socialist revolution in Russia—and perhaps world revolution too—was within reach. The Provisional Government of Russia, he wrote,

> is in no condition to escape collapse, for it is impossible to tear ourselves out of the claws of that terrible monster begotten by world capitalism—the imperialist war and the famine— without leaving the soil of bourgeois relations, without going over to revolutionary methods, without appealing to the greatest historical heroism of the proletariat of Russia and the whole world.

He arrived in Petrograd toward the end of April, 1917, after having crossed Germany with the assistance of the German government. At once he set the course of his small band of followers toward the seizure of power in the name of the proletariat, staking all on the monstrous effects of the war.

VI

1917: MARCH TO NOVEMBER

★

1917 WAS A YEAR of agony and mounting crises for all European belligerents. The strain of war, now stretching from the third into the fourth year, became well-nigh unbearable. England, governed since December 1916 by Lloyd George's strong war cabinet, was brought to the verge of starvation by German submarine warfare. France, after the failure of the Nivelle offensive in May, saw its troops mutiny on critical sectors of the front and its government falter until, in November, Clemenceau (the Tiger) took over the reins. In Germany, where more than elsewhere the exertions of the war had caused drastic government control of the economy and, under the "Hindenburg program" of December, 1916, of manpower as well, the ravages of the "turnip winter" reopened and deepened the prewar political schism. As a result, the government became a virtual dictatorship under the High Command. For Italy the year, which had witnessed much demoralization and unrest, ended with the disaster of Caporetto. As for Austria-Hungary, which of all major powers resembled Russia the most, the situation was summed up by the advice which Count Czernin, under the impact of the news from Russia, gave to the new Emperor Charles: "If the monarchs of the Central Powers cannot make peace in the coming months, it will be made for them by their peoples." The Emperor's Czech, Croat, and Italian soldiers were indeed hastening the peace by deserting to the enemy.

While stalemate on the western front persisted despite the use of ever more savage weapons, there was still hope of victory: for the allies in their association, after April, with the United States; for the Central Powers in the imminent collapse of Russia. This hope, combined with a patriotism often bordering on hysteria, produced in England, France, Germany, and—after Caporetto—in Italy the grim determination to endure to the end. Elsewhere defeatism rapidly gained ground. Among the countries that stood up under the strain, government became more authoritarian or dictatorial. At the same time war propaganda became more messianic. At the start of the war, men had thought of its aims in concrete terms of territories or boundaries. As it dragged on, they began to think of it ideologically, as a war for human freedom and justice, and even a war to end all wars, involving the very future of civilization or of mankind. After the entry of the United States into the war, Woodrow Wilson became the leader of the ideological crusade. Yet while they talked of humanity, governments and people became self-centered as never before, sacrificing the last shred of cosmopolitanism to the furies of combat. Russia could thus expect little sympathy from even its allies for its agonies in this decisive year.

Never did the Russian people enjoy greater political freedom or civic equality than after March, 1917. Apart from the pressure of the German and Austro-Hungarian armies (which remained passive for most of the year) and of increasing political and economic disorder at home, they were masters of their fate. In their new freedom—freedom from autocracy and freedom from concurrent western influences (except German power)—would they be able to manage bringing state and society into alignment and constructing a more effective government? Would they be able to raise the strength and prestige of Russia in the world? Out of the efforts of the heirs to cope with these key questions arose the next and more drastic revolution.

The new regime, as we have seen, did not get off to an auspicious start; the government which took over in March was deeply divided. Until the meeting of the Constituent Assembly, the Provisional Government considered itself the legitimate successor. It staffed the ministerial posts, made plans (many of them eminently sensible and necessary), formulated policies, and tried to carry them out as best it could without civil service or police. It was the government in everything except the essence: executive power. This attribute was rather in the hands of the other government, the Petrograd Soviet, which derived its mandate from the garrison and workers of the capital who had made the March Revolution. Its leaders, moderate socialists all, repudiated any thought of the Soviet taking over the reins of government. They conceived of the Soviet merely as the guardian of the toiling masses under a regime which was bourgeois in nature. Yet, under pressure from their constituents, they were all too often forced to assume the functions of government in crucial issues of domestic and foreign policy.

The solitary link between the uneasy partners was Alexander Kerensky. As an important member of both bodies, he became the central figure in the new era (although not prime minister until July). A young man of inexhaustible energy, an idealist of moderate Social Revolutionary views, gifted with superb powers of speech, and driven by an exalted sense of mission, he alone was capable of whipping up the consensus of moderate opinion necessary for a democratic regime. He was the first of the great orators of revolutionary mass politics in the modern age. The exalted quality of his appeal, so lofty and yet so devoid of political realism, fitted the mood of expectancy which reigned in the early weeks:

> New fires of hope and aspiration were kindled and the masses were drawn together by mysterious bonds [he reminisced in exile about the dawn of the new era]. We have lived through many beautiful and terrible events since then, but I can still feel the great soul of the people as I did in those days. I can feel their terriffic force which may be led to perform great deeds or incited to horrible crimes. As a flower turns to the sun, so the newly awakened soul of the people longed for light and truth. The people followed us when we tried to raise them above material things to the light of high ideals.

Yet persuasive as Kerensky's oratory was in those days, it could not close the gap of ideology and outlook that separated the Provisional Government from the Petrograd Soviet. From the outset, conflict between them was continuous, erupting in a series of crises. The first of these arose in early May over foreign policy. Miliukov, who had taken control of foreign affairs, favored continuing the policy of the tsarist government, its alliances and secret treaties (one of which promised to Russia the Straits of Constantinople). He—and all moderates—assumed that Russia would fight on to victory. The Soviet, however, fearful of unnecessarily prolonging the war and for the wrong ends, entertained a different conception. Already in late March, it proclaimed:

> Conscious of its revolutionary power, the Russian democracy announces that it will, by every means, resist the policy of conquest of its ruling classes, and it calls upon the peoples of Europe for concerted, decisive action in favor of peace.

This was the first of the revolutionary appeals for peace which "Russian democracy" (a title the Soviet arrogated to itself despite the fact that it represented only soldiers and workers) addressed to the toilers of all countries. When Miliukov persisted in his course, the Soviet became restive. On May 6, the enraged soldiers and workers poured into the street and demanded not only the ouster of Miliukov but peace at once, without annexations and indemnities. The crisis ended with Miliukov's resignation and the reorganization of the Provisional Government, which now included six members from the Soviet executive committee. The moderate socialists thus entered into an uneasy coalition—the First Coalition—with the "capitalists," a move which constituted a drastic departure from socialist etiquette (at least as practiced in Russia).

Even the new arrangement did not overcome the dualism which frustrated the conduct of government just when a strong central authority was urgently needed. The cause of the split lay deep in the nature of the two institutions. The Provisional Government tried to represent the will of all Russia until the Constituent Assembly would relieve it of its task. As an interim government it felt itself debarred from settling the basic issues, such as the form of government, the land question, the position of the non-Russian nationalities, or war and peace. It should, of course, have conducted elections for the Constituent Assembly at the earliest moment. But considering the state of the country, were the people quite ready yet for deciding their future calmly and fairly? Sound liberal instinct led to one delay after another, until it was too late.

The Petrograd Soviet, on the other hand, particularly after it was reinforced in June by a delegation from the first All-Russian Congress of Soviets, could never give its full support to a representative government. By origin and composition it was a class institution, bound to maintain its separate identity as spokesman of all the revolutionary soviets that mushroomed throughout the country in the wake of the March Revolution. And how they multiplied: four hundred in May, six hundred in August, nine hundred in October!

The rift in the government proved unbridgeable because, in the last analysis, it had its cause in the age-old division of Russian society itself. On the side of the Provisional Government we may group the public institutions of educated Russia, foremost the town dumas and the zemstvos, now reconstituted on a democratic basis, and with them all educated and Europeanized Russia; in short, "privilege Russia." On the other side we find "soviet Russia"; i.e., the peasant masses consisting of the peasants themselves, the peasants in uniform (the soldiers), and the peasants in the factory (misnamed, for the most part, proletarians).

"Soviet Russia," to be sure, formed by no means a uniform pressure group. The peasants set up their own soviets, hesitantly and under the prompting of citified elements. They did not really need soviets for what they wanted from the revolution. Under SR leadership, however, they rallied in periodic all-Russian peasant congresses in order to safeguard their political interests. The soldiers at the front banded together in their own soldiers' soviets. Garrison troops, however, most commonly sat together with the workers, the soldiers outnumbering the workers, particularly at the outset, and the workers by an even larger margin outnumbering the peasants, when eventually the latter were included. What mattered, however, was not proportionality of representation but authenticity of opinion. Deputies who ceased to reflect the temper of their constituents were apt to be recalled at once. Thus the moderate spokesmen commonly drawn from the educated classes after March were by summer and fall replaced with men from the ranks of extremist intellectuals.

As may be imagined, the soviets were huge and unwieldly bodies; for a time the Petrograd Soviet numbered about three thousand members. The proceedings, too, were apt to be chaotic, which at an early point caused the withdrawal of the decision-makers into the executive committee or even smaller caucuses. Each soviet, and particularly the Petrograd Soviet, which in June absorbed the executive committee of the first All-Russian Congress of Soviets, created its own administrative apparatus. This, unfortunately, tended to remove the leaders from close contact with the masses. The real strength of a soviet always lay in its identification with the local community. There were weak and strong soviets, the latter arrogating to themselves ever more functions of local government, some becoming veritable tyrants. And the soviets always displayed more zeal and energy than the town dumas and zemstvos in the same area, and more contempt too for legality and public order. At worst they became an instrument of class war at its most ruthless. Yet all soviets acted on the assumption that in them, and in them alone, resided "Russian democracy"; the other groups, which had shared with autocracy the burden of modernizing Russia, were exploiters, "capitalists," parasites. The distinction implied a clear repudiation of the Europeanized upper strata and of much they stood for.

It was for these reasons—their class character and their turbulence—that the soviet leadership (and Kerensky too) did not predict a long life for the soviets as an institution. They were unfit for government and would disappear when the Constituent Assembly had done its work.

The split between "privilege Russia" and "soviet Russia" was the most dangerous rift in the body politic but, unfortunately, not the only one. All existing fissures were opened up and widened. In her new freedom, Russia suddenly experienced all the frightening consequences of modern mass politics. Never before had there been such political fermentation. For the citizen, particularly the semiliterate simple man, life became an unending series of meetings, assemblies, and debates. He was bombarded with political appeals by pamphlet, poster, newspaper, or speech, all flattering him with a new importance. The western democratic values in the programs of the parties now holding sway were broadcast as a thousand tiny explosives shattering old habits of submission or apathy. Every view, every feeling hitherto unnoted became articulate and called for action. After March, Russia thus witnessed a gigantic awakening of heady political fantasies. Old hopes and resentments were mobilized and reinforced by present hardships of hunger, cold, uncertainty, and a thousand frustrations. Out of this awakening, a new age of rampant political spontaneity was born.

Everybody now spoke his mind, bluntly and imperiously as had been the custom of the authorities in the past. The resulting cacophony revealed how weak under the autocratic monolith had remained the bonds of community and how small the fund of political rationality. The conservatives, to be sure, lay low for a while; their Russia was discredited. All the others pressed their rival claims on each other *fortissimo*: manufacturers and workers, landlords and peasants, liberals and socialists, moderates and extremists, Russians and non-Russians (sometimes the non-Russians among themselves), Christians and Jews, fathers and sons. The arguments soon ceased to be reasonable. Everywhere one could detect a penchant for maximalism, an irresistible urge to go to the limit. Why else should a prominent employer have threatened his striking workers with "the bony hand of hunger" to bring them back on his terms, or a powerful landlord have preferred Black Partition to a timely accommodation with his aroused peasants?

The maximalism poured acid into the tidal wave of spontaneity which, from late spring onward, spread from the capital and the urban-industrial centers into the length and breadth of Russia, stirring its 150,000,000 inhabitants to their very depths. Its corrosive effects were strongest where the accumulated grievances were greatest and current suffering most acute. The pain brought to a boil all the ugliness of temper which centuries of humiliation and degradation had engendered. Russian politics from May, 1917, to the spring of 1921, when the riot of spontaneity died out in utter exhaustion, cannot be understood by the concepts of western democratic practice. They must be viewed primitively, in terms of Hobbesian social mechanics, in terms of crude violence among masses uprooted by war and revolution.

In the late spring and early summer, the peasants grew restive. They craved to be masters of the countryside at last; they wanted the land right away. Hesitantly at first and then more boldly they began to seize it by themselves, deporting their landlords or hanging them by their necks. By fall, all restraints were thrust aside. No force on earth could have stopped the vast agrarian revolution (which, in the end, netted the peasant only a minute increase in his holdings). The soldiers, meanwhile, had become active too. They deserted in large numbers, "voting for peace with their legs," as Lenin called it.* They—and most of the population— were sick of the war, regardless of the consequences for Russia (and who cared about the Allies?). No restoration of the death penalty could restore army discipline. Other groups likewise took the law into their own hands, workers throwing out their employers, or national minorities preparing for independence.

The temper of the times may be illustrated by a cruel tale about a group of soldiers who sometime during these months shot their officers, mutilating some of them beforehand by cutting off their noses. When asked about the noses, they explained that during rifle inspection in the old days these officers had put their fingers first into the muzzles of the rifles and then on the soldier's nose. If there was soot on the officers finger, it showed up on the soldier's nose. "You must have felt deeply offended," the Countess Kleinmichel (who told this story) said to a soldier, trying to fathom his motives. "Oh no," said he, "in those days nobody felt offended. We did not think about it. But later"— and here he drew himself up—"later we understood that it was an offense to our dignity." Indeed, by the new values much in the Russian past had been an offense to human dignity. Some

* By October the number of deserters had swelled to about two million.

months later, after the Bolshevik *coup,* the sailors of Sevastopol seized anyone with clean fingernails who crossed their path, stood him against a wall as a *burzhui,* a "capitalist," and shot him dead. The worm was surely turning.

That was the tide with which the soviets of soldiers, workers, and peasants were swimming. Here lay their strength. Conversely, the weakness of the Provisional Government and increasingly also of the moderate leaders in the Soviet bureaucracy lay in their aloofness from it. After the May crisis, the chief problem in Russian politics was whether that tide would destroy Russia or whether, perhaps, it could be checked before it had run its fatal course.

The hope that it might be checked emerged as a result of the next great crisis, the "July days," in which, for the first time, the masses of the capital were pitted against both the Provisional Government and their own moderate leadership in the Petrograd Soviet. They had reason to be angry. Since May, no progress had been made in any of the issues crucial to the workers, peasants, or soldiers. Their impatience grew as economic conditions deteriorated and the war continued. Furthermore, on July 1, Kerensky, who in May had taken over the War Ministry, launched a powerful offensive against the Austrian army. In its political aspects it was intended to consolidate the Provisional Government and to reassure the Allies (now including the United States), whose economic aid was badly needed. Yet at the height of the offensive, the government coalition patched together in May collapsed. The "capitalist" ministers suddenly resigned over an issue of agrarian policy, and on the following two days, July 16 and 17, the soldiers, sailors, and workers again poured into the streets. About half a million strong they made their way, shooting and looting, to the Tauride Palace, demanding that the Soviet take power from the Provisional Government. When they discovered that the Soviet leaders opposed such a step, they nearly lynched Chernov, who tried to calm them. Yet their fury spent itself vainly, for not even the Bolsheviks, who reluctantly had furnished some leadership for the uprising, felt that the time for action had come.

The reckless outburst had its effect on "privilege Russia." As the revolutionary masses withdrew, the propertied elements likewise took to the street and vented their wrath on the Bolsheviks, who as a result were driven underground. Thus the drift to the extreme left was halted for a while. Yet the period of reaction which ensued hardly bettered the position of the government. The Kerensky offensive collapsed, as it was bound to, and Kerensky, soon raised to the prime ministership, met with great obstinacy in shaping a new cabinet. It took him nearly three weeks—three weeks while Russia hovered on the brink of anarchy—to bring the liberals and moderate socialists into alliance again. The delay demonstrated how deeply the forces of liberal democracy were divided among themselves. Nor did they command mass support, as the July days had conclusively shown. They were powerless in the face of the tidal wave of revolutionary spontaneity. In these fateful weeks, the competition for the succession to the tsar was decided against the Cadets, the Mensheviks, and the run of Social Revolutionaries—against all the truly democratic parties.

Liberal democracy in Russia—using the term broadly—had proved unequal to the task. Since March it had given the country every opportunity to speak its will, and the result had been division, violence, and a breakdown of government. Spontaneity, leaving the population to its own devices, had produced anarchy. The invisible resources of unity and social discipline, which in the western democracies restrained liberty from degenerating into license and made possible not only effective government in peace but also unprecedented voluntary sacrifices in war, were found wanting in Russia. A few years later they were equally found wanting in Italy, Spain, Poland, or Germany (to mention but a few parallel cases). None of these countries had had a chance in the past of knitting the tight habit of subconscious unity before they copied western democracy. Russia was merely the first case in a long series of similar breakdowns, the one that occurred under the most exceptional circumstances.

Viewing the events of the summer of 1917 in this perspective, we must conclude that the failure of democracy in Russia was inevitable, if not in 1917 then surely in the years following (as suming that a Russian state still survived). Only decades, if not centuries, of relative immunity to the pressures of power politics and an active internal melting pot might have helped the discordant elements to grow together. Now there was no time. In the extreme moments of the twentieth century, a country either possessed that cohesion or had to create it artificially, if it did not want to fall apart.

After the July days, the sole question of Russian domestic politics was whether the heir to autocracy would be a dictator of the right or of the left. The wave of reaction favored the former. It brought to the fore General Kornilov, a distinguished officer whom merit had raised from the peasantry to his high rank and who was by no means a reactionary. He was convinced that only a military dictatorship could save Russia from Germany and from disintegration, an opinion which by now many members of "privilege Russia" (including some socialists) shared. With such backing he began, toward the end of August, to move supposedly reliable army units toward Petrograd, ostensibly in order to strengthen Kerensky but secretly prepared to go further if opportunity opened. Yet as his men approached the capital, they were met by agitators sent by the Soviet, under whose persuasion even the most loyal soldiers lost heart. Against the Petrograd Soviet, Kornilov's troops melted away as had the armies at the front, and his *coup* collapsed. No dictatorship of the right could stem the tide of revolutionary spontaneity as embodied in the soviets. On the contrary, Kornilov revived its impetus, somewhat checked after July, and prepared the way for the dictatorship of the left.

The dictatorship of the proletariat had, of course, been the goal of the Bolsheviks ever since Lenin returned to Russia. At every opportunity, he pressed home the argument that the war was an imperialist war and that it could be stopped, with all its savage hardships, only if the "capitalist" governments in Russia and elsewhere were overthrown. In his eyes, all those Russians who sought to continue the war—and this included Kerensky, the Mensheviks, and most Social Revolutionaries—were "capitalist" warmongers. He gambled on the inability of the provisional Government to carry out its staggering tasks and on the growing revulsion against the war.

Of all political parties, thus only the Bolsheviks cast their lot with the revolutionary torrent. Their slogan was "All power to the Soviets" until July, when the Soviet leadership turned against the masses. Then they allied themselves with the more radical elements represented in the Petrograd district soviets and the factory committees. In the fall, when they gained control of the city soviets in many parts of Russia, they proclaimed as their goal the dictatorship of the proletariat. They alone dared to profess what the unruly masses wanted and were already trying to achieve by themselves: immediate peace for the soldiers, land to the peasants by Black Partition, self-determination for the minority groups, bread for the hungry, and social justice on their own terms for all those who felt oppressed and exploited. They alone were willing to descend to the language of the *Lumpenproletariat* and, when necessary, to incite its passions to fever pitch. "The Bolsheviks," Trotsky wrote in retrospect, "not afraid of those backward strata now for the first time lifting themselves from the dregs, took people as history had created them." Mercilessly they exploited the ignorance of the masses.

Yet while they placed themselves midstream in the revolutionary tide, they would not be carried away by it. As a revolutionary elite, they had a will of their own. They thought of themselves as the engineers of revolution, harnessing the revolutionary steam power created by the historic conditions of the moment to its true purpose which only revolutionary Marxists could perceive. Whatever the Bolsheviks would do, for their own benefit and that of Russia, they would do through the masses, never against them. But they would also remain inwardly apart, as manipulators, not agents, of the popular will. In this manner, they solved the first of the underlying necessities of modern Russian development, identifying the people with their government and in turn identifying themselves with the people.

Falling in line with the drift toward the extreme, the Bolsheviks (who still were taking German money) were able to grow from a small minority to the dominant party in the soviets. In May they already controlled the majority of the soviet at Kronstadt, the naval base near Petrograd. Their big windfall, however, came in the wake of Kornilov's march on the capital. The Bolsheviks led in the defense of the city and, as a reward, soon controlled the Soviet. The trend was reflected in the changing membership of practically all soviets throughout Russia. On the eve of the second All-Russian Congress of Soviets, meeting in early November, Lenin's party could claim majorities in the soviets of Petrograd, Moscow, and the great industrial centers, of the Ural towns, and of the garrisons of the north and northwest. In Siberia they shared control with the SR, whose left wing throughout the country inclined toward the Bolsheviks. The latter lagged behind the SR, their closest rivals, only in the central black soil provinces, the Ukraine, and the western and southwestern fronts. The Mensheviks had completely dropped out of the running, except for their stronghold in Georgia. The trade unions, apart from the railway, post, and telegraph workers, went over to the Bolsheviks. Even in the city dumas of Petrograd and Moscow they made impressive gains, proving the strength of their appeal in the metropoles. There was no reason to doubt that the majorities would increase and the trend extend into all the regions of Russia. By the indices of practical politics, the time was ripe for the Bolshevik seizure of power.

Yet by the traditional indices of Marxist orthodoxy, Russia was still a backward country unfit for a socialist revolution. The Russian "proletariat and the poorest peasantry," to use Lenin's term for the forces at his disposal, were too weak a basis for building the most advanced social system. And even if the Bolsheviks succeeded in taking power now, they could not hold it for long, except by non-Marxist methods of terror. What was the benefit, so the "softs" asked, of such irresponsible adventurism?

Arguments like these, however, did not detain the impatient Lenin. He saw the straws of evidence from the West all pointing toward a general conflagration. Everywhere in Europe the people wanted peace; they would achieve it by revolution. A Bolshevik revolution might indeed provide the spark, as he had argued earlier. Much of the confidence which buoyed the Bolsheviks in these months—and years—stemmed from their anticipation of a European revolution. But Lenin also pursued another line of thought. The war itself, he argued while still in Switzerland, was preparing socialism by imposing ever more drastic controls. This was happening in Germany under the "Hindenburg program" and would happen in Russia, too.

> These steps are quite inevitably prescribed by those conditions which the war has created and which the postwar aftermath will make even more acute in many respects; and in their totality as well as in their further development, these steps would be a transition to socialism, which cannot be realized in Russia immediately, with one stroke, without transitional measures, but which is perfectly feasible and scientifically necessary as a result of such transitional measures.

Lenin, then and later, was never very precise about the prospects of socialism in Russia,* but he did offer concrete ideas as to what he would do if the Bolsheviks came to power. He expected to have the bulk of the population behind him. The dictatorship of the proletariat would therefore be an even more democratic regime than capitalist democracy, which benefited only the rich. He also would find at his disposal the vast creativity of the Russian people, liberated for once from all exploitation, and the newly created administrative machinery of the soviets for putting it to work. "Capitalist" techniques, he announced, had so simplified modern administration that even proletarian housewives would take their turn in the central offices. Lenin, moreover, intended to nationalize the banks and syndicates, utilizing their organizations and skills for running the economy. Experts in all fields would flock to Soviet power, because of the greater oppor-

---

* Leninism was never a single-strand doctrine, but one woven of many related (and sometimes contradictory) lines of argument. It was a matter of choice, on Lenin's part or that of his successors, with which particular strand the party line was to be brought up to date.

tunities for constructive work which it offered. In addition, he would make use of the "best models from the experience of the progressive countries." It seems incredible that so tough-minded a thinker as Lenin could indulge, with patent sincerity, in such utopian fantasies.

But his Bolshevik hardness had not left him. For those who would not cooperate, Lenin hinted, the shackles of social control were ready: food rationing and compulsory labor service. Still more ominous was his statement that under the new regime "all citizens are transformed into hired employees of the state which is made up of the armed workers. All citizens become employees and workers of one national state syndicate." The emphasis, one notes, rested on the overriding power of the state under a dictatorship which would wither away only when the superior social discipline which it required had become the self-discipline of the individual citizen.

The combination of utopianism with the harsh practicalities of power indicates the central paradox in the Bolshevik program. On the one hand, the dictatorship of the proletariat, so it promised, would launch the Liberation of Man. On the other, it called for discipline and restraint, for closely intermeshed cooperation in the huge workshop of socialist society. It held out freedom as the goal but took away its essence, the spontaneity of the natural man. Thus Lenin prepared his party for coping with the second of the overriding necessities of Russian development, the necessity for rapid updating of state and society. And no mean future he envisaged for his country:

> Owing to her revolution [so he wrote in September, looking back to the fall of the monarchy], Russia in a few months has caught up to the advanced countries in her political organization [a fine bit of megalomania]. But this is not enough. War is inexorable and puts the question with unsparing sharpness: either perish or catch up and overtake the advanced countries economically as well.

In short, a Bolshevik Russia, unwilling to perish, was to surpass the glories of the "capitalist" countries which had been the global

models for so long. It was Soviet Russia then that would spear-
head the human advance to freedom and justice. Thus, Lenin
competed with Woodrow Wilson as a savior of mankind in the
darknesses of the War.

With thoughts and assurances like these, Lenin spurred his
party to take the fatal plunge. On October 23, with some hesitation and after the defection of several doubters—even now the
party lacked the unity for which Lenin had pleaded since 1902—
the Bolshevik Central Committee voted for the seizure of power.
The preparation and execution of the *coup,* however, were not to
be Lenin's work—he remained in hiding from the end of July
until early November—but Trotsky's.

Liov Davidovich Bronstein, alias Trotsky, was a far more dash-
ing and versatile revolutionary than Lenin. He had escaped from
Siberia twice, had been president (for a time) of the St. Petersburg Soviet in 1905, had traveled farther and kept his eyes wider
open to the fascinations of life than Lenin. He lacked Lenin's
doggedness and practical common sense, being apt to carry points
of doctrine to an extreme, but he outshone him as a writer and
speaker. If Lenin may be called the Grand Strategist of the Revolution, Trotsky in these weeks was the Grand Stage Manager, an
artist of genius in revolutionary action. As skilled a dialectitian
as any Marxist, he excelled as a revolutionary journalist and pam-
phleteer; as a revolutionary orator, he still has to find his equal.*
He could throw himself wide open to the varieties of human experience and fuse them into service to the Revolution; he could
fall in with the mood of any audience, capture it, and bend it to
his will. In his words, the abstractions of Marxism came alive
with the body warmth of humanity. Yet despite his almost febrile
sensitivity he was a brilliant organizer of action, as hardheaded
and cruelly cold-blooded in the crucial moments of revolution as
Lenin. The one great flaw in this plethora of gifts—apart from
the repulsive fusion of idealism and expediency—was his pride.
He could not depersonalize himself as a Bolshevik should and
never inspired the selfless loyalty which bound men, includ-

---

* In this respect he surpassed Lenin, who was no mediocre orator
himself.

ing himself, to Lenin. Yet in these weeks Trotsky was at his best.

The "objective conditions," he agreed with Lenin, were right for revolution. The Provisional Government was discredited. Kerensky's rhetoric, now strained sometimes to the point of incoherence, had lost its spell over "the great soul of the people." The stalemate within the moderate center was more frustrating than ever. As a leading Menshevik observed in mid-September during the Democratic Conference, one of several *ad hoc* public bodies convoked to bolster the Kerensky regime, "The praesidium . . . has unanimously decided that there is within the organized democracy no unanimity of will that could be translated into action." Could there have been a more damning admission? Meanwhile, the German army was advancing on the Baltic coast, which heightened the sense of crisis in the capital.

If the Bolsheviks did not seize the propitious moment now, another and more successful Kornilov might arise. Under the pretext of defending the masses against the forces of reaction Trotsky set to work. Using the machinery of the Petrograd Soviet, regardless of the opposition of the moderates, he armed the Red Guards (the Bolsheviks' own fighting force), won over wavering units of the garrison, and incited public opinion to fever pitch by ruthlessly fanning the phobias and hopes of the masses. An eyewitness has left us an account of Trotsky's power over his audience in those days:

> Around me was a spirit close to ecstasy. It seemed that the crowd would, at once, without any urging or leadership, sing some sort of religious hymn. . . . Trotsky formulated some sort of short general resolution, or proclaimed some sort of general formula like "we will stand for the cause of the workers and peasants to our last drop of blood."
>
> Who is in favor? The crowd of thousands, as one man, raised their hands. I saw the raised hands and the burning eyes of men, women, youngsters, workers, soldiers, muzhiks, and—of typically lower middle-class persons. Were they in a soulful passion? Did they see, through the raised curtain, a corner or some sort of "holy land" toward which they were

striving? Or were they imbued with a consciousness of the political moment, under the influence of the political agitation of the socialists?

The *coup* was planned for the eve of the second All-Russian Congress of Soviets, known in advance to have a Bolshevik majority. The Bolsheviks did not wish to be given power by that congress, but to take it by themselves and to present the delegates with the *fait accompli*. They were determined to preserve their separate identity.

While the preparations were in progress, Kerensky remained inexplicably passive. He did not seem to be worried by the ill-concealed talk of insurrection. When at the last moment he took a few precautions, it was too late. Through the Red Guards and a few radical elements in the garrison, the Bolsheviks, early on November 7, occupied the key points of the city and after much hesitation late on the same day laid siege to the Winter Palace, the seat of government. There followed some aimless shooting, yet before long they gained entry peaceably and arrested the ministers whom they found there drafting and redrafting an appeal to the people of Petrograd (Kerensky had already left to seek help outside the city). Little blood was shed, and the city was spared the terror that had characterized the July days. Indeed, life in Petrograd remained strangely normal, for the deed was done, on the whole, according to schedule—with some competence, as befitted a revolutionary elite, although hardly with the precision and command of the situation of which party history was to boast subsequently. In Moscow, however, the Bolshevik seizure of power took place only after a week of bitter fighting. The country was far from won.

On November 7, even before the *coup* was completed, Trotsky announced to the Petrograd Soviet that the Provisional Government was overthrown, and Lenin, appearing again in public, gave a brief explanation of the meaning of these events:

What is the significance of this revolution? Its significance is . . . that we shall have a soviet government, without the participation of the bourgeoisie of any kind. The oppressed masses will of themselves form a government. The old state machinery will be smashed into bits and in its place will be created a new machinery of government by the soviet organizations. From now on there is a new page in the history of Russia, and the present . . . Russian revolution shall in the final result lead to the victory of socialism.

On the same day, the second All-Russian Congress of Soviets assembled in the Smoĺny Institute, a former school for aristocratic young ladies which also served as the Bolshevik headquarters (despite Lenin's quip that the party was no girls' dormitory, there was a girls' school in the revolution after all!). The congress was no longer a gathering of the cream of the revolutionary intelligentsia, as it had been in June, but of the unwashed, suspicious, and sullen "black people" from the depths of Russia who, as Trotsky put it, "grasp a phenomenon wholesale, not bothering about details and nuances." As the delegates, among whom the Bolsheviks comprised slightly more than half, voted a Bolshevik Central Executive Committee, the Mensheviks and moderate Social Revolutionaries (but not the left SR) walked out in protest. "So much refuse thrown into the garbage pail of history!" Trotsky shouted after them. During the following night, November 8-9, Lenin, stepping into his role as head of the new government, announced two decrees, the first declaring the war at an end, the second handing the land to the peasants largely on their own terms. The third and last item of business, after which the delegates were sent home again, was the ratification of the Council of People's Commissars, the new executive organ that was to carry out all the other promises of the Bolsheviks.

Let us ignore at this point the fact that the Bolsheviks were not firmly established for several years, but rather draw a few conclusions about their ascent to power. In the first place one can hardly deny that theirs was a democratic revolution. It established a government that could hope to speak—at least at this fleeting moment—for a majority of Russians. It was a government of "soviet Russia," as this term has been used here, close to the political instincts of the bulk of the people.

Secondly, the overthrow of the Provisional Government—and of "privilege Russia" in general—was not entirely of the Bolsheviks' own making. It was the result of the elemental torrent of liberation that had broken loose after March. The existing bonds of government and society were all snapping by themselves, in the countryside, the army, the factories, the national minorities, everywhere. No authority was strong enough to stem that tide. All that could possibly be attempted—and that with great difficulty—was to direct it from within until it had run its course.

Thirdly, the elemental revolt aiming at the smashing of the old state machinery was a phenomenon possible only in Russia (or underdeveloped countries like China). Only there did the run of the population still live in relative self-sufficiency, with hardly a stake in the government. "Soviet Russia" had little to lose from the overthrow of the government, neither protection of property or status, nor social security, nor extensive public education, nor any other boon of government.* In urban-industrial Europe, on the other hand, the majority of the population had long since acquired such a stake. State, society, and the economy were interwoven a thousandfold; all citizens were patently interdependent for their very livelihood. Thus nearly everyone had a vested interest in order and security, regardless of his political views. Threaten him, in time of crisis and internal disunity, with the overthrow of the government and he would rush headlong into the arms of a Mussolini or Hitler. And if he longed for a change of regime, he would still insist that the transition be accomplished "legally," without disturbing the continuity of the public services. There would never be a chance, in other words, of a Bolshevik revolution in the West.

The Bolshevik seizure of power—to take at this point a long look both backward and forward—marked for Russia the end of

---

* Those groups which depended on public order or were aware of the technical problems of government were unanimous in their condemnation of the Bolshevik *coup*.

an era of revolution from below. The tide of liberation, which assumed hurricane proportions in the fall of 1917 and continued to rage for several years more, had been rising since the start of the century. Autocracy had sacrificed the "Witte system" to it but had itself been forced to give ground in 1905. While seemingly recovering most of its losses, it never succeeded in reestablishing its authority. The trend continued to run against it, even under the pressure of the war. The defeats deepened and strengthened the upsurge until it finally broke all bounds after the sudden fall of the monarchy.

The new freedom liberated the long-suppressed spontaneity of the peoples of Russia. It did not lead, unfortunately, to the self-discipline needed for an effective democratic polity or an industrial economy. Liberation meant throwing off the hated restraints of the old order and being able, for once, to act according to one's deepest feelings.

The war, on which the Bolshevik victory is so often blamed, had rather little to do with that extremist turn of events. It may have contributed to the savagery of the revolt, but it destroyed neither liberal democracy nor Russian "capitalism." Freedom, the heady freedom of the new regime, did that. Given its own ideals, liberal democracy in Russia could never have been more than a brief transition phase. It would always have led to "soviet democracy," the freedom of the "black people," which signified, under existing conditions, spontaneity carried to the point of anarchy.*

By the same logic, however, freedom was bound to destroy itself. If Russia was to survive as a Great Power, with the same universal appeal as the others—these were the harsh terms of the competition—it needed the discipline of cooperation under both government and an industrial economy.

Here lay the central quandary of modern Russia. It was a

* Traditionally, the Russian concept of freedom has always tended toward anarchism. Many are the cases, before and after the Revolution, of Russian travelers hoping to find "freedom" in western Europe and being bitterly disillusioned by the tight cake of custom encrusting western life and making a mockery of freedom as they had expected it.

backward country at the mercy of powerful neighbors. The essence of its backwardness rested in the fact that its people, left to their own devices, could manage neither effective government nor a productive modern economy. Was the Russian Empire then to be dissolved? For the Bolsheviks, at any rate, and many non-Bolsheviks as well, the answer was a passionate No! They craved power for their own survival, for the future of world socialism, and for the integrity of their territorial base in Imperial Russia which they dearly loved. Thus from November, 1917, onward the suppression of spontaneity began anew, slowly at first under Lenin, furiously at last under Stalin. The new harness of Communist rule proved to be far tighter than the tsarist one. The dangers to the country were greater, the ambitions of its rulers bolder, and the progress of the "advanced" countries undiminished; they would not mark time while Soviet Russia tried to catch up.

The essence of industrialism, which stands at the base of modern power, is interdependence and voluntary cooperation throughout the length and breadth of society. Lenin's sociology, although clumsy and extreme, took its cue from the "capitalist" order. Every advanced industrialized society constitutes a vast workshop. Its members voluntarily coordinate their activities under a common law and government—never perfectly, to be sure, yet sufficiently so as to produce a remarkable flow of goods and services.* They do this with no more drastic compulsions than submitting to majority rule and earning a living, and sometimes with much nonpecuniary zeal. Submitting to the discipline of their jobs and their political order, they ordinarily do not even feel constricted in their freedom; they are spurred on by the opportunities (the current talk of alienation notwithstanding).†

---

* It should be emphasized that modern industrialism requires for its effective operation the discipline both of steady habits of work in shop or office and of government by discussion. In pre-Bonn Germany, for instance, one could find the first but not the second, with the result that social and political conflict constantly interfered with production.

† It is to be noted that the philosophy of alienation from Marx to Freud originated in central and eastern Europe, where resistance to the

Woe now to a country that requires the results of modern industrialism without possessing among its inhabitants the necessary motivation and self-discipline. It has no choice but to replace the spontaneous self-discipline of the West by a process of deliberate substitution replacing lacking motivation by compulsion. The scope of Communist totalitarianism, as it developed over the years, indicates to what extent, in the judgment of its leaders, the Soviet population still lacks the spontaneous motivation needed for competitive power in world affairs. What it lacks has to be replaced by an artificial, external discipline.*

The Bolsheviks would never admit, of course, that they were sacrificing freedom for the sake of power. Their determination to become a superior universal model required that they make an additional effort to represent their Russia as the embodiment of a freedom greater than that found in the "capitalist" West. They had to overtake their model in *all* attributes of superiority, even as the price of stretching the vocabulary of freedom and spontaneity beyond all recognition.

---

discipline of urban-industrial life was greatest. To this day, it is sustained by intellectuals from the fringe areas of industrialism rather than by the hardened natives of Manchester, Detroit, or Chicago. Unfortunately, this essay cannot deal with the hidden psychological and spiritual counter current to the outreach of western rationalism connected with the influence of Dostoevsky, Nietzsche, Freud, or the Indian mystics. This current, which is moving from the periphery toward the center, has not (or not yet) significantly influenced the course of global politics. Yet, it is rising to prominence in the United States, creating a state of mind resembling that of the Russian intelligentsia in the nineteenth century. There is, however, a basic inconsistency in the attitude of the alienated: While they turn their backs on the relentless organization of urban-industrial society, their life style, nevertheless, remains closely dependent on its products and services (like The Pill).

* This line of argument implies that in analyzing the causes of modern totalitarianism we can make no distinction between polity and society, between the political system and the totality of individual and social motivation. What counts is the totality of the organization and distribution of human vitality in the body politic, programmed, as it were, into the volition of each separate individual.

VII

THE FIRST MONTHS OF THE SOVIET REGIME

THE BOLSHEVIKS, to return to the story of the Revolution, had seized power; the Communists, as the Bolsheviks under Lenin's urging now began to call themselves, had to hold and consolidate it throughout the Empire and spread it beyond if they could. What they had learned in their struggle against autocracy and the Provisional Government they now had to apply even more recklessly and on the grandest scale. They aimed at nothing less than overthrowing the entire world order, both in the capillaries of socioeconomic relations and in the coarser tissues of global politics, and replacing it by a superior, more finely meshed society and a more advanced civilization suited to the highest potential of man. As they saw it, mankind was entering a crucial phase of development. The age was one of final solutions: capitalism was giving way to socialism with all the bloody alarms of a great historical earthquake. Taking this heroic view, the Communists were emotionally steeled for the grimness that lay ahead. Were the Wilsonians in their rosier vision of the future better prepared?*

* At this point, we should briefly consider the view that the Communist vision was a case of self-fulfilling prophecy: by raising their sights to the magnitude of final solutions and preparing for them, they brought about, or at least helped to bring about, the conditions that they had foretold. A reasonable case may be made for this view. Communist doctrine and agitation certainly assisted in the rise of fascism and national socialism; they thereby contributed to the holocausts of World War II. Yet, this view makes the influence of Communism appear stronger than it actually was. Seen in more comprehensive perspective, there were a great many other forces at work in Europe and the world contributing as much (or more) to the subsequent catastrophes. In

Communism's greatest asset for the realization of its far-reaching ambitions was no doubt its ideology. Marxism-Leninism was a true myth, as Georges Sorel, the advocate of violence, had used the term, a potent capsule mixing vital political insights with profound psychic drives and releasing spectacular energies for revolutionary action.

Many ingredients recommended this myth to the condition of Russia. Marxism was an ingenious mixture of German romanticism with British industrialism, a fusion of the slow and moralizing mentality of an agrarian (or pre-industrial) society with the fast rationalism of a superbly integrated and technically oriented community. Modern Russia found itself in a transition ever more rapid than that through which Germany had passed in the days of Marx; it wanted an appropriate ideological synthesis. Marxism also offered concrete advantages. It was most knowledgeable in fields in which the tsars had been notoriously deficient: economics, sociology, industrial relations, and mass politics. To their Marxist inheritance, the Bolsheviks added their own store of revolutionary experience and their insight into the psychology of frustrated idealists, displaced and uprooted factory workers, and the underdog in general.

Marxism-Leninism also supplied certain useful specifics. To mention but two: Its concept of the classless society justified the elimination of all the accumulated divisions and schisms in Russian society. It recognized only one class—the proletarian toilers regardless of race, religion, nationality, or level of culture. Its slogan of the dictatorship of the proletariat, moreover, allowed for a far more vigorous assertion of governmental leadership than had been possible under the recent autocrats. At the same time, it stressed the identity of the rulers and the ruled. The new regime had grown out of an uprising of the masses. The Communists were determined never to lose touch with that base.

New opportunities were also contained in the more general

---

other words, like other groups of men in the twentieth century the Communists were victims as much as makers of circumstance, anvil as much as hammers of destiny.

concept of Marxist-Leninist philosophy. More temptingly than the church, it held out hope for a better life for all mankind. And in stressing the interdependence of all social phenomena, it opened up vast vistas for experiments in social engineering designed to give reality to that hope. The economic base and the superstructure of government, law, art, literature, religion, the family, education—of the entire culture and the innermost consciousness of the individual—were all of one piece. Change the first and you would have license to tamper with all the rest. By its very nature, socialist sociology encouraged totalitarian practices.

Marxism-Leninism, moreover, provided a principle of international organization. Its doctrine of imperialism gave militant expression to the yet vague longings for independence in nonwestern countries overrun by "capitalist" civilization. It dignified their quest for prestige and power with a global significance, offered an outlet for action, and held out, in the vague distance, a promise of world government capable of guaranteeing peace and prosperity for all. The greatest reassurance in the Communist myth was reserved to the Russians themselves (if they could but convince themselves of its reality!). They now assumed leadership in the global antiwestern revolt, proud of having been the first to leap forward into the new era of human history, sure of possessing the foundations for the most advanced social order in the world. Both their myth and their nationalism compelled them to concentrate all their energies on catching up to and overtaking the "capitalist" countries, not only politically but in every other respect as well.

The appeal to Russian patriotism could be lifted out of the Marxist-Leninist context and be used separately, like a second language, for communication with those whom the myth could not reach. Yet the traditional pride of country could not supply the myth's universal sweep. Nor could it bestow the victorious uplift imparted by Marxist dialectics, which were the myth's most powerful ingredient. Marx, so the myth read, had discovered the laws of historical evolution, and his followers—his true followers like Lenin—could employ these laws with scientific accuracy in order to guide the world toward its socialist goal. This faith gave the Communists their arrogance and their imperviousness to failure. If history was with them, who could prevail against them in all the tempests of history?

The suitability of this myth for Russia's condition lay in the grand conceptions articulating government and society, Russia and the world, reality and ambition, in a manner inspiring self-confidence and a will to action. Yet there was one crucial proviso attached to it. While there might be slight adjustments in detail, the myth capsule had to remain intact. The irrational resolve to succeed must never be relaxed. Reasonableness and softness in any form quickly corroded the potency of the myth and were to be shunned like poison. If one ingredient gave way, the others lost their savor too. And if the myth collapsed, the revolutionary determination would wither, the dynamic drive stall, and all be lost. The preservation of the myth was the central condition for Communist survival.

The rigid ideological dogmatism, however, would never have sufficed for survival had it not been mated with an amazing pragmatic flexibility in the development of suitable political techniques. This continued unscrupulous agility in the choice of means bordering on adventurism was the result of several factors: the acute danger to their power which for years harassed the Communists; the continued discrepancy between their ambition and their resources; and finally, and perhaps most important, the wholesale rejection of all liberal-democratic models, which left them with only their own wits to face Russian realities. Not even Marxist doctrine offered concrete guidance for the construction of a socialist society. The constant improvisation in Communist practice brought into Russian statecraft an element of originality typical of that brief era of rampant spontaneity in Russian history.

The Communists' capacity for social and political experiment was put to a severe test after November, 1917, not only in Russia but in the world. Their very first act as a government, the decree on peace, placed their revolution in the global context.

While bidding the governments of the belligerent countries arrange an immediate armistice, it incited their subjects to revolution. All warring governments at the time were fomenting strife behind the enemy lines; the German gamble on the Bolsheviks had indeed paid off most brilliantly! Why should the Communists not play the same game? They were better apprenticed in the arts of subversion than any liberal or conservative regime. And years before, Lenin had already set the basic course: revolution in Europe and in Europe's colonies and dependencies throughout the world. Now the chance had come to put the revolutionary myth into effect and build up the counter power to European imperialism in all its forms.

In this foreign policy, Lenin played a double game. He dealt with the "capitalist" governments so long as they possessed effective power. But over their heads he also pushed for revolution by any means at his disposal. Immediately after taking power, he published the secret treaties of the Allied governments in order to expose their imperialist character. He sent out inflammatory radio appeals and put agitators to work on the soldiers of the Central Powers through both fraternization at the front and indoctrination in the prisoner-of-war camps. Where diplomatic channels were available, he used his ambassadors (or lesser emissaries with diplomatic immunity) as agents of the revolutionary contagion. In fomenting revolution everywhere, the Communists drastically broke with the social solidarity of the European state system that had become customary in the nineteenth century.* They set themselves apart as the center of a new global order, thereby also settling old scores in the field of foreign relations. With what relish they repudiated the foreign debts of their predecessors (which most likely would have been cancelled anyway)! With what insolence they addressed the "capitalist" governments when they thought they could do so with impunity!

---

* For the sake of perspective, however, we might keep in mind Bismarck's view of British foreign policy in the age of Palmerston and Gladstone: "For a good many years England has made it her business to threaten foreign countries with revolution."

And how they railed against the "colonial exploiters"! Within less than a month, they issued a rousing *Appeal to the Working Moslems* (among whom in their zeal they included even the Hindus of India):

> The working people of Russia burn with the sole desire to get a just peace and to help the oppressed people of the world to conquer freedom for themselves. . . . Russia is not alone in this cause. The great watchword of liberation . . . is caught up by all the workers of the West and the East. . . . The reign of capitalist pillage and violence is crumbling. The ground is burning beneath the feet of the bandits of imperialism. . . .

Thus began the deliberate mobilization of all dissatisfaction and bitterness throughout the world that could possibly be put to political use. The Communists drew on the widespread postwar pacifism; they probed into the deeper layers of disaffection with "capitalist" society which Sorel, Spengler, and others had expressed before the war; and they cultivated the frustrated ambitions of the native intelligentsia of Asia.

In times of stress, modern mass politics tends to become psycho-politics; it favors the absorption of the emotional needs of an aroused and often bewildered populace into political programs and political action. The Communists were pioneers in the arts of activating and manipulating the fears and hopes of the common man. They raised extravagant illusions and held out a promise, certified by the laws of history to become true, of a world order free from anxiety, hunger, exploitation, injustice, and, most important in these years, from war. They even appropriated the pacifist ideal of a peaceful world federation and incorporated it into their first constitution. Said one speaker in July, 1918, while commending that document:

> Our constitution is of world-wide significance. As the workers and peasants from different countries take advantage of favorable circumstances and follow the example of Soviet Russia, the Russian Soviet republic sooner or later will be

surrounded by daughter and sister republics, which united will lay the basis for a federation first of Europe and then of the entire world.

There would be no occasion for war in the commonwealth of peaceful toilers.*

In terms of modern power politics, the emotions of the masses were novel political raw material. No one could accurately gauge their strength in the final stages of an unprecedented war and in the agonies of its aftermath. The war had created a new climate of politics. As the clash of arms ended, the clash of political creeds mounted and new political armies descended into street and parliament. The Communists set high hopes on the effectiveness of the new instruments of power, and apprehensive conservatives often flattered them by taking their estimates at face value. The manipulation of public opinion abroad was the most effective foreign policy instrument which Lenin had at his disposal when all conventional tools of Russian power had been dissolved by defeat and revolution. He was determined to employ these tempestuous weapons as much as the blockade of Soviet Russia and its limited resources would permit, particularly as the Communist experiment within Russia encountered many unexpected obstacles.

As it turned out, the Bolshevik seizure of power in Petrograd was a rather minor event, important only in retrospect. The Bolsheviks could not overthrow the previous regime by telegraph as the Provisional Government had done in March. They had to conquer power in every locality afresh. This was fairly easy where they possessed solid support in the Great Russian heartland. But the course of events ran differently in the rural expanses along the mid-Volga, the Ukraine, the south and southeast, in Siberia, and in the fringe territories inhabited by

* Soviet federalism, incidentally, was not extended to the countries that fell under Communist rule after the second World War. Communist China, like Yugoslavia, remained vigorously independent; the others (Poland, Czechoslovakia, Hungary, and Rumania) retained legal sovereignty as People's Democracies.

non-Slavic peoples. And even where they held power, they did so tenuously, having to combat not only political enemies as desperate as themselves but also incredible disorganization, hunger, cold, exhaustion, explosive anarchy, and all the miseries of backwardness compounded by defeat and revolution. The tidal wave of popular spontaneity, which was to make the dictatorship of the proletariat a truly democratic regime for the vast majority of the inhabitants of the Empire and release untold creative social energy, soon proved to be a tricky, many-channeled, chaotic flood whipped to white fury by the acts of the new regime. How under these conditions was a small minority like the Communist party to make itself master of Russia?

There was unexpected trouble from the start. The new regime was boycotted by the entrenched civil servants in the ministries and banks on which it still had to rely. Step by step, it was forced to turn on them, and on their allies among the public, the terror edge of the proletarian dictatorship. It suppressed the liberal press and instituted what it called revolutionary justice, summary proceedings against all class enemies. It even created a new political police, the dreaded Cheka, to fight the counterrevolution whose leaders were drifting to the Don Cossack territory to prepare for civil war. Among fellow socialists, too, Lenin met with rancorous hostility which was not so easily countered. The moderates who had walked out of the second All-Russian Congress of Soviets set up their own Committee of Salvation. Through the Menshevik-led railway workers union, they controlled the chief means of communication and threatened a general strike. Even some of Lenin's closest followers voiced uneasiness over the rashness of the Bolshevik *coup*. Faced with such opposition within the Soviet ranks, Lenin bowed to political necessity and formed a political coalition of Bolsheviks and left Social Revolutionaries in order to give a somewhat broader base to his regime. Yet the smallness of even that foundation was soon made painfully evident.

Having joined, for propaganda reasons, the clamor for elections to the Constituent Assembly before he came to power, Lenin could not afterward prevent their being held. Nor could he rig them to hide the fact that majorities in these soviets of soldiers and workers did not signify majorities among the population at large. The results, as he anticipated, were distinctly disappointing. "Privilege Russia," to be sure, was completely routed (and not alone because of the political pressure against all *burzhui*). Even the Mensheviks had come off very poorly. The Social Revolutionaries (of all shades) and Bolsheviks together counted for four fifths of the vote, which again showed where the majority of Russians stood. But the bulk of that block belonged to the Social Revolutionaries, the Bolsheviks reaping slightly less than a quarter of the total. The left SR had not run separately from the SR party; hence the numerical strength of Lenin's Bolshevik-left SR coalition could not be tabulated. But as the few ballots of the Constituent Assembly subsequently indicated, it clearly did not command a majority.

Nor could Lenin, who had no use for parliamentary institutions, prevent a meeting of the Constituent Assembly. After much sparring, it was allowed to gather on January 18, 1918, in the Tauride Palace, surrounded by Red Guards. It at once showed its anti-Bolshevik orientation, whereupon the Bolshevik delegates walked out. The remaining members did, however, endorse the Bolshevik decree on land and declare Russia a democratic federative republic. When the session dragged on into the early hours of the next day, the commandant of the Tauride Palace informed Victor Chernov, who happened to be speaking, that the guards were tired and wanted to go home. Thereupon the assembly adjourned. When the delegates returned, they found the doors barred by order of the Central Executive Committee of the second All-Russian Congress of Soviets, which, meanwhile, had declared the Constituent Assembly dissolved. Thus ended the brief experiment of democratic parliamentarism, the posthumous child of the Provisional Government.

Was there any possibility that it might have succeeded where its parent had failed? It would hardly appear so. The Social Revolutionary party, to be sure, would doubtless have been able to form a government of its own, thus escaping the wrangles of coalition. But modern peasant parties have been notoriously weak and unsuccessful, and neither the SR party's program nor its organization held out a promise of superior efficiency (to put it mildly).* Moreover, the weakness and disunity of the moderate elements in general and the absence of a common set of convictions, which had destroyed the Provisional Government, would still have troubled any parliamentary regime emerging from the Constituent Assembly. In short, even though the tide of spontaneity no longer favored the Bolsheviks as it had before their seizure of power, their dictatorship still represented the best balance of social and political forces possible under the circumstances. The suppression of the Constituent Assembly did not, therefore, alter the political scene, although it made the dispossessed opposition more militant and thereby contributed to the outbreak of civil war. Afraid of such repercussions, Lenin immediately afterward convoked the third All-Russian Congress of Soviets which passed a "Declaration of the Rights of the Toiling and Exploited Peoples" designed to reassure the Soviet masses. And soon more urgent problems, requiring a strong and resourceful government, moved into the foreground.

For now the negotiations for peace were in their final stage. Lenin's call for a general armistice had been accepted only by the Central Powers. If the Communists wanted to end the war, they had to break Russia's treaty obligation to its allies not to conclude a separate peace. The negotiations with the German government were held at Brest-Litovsk in eastern Poland. They continued for several weeks, under the full glare of publicity, for the Communists wanted to practice what they proclaimed to be the people's choice in international relations: open covenants openly arrived at. And with the help of Trotsky's quick tongue they often managed, in the drawn-out exchanges, to best the German generals and diplomats, laying bare their aggressive designs.

The German conditions were indeed stupendous. Russia was to lose its Baltic provinces, all of Poland, the Ukraine, and vital

* After the influx of many nonpeasant elements in the wake of the March Revolution, the Social Revolutionary party was a deeply divided organization (if organization it could be called).

territories in the Caucasus, which were to be ceded to Turkey. Against these demands Lenin played for time in order to let the German Revolution, on which he had staked much, come to his aid. Despite the publicity of the negotiations, however, the German proletariat did not rise against its imperialist masters. In late February the German High Command, impatient with the Communists' procrastination, ordered the German armies to march deeper into the defenseless country. Thereupon the Communist leaders, who in fear of being captured had just moved the capital from Petrograd to Moscow, were forced to come to terms. The delay had already cost them dearly. It had given the Germans a chance to conclude a separate peace with the government of the Ukraine, which had seceded from Russia after the November *coup* and had not been brought to heel again by the Communists. Thus, for the time being, the Ukraine escaped from Soviet control seemingly by self-determination rather than by German power.

Signing the peace was a painful decision for the Bolsheviks.* Their party was deeply divided over the issue. The most militant elements preferred what they called revolutionary war—fighting the Germans by any means that came to hand and kindling among the entire population the passions of a last-ditch stand. In this they had the support of the left SR. Lenin, on the other hand, argued that a disastrous peace was still preferable to further chaos in Russia. He was not willing to risk the tenuous position of the Communist regime in an all-consuming holocaust which, in any case, might not stop the German juggernaut. On his plea the treaty of Brest-Litovsk was signed and ratified in early March, 1918.

A greater humiliation could hardly be imagined. By its provisions Russia lost the gains of two centuries of expansion, its greatest and most modern industrial center (which included most

* It was in these weeks, apparently, that the German subsidies to the Bolsheviks came to an end. Yet the parallel course of German and Bolshevik self-interest still continued. The German government accepted the Soviet regime as the most cooperative one which it could hope for in Russia. The Bolsheviks, in return, could send an old revolutionary as their ambassador to Berlin.

of its coal and iron), its food basket, most of its oil, and almost one third of its population. It was reduced, in terms of traditional power at least, to third-rate significance.

Thus did the peace treaty reveal the hollowness of Imperial Russia's great power pretension, as realists like Witte had prophesied long ago. The Germans roamed freely through the richest parts of the Empire, for a brief while even occupying Baku. And at home German industrialists laid their plans for the economic penetration of Soviet Russia as well, through the control of her means of communications. In the East, indeed, the German dream of a powerful *Mitteleuropa* seemed to have come true. Soviet Russia could consider itself fortunate that it had not lost far more. Had the bulk of the German armies not been diverted to the western front by the combined onslaught of France, England, and the United States, a sovereign Russia might have ceased to exist at all.

The peace of Brest-Litovsk was an exceedingly grim event in Russian history. But Lenin, whose work had braced him for just such situations, knew how to draw strength from its very grimness:

> We must plumb to the very depths the abyss of defeat, dismemberment, bondage, and humiliation in which we have been plunged. The more clearly we understand this, the more firm, hardened, and steeled will be our determination to achieve liberation, our striving to rise once again from bondage to independence, and our indomitable resolve at all costs to make Russia cease to be wretched and feeble and become mighty and abundant in the fullest sense of the term.

Fortitude was indeed sorely needed. While the treaty of Brest-Litovsk represented the nadir of Russian state power in modern times, there was still worse to come for the Communist regime. It was an evil omen that as a result of the peace the left Social Revolutionaries drifted away from the Communists, who henceforth carried the burden of power alone, thereby hastening again the outbreak of the civil war.

THE FIRST MONTHS OF THE SOVIET REGIME

For a moment, however, the treaty of Brest-Litovsk allowed Lenin a brief breathing spell. By mid-March the Communists had concluded peace, given the land to the peasants (albeit with many mental reservations), and made some progress toward the recasting of Russian government and society according to their program. In the spring and early summer, despite a gradual deterioration of the regime's position, the outlines of the new order were beginning to show. The institutions of "privilege Russia," zemstvos, town dumas, press, universities, learned societies, clubs, and social centers—the whole web of its economic and social power—were demolished. The *bourgeoisie* was harrassed, terrorized, subjected to special capital levies, drafted for compulsory labor, treated like outcasts, and annihilated as a class. Thus began a long martyrdom for the Europeanized upper strata of Russian society. They suffered not only with their bodies but in their souls as well. The great majority of them had been patriotic Russians. Why should the impersonal sins of Russian history (which so few of them understood) be suddenly visited upon those who felt entirely innocent? Some of them turned against the Communists and fought back. Others—more than is commonly realized—succeeded in seeping into the Soviet establishment where their skills were wanted, a few even attaining important positions. None, however, could escape being dragged down into the gray, shapeless Soviet masses.

The egalitarianism of the communal tradition now began to set the official tone of the Soviet regime. No one was allowed to rise above his fellows. Even the People's Commissars, the ministers in the Soviet government, were paid only a skilled worker's wage (exceptions were made, however, for famous specialists or artists). No individual was allowed to enrich himself by the labor of others; only the state was permitted to hire and fire workers.* In other respects, too, the "black people" began to call the tune.

---

* The Soviet regime, however, never tampered with the right of individuals to own a minimum of private property such as household furnishings, books, a bicycle, and, later on, a savings account or even an automobile.

The former instinctive receptiveness to western influences was replaced by a deeper tradition of xenophobia and suspicion of all things European (the abstract internationalism of many leading Communists notwithstanding). Speech, rhetoric, fashion, and a thousand other details of life and thought changed flavor as the new regime adapted itself to the mentality of the Soviet masses. It was a shocking descent from previous standards, yet an inevitable corollary of modern mass politics, with some parallels in western Europe (as for instance the decline of journalism from *The Times* to the yellow press). Soviet teachers, writers, scholars, and the Party itself, were now faced with the endless uphill struggle to educate, refine, and civilize those who had hitherto distrusted all culture as the work of aliens or exploiters.

The new order was formally embodied in the Soviet constitution promulgated in July, 1918, for the territories left to Soviet rule, now called the Russian Soviet Federated Socialist Republic (RSFSR). It created a hierarchy of soviets as the basis of government, continuing the heavy overrepresentation of the workers and the system of indirect representation, both of which had evolved in the previous year. Various local councils at the base sent delegates to the provincial councils, which in turn were represented in the regional councils; these elected the members of the periodic All-Russian Congress of Soviets at the apex, the source of popular sovereignty (in theory), whose permanent organization was its All-Russian Central Executive Committee (VTsIK), a rather large body itself. Representation thus proceeded from the grass roots upward. Yet government authority descended strictly in the opposite direction. The Council of People's Commissars, the true executive in the Soviet system, acted with quick dispatch, submitting its decrees and actions to VTsIK at the latter's infrequent meetings merely for summary approval. The decisions of the Council of People's Commissars were binding on the executive committees of all lower soviets. They and their staffs constituted the new Soviet bureaucracy, in which one could recognize quite a few familiar faces held over from the old Russia, as well as its red tape and officiousness. In this manner the government of Russia became a strictly centralized Soviet government backed up, of course, on every level, by the Communist party.

At the same time, the Communists also brought Russia up to date in the relationship between church and state. They dissolved the monasteries and confiscated their properties (as once upon a time Henry VIII had done in England), made religion a private concern of the citizen, and left to the clergy and their flock only the church buildings (and often not even those). As militant atheists, the Communists were more ruthless in pruning the power of the church than the French radicals had been in the aftermath of the Dreyfus affair. Moreover, they made their fight against the church into a war against all religion,* avenging all the sins into which the Russian state—or Russian history—had led the Orthodox church. But knowing full well that the church is strengthened by the blood of the martyrs, they pressed their persecution with some caution.

Other innovations were legal equality for women; greatly liberalized laws on marriage, divorce and abortion; solemn safeguards against racial discrimination; constitutional pledges of extensive social services, of free education, and of improved housing, all guaranteeing the toilers access to the best of contemporary civilization. Needless to say, most of these measures remained on paper because of the continued penury of the state. The Communists also introduced, at long last, the Gregorian calendar, bringing Russian chronology up to that of the "capitalist" West by skipping thirteen days. Even the alphabet was simplified.

The Communists, finally, began to feel their way toward a socialist economy. The great banks were nationalized and industry (some of it in private hands until the summer of 1918) grouped by branches into syndicates under the authority of a new Supreme Economic Council. In economics, too, the Com-

---

* The Marxists followed the same eighteenth century "scientific" attitude toward religion which also guided men like T. H. Huxley or Freud. The Communists, as usual, were more zealous than the run of "enlightened" atheists.

munists pursued ambitious goals. Marxist doctrine had long proclaimed the superiority of a centrally planned economy over the anarchy of the capitalist market. Its heirs were now preparing to draw up a general economic plan for a Soviet Russia. We need not take too seriously, however, their pride of authorship of modern economic planning. Ever since the Witte system many Russian economists, industrialists, and scientists had recognized the necessity of central planning as a means of developing Russia's lagging economy and argued about its details. Only in one respect did the Communists far exceed their prerevolutionary predecessors: They were ready to extend their economic plan to all other peoples who might adopt the Soviet socialist system. This was the economic corollary of the constitutional provision for expanding the political federation. What gave actuality to such trust in planning was the model of German "war communism," which from the start had been intensively studied in Russian Marxist circles. Lenin himself, however, fancied a somewhat plainer scheme (also derived from a German source). He was to advance the socialist economy by providing cheap electricity to the whole country, arguing rather naïvely that Soviet rule plus electrification produced communism. All these schemes, however, remained only vague expectations. Effective planning required a more integrated and stable community than the Communists possessed in 1918 (or for years to come). The immediate problems were more elementary.

The economic deterioration which had begun with the war still continued, and at a disastrous clip. In the spring of 1918, the Russian economy was approaching the point of complete collapse. Money lost all value; manufactured goods disappeared from the shops; the shops themselves closed down as the normal channels of trade ceased to function; speculation and corruption were rife. The greatest need in the urban-industrial centers, where the Communists enjoyed their most solid support, and in many other places as well, was for food. More bread was the one item in their prerevolutionary appeals which the Communists had not been able to provide.

Supplying food for the urban population was not only a matter of central control over distribution and consumption, which was begun by the Provisional Government and carried to an extreme by the Communists, but above all of stimulating grain production in the villages. But when "boughten" goods could not be obtained even by barter, why should the peasants raise food for the market? In their extreme need, the Communists soon took to extorting what grain there was in the villages, using "committees of the poor" to pry it from the more prosperous peasants or, even more drastically, sending armed workers into the countryside to take it as a prize of war. The effect of these measures on the peasantry can be imagined; yet they lasted until 1921.

The proper remedy, obviously, lay in stimulating industrial production. But here the Communists encountered another serious problem. How could the revolutionary workers, who had just seized the factories, be persuaded to work even harder than under capitalism and for a smaller return? In the last analysis, as Lenin was fully aware, socialism had to prove its superiority over capitalism by outproducing it at lower cost. Labor productivity was the crucial issue that loomed behind much of Soviet domestic policy from 1918 to the present.

In theory, there should have been no difficulty. The destruction of the capitalist system was presumably carried out by a proletariat which, having learned the best that capitalism could teach, stepped forward with a superior discipline. Russian realities, however, did not fit the doctrine. As Lenin himself admitted in April, 1918, "The Russian worker is a bad worker compared with the workers of the advanced countries." The Soviet regime thus had to instruct its toilers how to work properly. And this meant using, in the name of the higher stage of development, all the tricks of the capitalist employer: piece wages, competition between work gangs, and time-and-motion studies according to Frederick W. Taylor. Lenin's advice to workers' delegations in these months might well have shocked less flexible Marxists. "Now we'll learn from the capitalists, because we don't know enough." And he treated his listeners to a dose of the Protestant ethic to boot: "Keep books punctually and conscientiously, manage economically, don't be lazy, don't steal, preserve strictest discipline in your work." How, one wonders, were the Russian workers to imitate the skills of capitalism without stumbling into the pitfalls of "petty-bourgeois spontaneity" of which Lenin emphatically warned them?

But he used still another and more ominous line of thought. As he put it, modern large-scale industry, by which the Communists set such store, required an "absolute and strict unity of will which directs the joint labor of hundreds, thousands, and tens of thousands of people":

> The revolution has only just broken the oldest, most durable, and heaviest fetters to which the masses were compelled to submit. That was yesterday, but today the same revolution demands, in the interests of socialism, that the masses unquestionably obey the single will of the leaders of the labor process.

Almost simultaneously, the seventh Communist party congress with its usual Bolshevik shrillness demanded "the most energetic, unsparingly decisive, draconian measures to raise the self-discipline and discipline of workers and peasants." These were alarming prospects for the Russian toilers. It was one thing to bring Russian state and society into alignment and do away with all class barriers. But it was quite another to train the Russian proletariat for industrialization.

Obviously, the Russian proletariat was not yet ready to submerge its newly awakened wills into one single will, or, more generally, to assume its governmental duties. A deep disappointment over its response to the Communist dictatorship runs through Lenin's speeches in the spring and summer of 1918. As he observed in July:

> The workers and peasant masses possess greater constructive talent than might have been expected. . . . But at the same time we have to admit that the chief shortcoming of the masses is their timidity and reluctance to take affairs into their own hands.

Two weeks later he admonished party workers, "We must broaden our sphere of influence among the working class masses." The spontaneity of the latter, alas, left much to be desired. What Lenin really meant was, to paraphrase one of his classic statements, that the Russian proletariat, exclusively by its own efforts, was apt to develop only the petty-bourgeois habits of backwardness. The social energy released by the revolutionary masses, by those "backward strata now for the first time lifting themselves from the dregs," was not by itself going to build socialism. His Menshevik critics had been right after all: On such foundations no socialist order would last.

Yet the impatient Lenin was to be stopped neither by the Russian workers' spontaneous trade-union consciousness nor by their backwardness. The obstacles merely affirmed his determination. As he announced in what was probably the crassest statement of Leninism:

> The habits of the capitalist system are too strong, the tasks of reeducating a people educated in these habits for centuries is a difficult job which demands a lot of time. But we say: our fighting method is organization. We must organize everything, take everything into our hands. . . .

Ever more total organization and comprehensive social engineering were Lenin's ultimate answers to the staggering problems facing a Communist Russia.

All the innovations decreed in these early months were, however, only glimpses of things to come. In the spring and summer of 1918, the time was hardly ripe for the total reorganization of Russian society. Lenin's regime was still caught halfway between the constructive discipline required for even the most elementary functions of government (not to mention socialist reconstruction) and the destructive revolutionary spontaneity which had helped the Bolsheviks into power. As Lenin constantly stressed, the overthrow of a social order entrenched for centuries called for a protracted effort. In order to survive, the Bolshevik Revolution had to plow exceedingly deep.

Oh, for that visceral, anarchic excitement of revolution set off by the Bolshevik tocsin!

Life is only worth living when we make immense demands on it. All or nothing! A faith, not in what is not found upon earth, but in what ought to be there, although at present it does not exist and may not come forth for quite a while! . . . A true revolutionary cannot aim at anything less, though we cannot yet say whether this aim will be accomplished or not. Its cherished hope is to raise a universal cyclone which will carry to the lands buried in snow the warm winds and the fragrance of orange groves, and will water the sun-scorched plains of the south with the refreshing rain from the northern regions. Peace and brotherhood of nations is the banner under which the Russian revolution marches on its way. This is the time of the roaring flood. This is the music which he who has ears should hear.

In the early stages of the Revolution, such exultation was a source of Communist strength, particularly among the intellectuals. It added a sheen of pure idealism to Bolshevik expediency. Before long, however, it was apt to turn either into revulsion (as in the case of the poet Alexander Blok, who wrote the lines just quoted) or into irresponsibility. Idealists are worshipers of spontaneity, which makes them poor organization men.

For coarser and more easily guided natures, the Communists unhesitatingly beat the vile drums of greed, hatred, and sadism. Lenin wholeheartedly endorsed the slogan, coined by an anonymous revolutionary, "Let's loot the looters." He also recommended revolutionary justice carried out on the spur of the moment, without process of law. And he did not shrink from putting the revolutionary dynamite into the deepest bonds of social life.

In granting freedom and equality to all women, the Communists made the ambition of women and the discontent of wives into a powerful political force. A Bolshevik virago was sometimes more frightful than the fiercest Red guardsman. They also revamped the traditional relationship between the sexes. Bourgeois marriage was a fraud, the Communist Manifesto had declared. It was now to be replaced by "the free union of men and women who are lovers and comrades," in the words of Mme. Kollontai, the Communist authority on the "woman question" (who freely practiced what she preached). Marriage in times of revolution was bound to suffer. But the new gospel helped to undermine it even more.

As for the care of children born from these free unions, Mme. Kollontai supplied the following answer:

> The worker mother who is conscious of her social function will rise to a point where she no longer differentiates between yours and mine; she must remember that there are henceforth only *our* children, those of the communist state, the common possession of all workers.

Alas for the socialist mothers; they must remember that the maternal instinct was merely a bourgeois relic (even *their* spontaneity was not suited to the new age)! And alas for the waifs entrusted to the care of a society at war!

The new regime also tended to set the children against their parents, particularly if the latter did not belong among the toilers, and the pupils against their teachers. The teachers, by Lenin's own admission, felt rather lukewarm towards the Revolution. For the most part they belonged to the old Russia, a fact of which their charges were quick to take advantage. For years, Russian education was treated as a tool of revolution, and the curriculum as well as classroom discipline suffered. Needless to say, the institutions of higher learning, now open only to the toilers, lost all their former luster.

Thus the universal cyclone began to take its toll. But deliberately unleashing it against all customary order and stability was a dangerous game. It nearly brought down even the Communist regime.

VIII

THE UNIVERSAL CYCLONE, 1918–1921

✪

THE BREATHING SPELL after Brest-Litovsk barely gave Lenin time to come to grips with basic issues of socialist reconstruction before he was confronted with all the unfinished business of revolution now grown to gigantic proportions. By their unilateral coup in November and their continuous instigation of revolutionary terror, the Communists had set the example of deliberate violence. Under such prompting, the anarchic spontaneity of the previous year, already tending toward bloodshed, turned into an open and universal civil war. Starting in a minor way before November had ended, it smoldered under the surface during the following winter and spring. In May, 1918, the fury suddenly leaped into the open and raged for almost three terrible years in every community of the Russian Empire with unforgiving finality, pitting Reds against Whites (as the defenders of the old Russia were called), poor peasants against kulaks and Cossacks, city dwellers against villagers, uneducated against educated, socialists against capitalists, Bolsheviks against Mensheviks or Social Revolutionaries, non-Russians against Russians, Christians against Jews, men against men in the frenzy of raw spite. In this orgy of fratricide, certain clearly defined fronts stood out. In the border regions of the north, west, southwest, south, and southeast, non-Russians fought for independence or genuine autonomy. In Siberia and the same border regions, Reds fought Whites. In addition, peasant forces called the Greens fought both Whites and Reds in many parts of the country, but particularly in the Ukraine.

Oddly enough, the first and most dangerous threat to the Communist regime came not from the army officers who were gathering in the south or Siberia but from the Bolsheviks' former allies in the underground, the Social Revolutionaries. Excluded from power, they turned their conspiratorial methods against the Communist dictatorship. The left SR, in opposition after March, was even bolder, plotting within the Cheka (to which it had been admitted as member of the coalition) for an uprising in the capital.

The Social Revolutionaries, as well as other opposition elements, received aid from an unexpected quarter. A rather large contingent of Czech soldiers, sifted from the Austro-Hungarian prisoners of war for volunteer service in France, was to be evacuated via the Siberian railroad and Vladivostok. As the Czechs gathered in the latter part of May along that far-flung line, the Communist leadership, suspicious of their motives, suddenly demanded that they disarm. In reply the Czechs seized control of the Siberian railroad and thereby encouraged various opposition groups in the vicinity to similar defiance.* Now events moved thick and fast. In western Siberia, two anti-Communist centers sprang up. Closer to Moscow, in Samara, several prominent Social Revolutionary deputies of the Constituent Assembly created an anti-Bolshevik government of their own and began to rally an army. On July 6, a group of the left SR, after their party's final break with the Communists, assassinated the German ambassador at his Moscow residence and tried to seize the city. At the same time, some towns on the upper Volga ousted their Communist-led soviets. Elsewhere, factories revolted and railway workers threatened to strike. At the end of July, Lenin, thoroughly alarmed, declared "the socialist fatherland in danger."

---

* These events decided the fate of the Imperial family. Transferred in August, 1917, from Petrograd to Tobolsk in western Siberia, they were shifted in late April to Ekaterinburg, an industrial town under Soviet control. In the night of July 16, ten days before the Czechs occupied the town, they were murdered in the cellar of their house, together with their physician, two servants, and a spaniel.

To the internal uprisings, foreign intervention was added. In late June, the British government, eager to preserve the Russian front by any means at its disposal, reinforced the port of Murmansk, which British troops had occupied in March. In early August, with American help, it seized Archangel as well, thereby cutting off Soviet Russia from its remaining outlets to the sea. The British also dispatched a small force to central Asia, and, in order to speed the evacuation of the Czechs, the three western Allies and Japan occupied Vladivostok and the stations along the Siberian railroad as far west as the Urals, giving aid and comfort to all anti-Bolshevik groups on their way.

The climax of the crisis came in August. The month began with the capture of Kazan on the mid-Volga by the Samara regime. It ended with the assassination of Uritsky, the Petrograd chief of the Cheka, and the severe wounding of Lenin by an assassin in Moscow. Never was the Communist regime closer to collapse.

Pressed against the wall, the Communists fought back with cold fury. The reverses strengthened the discipline of the Red Army which Trotsky had begun to train after Brest-Litovsk; now it began to show its fighting qualities. The Cheka, too, swung into action. Large-scale terror became the order of the day, as thousands and thousands of hostages picked from all strata of society and all opposition groups were shot. Thus began the horrors of the civil war, destined to last until the spring of 1921.

By September, 1918, the Communists had successfully beaten off the uprisings of the Social Revolutionaries, only to encounter the more effective onslaught of the tsarist officers who now entered the field as champions of the dictatorship of the right; in Siberia, they established their first stronghold under the leadership of Admiral Kolchak. As "Supreme Ruler" of the Empire he claimed command over all armed forces of Russia. In the winter and spring of 1919, his troops were slowly advancing northwestward in order to achieve a junction with the British at Archangel, thus creating a second crisis for the Communists.

The German revolution in November, 1918, brought Lenin a blissful moment of elation, but little relief. The armistice in the West, which preceded the German revolution, annulled the treaty of Brest-Litovsk and reopened the Baltic and the Ukraine to Soviet forces. But at the same time it intensified western intervention, which now assumed a clearly anti-Communist orientation. While the retreating German troops guarded the Baltic littoral against the Red Army, British ships entered the Baltic Sea. British troops also appeared on the Caspian Sea, and French forces occupied key Black Sea ports.

The Communists succeeded in turning back Kolchak's offensive just in time to prevent diplomatic recognition of the "Supreme Ruler" by the Paris peace conference. But as his fortunes ebbed, the White "Army of the South," commanded by General Denikin, an abler man than Kolchak, began its advance into Soviet territory. In October, 1919, it drove to within 250 miles of Moscow, producing yet another spell of tenseness in the Kremlin, particularly as a third White force under General Yudenich, operating from the Baltic, simultaneously penetrated the outskirts of Petrograd. Comforted by the virtual withdrawal of Allied intervention in September, 1919, the Bolsheviks also survived these alarms. But as they drove Denikin's army to its doom (Yudenich never constituted a serious threat), the government of the newly established Poland declared war on Soviet Russia. After some amazing reversals of the fortunes of war, the Polish armies penetrated deep into Byelorussia before peace was made. The last battles of the civil war were fought during the fall of 1920 in the Crimean peninsula, from which General Wrangel, Denikin's successor and the most capable of all the White commanders, had conducted a futile campaign into the mainland before being evacuated with French help.

In the winter of 1920-1921, the war with the rebellious non-Russian minorities in the steppes and deserts of the southeast also came to an end. The Tatars and Bashkirs between the Volga and the Urals were granted a measure of autonomy under strict Soviet control, as were the Kirghiz people further to the southeast. Turkestan in central Asia was likewise subdued, although a few rebellious tribesmen still held out. It too received autonomy as a Soviet Socialist Republic. And in the Transcaucasian region the Red Army reconquered the three republics, Georgia, Armenia, and Azerbaijan, which had proclaimed their independence earlier in the civil war, and subjected them, as a Soviet Socialist federation, to Communist rule.

We cannot, however, view these murderous events in isolation, as is done in Soviet histories, for from the start the principal fronts of the civil war had been extended far beyond Russia. The Russian civil war was the center of the universal cyclone which shook all of Europe—a Europe wanly emerging from the war—and jolted the world as well, as Lenin had predicted.

What a dismal spectacle the chief regions of Europe presented at the end of the war, and what an opportunity for revolutionary agitation! In eastern Europe a great landslide was underway. The three empires which had given order and stability to the marches of Europe had collapsed (not to mention the Ottoman Empire, whose final dismemberment spread the cataclysm into the Near and Middle East). As a result, not only Russia (as we have seen) but the broad stretch of liberated lands· from the Baltic to the Black Sea and Mediterranean found itself in a profound state of flux, traversed by two revolutions.

The first was the revolution of national self-determination, which created a series of new sovereign states, Finland and the three Baltic republics, Poland, Czechoslovakia, and Hungary, and greatly augmented two older states, Rumania and Serbia (now renamed Yugoslavia). Constituting (or reconstituting) their governments, drawing their boundaries, and settling the fate of innumerable national minorities in regions which history had not predestined to form nation-states, were difficult if not superhuman tasks. In the process much blood was spilled.

The other revolution, compounding the first, was a social one. In the lands carved from the old Russia, Austria-Hungary, and Germany, the monarchical order of life was overthrown and western democracy introduced, yet not without some competition from the Soviet model. Particularly where large landed estates had been the rule, land reform was hastily pushed through lest it be accomplished, Soviet style, by the peasants themselves. In its wake peasant parties, akin to the Russian Social Revolutionaries, sprang up and gained numerous adherents. The Marxists, both "soft" and "hard," were also active, demanding a better lot for the workers in the scattered industrial centers, and clashing, like the peasants, with liberal and conservative parties. How the various social, regional, and national groups in the new parliaments could be yoked together under a democratic government capable of solving the problems of the postwar era was at best an open question, except in Czechoslovakia, where democracy really took hold. Unsatisfactory indeed was the subsequent history of the fragmented and weak *Zwischeneuropa* caught between Germany and the Soviet Union.

The vanquished peoples of central Europe were likewise shaken by social revolution. The defeat of their country and of their political ambitions in Europe and the world had come as a terrible shock to most Germans. It had set off not only a widespread revulsion against the Bismarckian system of government —this was the cause of the November Revolution which created a democratic republic—but also a clash of extremist groups on the right and left. The Bolsheviks had many allies among Spartacists, Shop Stewards, and Independent Socialists, but also fanatical opponents. At the outset the radical left took the offensive, staging many uprisings in the winter and spring of 1919. In April, a Soviet-type government ruled over Munich. Who in these months could have been sure that the German republic would not go the way of the Kerensky regime? And who, furthermore, could foretell whether the workers of Vienna would remain loyal to their moderate socialist leaders? In Hungary, indeed, democracy took the Soviet turn under the dictatorship of Béla Kun, one of the prisoners of war whom the Russian Communists had converted.

Not even the victorious Allies in western Europe were immune to the revolutionary fever. For a week in January, 1919, the red flag flew from the municipal flagpole in Glasgow, and at least one British radical ventured the hope that it would also be hoisted over Buckingham Palace. The British government, in addition, had its hands full with rebellions in Ireland, Egypt, and India, as Soviet propaganda gleefully noted. South of the Channel, Clemenceau was wounded by an assassin of anarchist leanings in February, while French workers were preparing, now that the war was over, to resume the class war. The federation of French trade unions declared a May Day holiday amounting to a general strike. It wanted "to impress the French public with the strength and the unity of the working classes." Red flags adorned many a local parade; in Paris bloody scuffles ensued. Plans were laid in the summer for a common general strike of English, French, and Italian workers (which, however, never took place). Italy, where the right and left clashed as in Germany, seemed even closer to revolution. Italian socialists staged sit-in strikes in the industrial centers of the north and talked of seizing power, profiting from the universal letdown of political morale.

Everywhere, demobilization produced a profound disillusionment. Wartime oratory had raised extravagant expectations of a better future, greater national glory, and a higher standard of living. But after the war all governments were hopelessly overburdened with debts, as the astronomical costs of the war were carried over into the peace through inflation, taxation, and widespread unemployment. Even victory was hollow; the promises could not be kept. The war, furthermore, had destroyed the interdependence of Europe on which everyone's prosperity depended. It would be years before the prewar levels of well-being could be reconstituted on a new basis. Meanwhile, men grew impatient. Their minds were agitated as never before by the problems of war and peace, prosperity and socio-economic organization, government and politics. In their ignorance they now searched for quick, soothing explanations of the recent holocaust and their present frustrations; they craved for culprits and scapegoats. The political irrationalism that had arisen before the war now found many new converts. The political passions thus aroused imposed a heavy strain on the democratic order inherited from prewar reforms or introduced, as a result of western victory, into all the defeated and newly created countries of central and eastern Europe.

Even the United States, which had saved the Allies from defeat and now entered global politics in full force, felt the tremors of the cyclone. In 1919, four million workers went on strike (which, however, signified far less revolutionary zeal than similar events in prewar Russia). In the Pacific northwest, the center of some of the most violent unionism in the country, the city of Seattle experienced a brief general strike in February. In the same months the "Friends of the New Russia" staged a dinner party in Washington. In September not one but two Communist parties were founded in Chicago (both tiny). And the year ended with a prolonged steel strike which brought William Z. Foster, the future leader of American communism, into national prominence. The anti-Communist rebound was even more vehement, as Attorney General A. Mitchell Palmer led the charge against "the red menace."

The unrest was felt even further afield. All around the world, perceptive observers sensed a break in the traditional global order. A new era was beginning in which Europe no longer stood at the center. The United States, Japan, the British dominions, and even the "colonial" peoples in Asia loomed larger now that Europe had demeaned itself by its great war. New hopes and ambitions were aroused. The Indian scene, as described by Nehru, was typical.

> The end of the world war found India in a state of suppressed excitement. . . . Political agitation, peaceful and wholly constitutional as it was, seemed to be working itself to a head, and people talked with assurance of self-determination and self-government. Some of this unrest was visible also among the masses, especially the peasantry. . . . The soldiers back from active service on distant fronts were no longer

the subservient robots that they used to be. They had grown mentally, and there was much discontent among them.

In China, the universal unrest flared up with unexpected suddenness. When on May 4, 1919, the news arrived that the Paris peace conference had failed to protect China against the Japanese demands that had grown out of the war, the people of Peking, led by the students, poured into the streets in violent protest. The agitation continued for months afterward and spread to other cities as well. The May Fourth Movement, as this first outburst of a new Chinese nationalism became known, eventually led to the formation of a Chinese Communist party. In short, the political ambitions of the western model, having already swayed Japanese society for two generations, were now beginning to influence Chinese life as well.

How discouraging were the toils of statesmanship under these conditions! At Paris, where in the winter and spring of 1919 the statesmen of the victorious powers and their clients were assembled, a multitude of baffling problems presented themselves. They ranged from guarantees of racial equality desired by the Japanese, the rules of guardianship for the emerging colonial peoples, and a new European order, to the prevention of another world war through the League of Nations. In March, 1919, Wilson, Lloyd George, and Clemenceau were deadlocked over the peace terms to be offered to Germany. Their subsequent compromise, which led to the "dictated" peace of Versailles, provided a basis for a fresh start after the war but hardly for a lasting settlement. Yet it was fortunate, perhaps, that the German representatives were not invited to that conference—and still more fortunate that the Communists were kept out. The participation of both, however conforming to precedent and general interest, would certainly have precluded any settlement whatsoever.

In the light of all these conditions it was no irresponsible fantasy to say, as did the program of the Communist International in March, 1919, that "the imperialist system" was breaking down.

> Ferment in the colonies, ferment among the former dependent small nations, insurrection of the proletariat, victorious proletarian revolutions in some countries, dissolution of imperialist armies, complete incapacity of the ruling classes to continue to guide the destinies of the peoples—this is the state of affairs throughout the world.

Against this somber background, the Communists projected their own apocalyptic oversimplification: "Humanity, whose entire civilization lies in ruin, is threatened with complete annihilation. There is only one force that can save it, and that is the proletariat."

At the height of the civil war in Russia, Lenin, appealing to his comrades on the extreme left of European socialism, created the Third International in order to guide the manifold stirrings of revolution in the direction of the Communist myth and to utilize them for the benefit of Soviet Russia. Within the next two years, the new Communist International (Comintern) won over most of the extremist elements in the European socialist movement, while the moderates rebuilt the Second International scattered by the war. Thus European socialism (always divided) was forever split and thereby robbed of its future. Despite the formation of the Comintern in 1919, one could hardly speak, however, of an international Communist conspiracy. What linked the various revolutionary plots and rumors of plots in those chaotic months was their common revolt against a discredited order and a vague identity of slogans and symbols. All left-wing groups desperately needed support and sought it in a common solidarity, despite profound differences in philosophy and organization. The Third International, paradoxically, became a reasonably reliable tool of Soviet foreign policy only long after the cyclone of revolution had subsided.

Yet it was clear from the start that Lenin viewed the revolutionary tinder elsewhere as a natural opportunity for extending

Soviet control. He was ready to ignite it by any means within reach, making little distinction between conventional power based on arms and revolutionary power derived from a genuine local revolutionary situation such as had existed in Russia in November, 1917. When Béla Kun's regime was faltering, Trotsky dispatched two divisions of the Red Army to succor it. And in the summer of 1920, when the Red Army for a brief moment besieged Warsaw and the Communists hoped for assistance from the Polish workers, Lenin quipped of "breaking the crust of the Polish *bourgeoisie*" with the bayonet. Sometimes the bayonet alone seemed to be the decisive factor. In October, 1918, hoping to liberate the territories still held by the Germans, Trotsky inspired the Red Army with bold talk of Communist expansion:

> Free Latvia, free Poland and Lithuania, free Finland, on the other side free Ukraine will not be a wedge but a uniting link between Soviet Russia and the future Soviet Germany and Austria-Hungary. This is the beginning of a European communist federation—a union of the proletarian republics of Europe.

Trotsky's ambition, incidentally, seemed almost like a Communist replica of Germany's *Mitteleuropa*.

The militant revolutionary outreach thus encouraged conferred another boon on the Russian Communists. It proved to them (who were acutely aware of their weakness) the accuracy of their myth and hardened their self-confidence. As early as the fall of 1918, Lenin wrote:

> Bolshevism . . . has shown by the example of Soviet power that the workers and peasants even of a backward country, even with the least experience, education and habits of organization, have been able for a whole year amidst gigantic difficulties and amidst a struggle against the exploiters (who were supported by the bourgeoisie of the whole world) to maintain the power of the toilers, to create a democracy that is immeasurably higher and broader than all previous democracies

[154]

in the whole world and to start the creative work of tens of millions of workers and peasants for the practical achievement of socialism.

Therefore, he proclaimed, "Bolshevism can serve as a model of tactics for all" proletarians in the whole world. In 1920, he presented the same point even more strongly:

> At the present moment of history the situation is precisely such that the Russian model reveals to *all* countries something . . . of their near and inevitable future.

This was the presumption underlying Lenin's relations with foreign socialists.

The Communist outreach into Europe was matched by "capitalist" intervention in the Russian civil war by France, England, the United States, and Japan. Their motives for this venture were exceedingly complex. Starting with a desire to maintain the second front and to forestall German capture of Allied war material stored in Russia or a German thrust toward India, the three western powers began to support any anti-Bolshevik force willing to continue the war. From this intermediary position they drifted, with varying degrees of conviction, into an openly anti-Communist policy. Needless to say, neither western statesmen nor their constituents possessed much understanding of the conditions of Russia nor of the necessities prompting its internal evolution. All they saw was a regime that proclaimed domestic policies outrageous to their sensibilities, flouted the decencies of international discourse, and fostered universal revolution. The Allied leaders faced troubles enough at the end of the war. The seemingly unlimited ambitions of the Communists to create further chaos only inspired deep revulsion.

In addition, the interventionist powers were guided by specific interests, France by its extensive investments in Russia, Britain by its political position in the Near and Middle East, Japan by its desire for a bridgehead on the Asian mainland. Only the American government, benefiting from past isolation, maintained a relatively impartial policy. Its intervention in European Russia was prompted by a need for cooperation with England and France; in Siberia it was to check the Japanese appetite. It was no wonder that those governments with concrete stakes in Russia should carve out, on paper, prospective spheres of influence and operations and exact from the White regimes humiliating pledges of future concessions in return for their aid. Like the treaty of Brest-Litovsk, these agreements testified anew to the weakness of Russia.

Measured in terms of the Allies' recent war effort, the extent of western intervention in Russia was ludicrously small. Yet in terms of the tiny weights needed to tip the scales of the civil war, of the traditional and well-nigh irrational Russian fear of western invasion, or of Bolshevik desperation, foreign intervention loomed large.* The presence of western troops and, more significantly, the grant of food and war material to the anti-Bolshevik forces did have its effect. Otherwise Denikin would never have come so close to Moscow. Nor would Trotsky have been forced to cancel the military aid to Béla Kun. British and French assistance to the Poles, furthermore, did stop the Communist advance at the gates of Warsaw and permit the subsequent Polish penetration into Byelorussia. Without British and German aid, finally, neither Finland nor the Baltic states would have been able to gain independence.

The advantages in this far-flung battle, however, did not all lie with the West. The Communists also scored some successes. They achieved the withdrawal of the French occupation forces from Odessa by thoroughly contaminating them with their propaganda. Through the sympathies which they had aroused among British workers, they stopped Lloyd George from sending more war material to Poland. And in a thousand other ways they profited from the universal war-weariness. Interventionist senti-

* Needless to say the Bolsheviks, then and later, engaged in deliberate and vile exaggeration on this subject. In 1958 the author saw in the Museum of the Revolution in Moscow a huge enlargement of a photograph showing a number of corpses scattered over a square in some town, said to be the work of American troops in Vladivostok. No such incident ever occurred.

ment, found particularly among conservatives, was defeated at the source of public opinion. And, last but not least, the Communists had the advantage of the unspeakable messiness of Russian civil war politics, which quickly disgusted all who were venturesome enough to meddle in it, Czechs, Frenchmen, Englishmen, and Americans.

Yet in the end, the revolutionary potential proved far less effective than Lenin had anticipated. In its periphery, the cyclone merely produced a mild disturbance. No red flag flew from Buckingham Palace or the Champs Élysées, no socialist revolution took place in central Europe where the chances had seemed so propitious. Nationalism rather than socialism and communism attracted the uprooted intellectuals. The bulk of the German proletariat was committed to the continuity of the state organization which rescued employment, social security, and all the other benefits of order from the defeat; it turned a cold shoulder to Lenin's overtures and, under Social Democratic leadership, became one of the pillars of the Weimar republic. In Austria, the moderate socialists, likewise, retained the leadership of the workers and played a prominent part in the early years of the new republic. In Hungary, Béla Kun's regime, unpopular even with the workers, was suppressed without much trouble, and Hungarian communism ceased to exist until the end of the second World War. Throughout eastern Europe, nationalism proved an effective rampart against communism. The Communists, to be sure, succeeded in gradually transforming the extreme groups among the European socialists into pliant and dependable Communist parties; but in the end they could not prevent a new era of "capitalist consolidation." Lenin's hopes for a revolution among the colonial peoples went likewise unfulfilled. Except for a few skirmishes, the masses of Asia were not ready to leap to arms. It was not so easy, after all, to build a counter power to European imperialism. Lack of response, however, did not stop Lenin from casting the Communist bread upon the colonial waters—for a profitable return, perhaps, in future years.

By the end of 1920, the Soviet experiment of matching the

revolutionary weapons of foreign policy against western arms and influence had run its course. A realistic equilibrium had been struck. Soviet Russia had lost Finland, the Baltic littoral, Poland, parts of Byelorussia, and Bessarabia. Yet it had retained the Ukraine and preserved intact the Middle Eastern borders of the Empire (except for small losses to Turkey) and, after the Japanese withdrawal in 1922, its Far Eastern boundaries as well. And thanks to the Communist International, it was still a force to be reckoned with.

Most important of all, however, the Communists were entrenched as masters of Russia. They had decisively won out over their domestic enemies, for many reasons. They had preserved control of the areas of their main strength, Great Russia and its industrial centers; they had also held on to their following in the Ukrainian heavy industries and in the Urals. They had retained the advantages of interior communications while their enemies, who could never coordinate their sallies, had to strike from the periphery. As heirs of the tsars, they had represented the integrity and continuity of the Russian state, claiming the loyalty of all patriots. They had shown superior leadership, too, and the ability to rally the fanaticism which upholds men under extreme strain. In addition they had excelled in organizational skill. The Red Army had emerged as a modestly respectable fighting force, superior to that of the Whites in the decisive engagements of the war. The Communists had even managed, by desperate measures that played havoc with all planning, to preserve a minimum of industrial production, to prevent mass starvation, and actually to dignify their economic improvisations by the term "war communism."

Under these conditions, the savagery of the civil war proved only that the political balance emerging from the fall of the monarchy was basically sound. The moderate groups were all but extinct; the dictatorship of the right had no chance. The political ineptitude of the old Russia dogged the anti-Bolshevik forces at every step. The Whites, who continuously quarreled among themselves,* could draw no mass support. They could never clear themselves of the suspicion that they yearned to turn the clock back or that they conspired with the foreigners (despite the fact that in their negotiations with the Allies they had obstinately tried to safeguard Russia's sovereignty). Faced with the stark choice between White and Red, the bulk of the population inclined toward the Red, the harshness of Soviet rule notwithstanding. And the many local nests of resistance were too anarchic and weak to offer a real threat. Once the Whites were defeated, the Greens were quickly snuffed out.

After three incredible years of emergency measures, the Bolsheviks managed to survive as the sole rulers of Russia. But they had saved little else. The country, which had lived so long on the accumulated capital of the prewar period—how fat the old leanness now appeared!—had reached the point of utter exhaustion. The biggest cities had lost almost half of their population, as city folk with relatives in the country had drifted back to the source of food (which showed again how closely the urban masses were still related to the village). Industrial production, likewise, had catastrophically declined. In 1920, large-scale industry produced only 14 percent of its prewar total. Steel production, which in 1918 was down to 10 percent of its 1913 level, sank to an all-time low of 5 percent in 1921. The harvest did not shrink quite so drastically but fell off enough to cause a searing famine in southeastern and eastern Russia during 1921-1922. So desperate were the conditions in the stricken regions that the Communists were forced into the humiliation of admitting Herbert Hoover's American relief organization, which, estimatedly, saved ten million lives.

Two events in 1921 brought home to Lenin the true state of affairs. The first was the collapse of a renewed effort of the German Communists to seize power in Germany, which proved

* At one point, cadets from the military schools refused to fight side by side with students because they thought the latter were "socialists." The lack of any sense of spontaneous cooperation was typical of the old Russia (and probably still prevails today).

to him that no outside support could be expected; the second, a series of strikes by Petrograd workers culminating in an uprising of the Baltic fleet at the Kronstadt naval base in March. It was an alarming moment when their erstwhile shock troops turned against the Communists and pointedly demanded Soviet but not Communist democracy. It also pointed to the danger of another peasant revolution. The Kronstadt uprising was put down with sickening terror, but it convinced Lenin that the time had come for a strategic retreat. After so many years of war, revolution, and civil war he had to give the peasants—and all inhabitants of Soviet Russia—a chance to catch their breath and to recuperate by their traditional remedies, with a minimum of government interference.

> Our poverty and ruin are so great [Lenin said in March, 1921] that we cannot at one stroke restore large-scale factory state socialist production. This requires that we accumulate large stocks of grains and fuels in the big industrial centers, replace worn-out machines with new ones, and so on. Experience has convinced us that this cannot be done at one stroke.

Thus began a new phase of Soviet rule, based on a New Economic Policy (NEP) which gave its name to the entire era from 1921 to 1928. It was designed to let the peasants sell most of their grain for whatever price it would fetch and thus stimulate the production of consumer goods in general through the incentives of the open market, as under capitalism. Private trade was thus allowed to revive, as was, under certain safeguards, the hiring of labor by private enterprise. Large-scale industry remained under state control, but even here capitalist accounting methods were introduced. Lenin was no longer trying to achieve socialism in a hurry. The timetable had to be revised to suit a country whose population consisted largely of peasants. Instead of taking the phantom Bolshevik express, Soviet Russia had to travel for a stretch by the old fourth-class carriages. Said Lenin:

> Our aim . . . is to prove to the peasant by deeds that we are beginning with what is intelligible, familiar, and im-

mediately accessible to him in spite of his poverty, and not with something remote and fantastic from the peasant's point of view; we must prove that we can help him. . . . Either we prove that or he will send us to the devil. That is absolutely inevitable.

Link up with the peasant masses, with the rank-and-file toiling peasants, and begin to move forward immeasurably, infinitely more slowly than we expected, but in such a way that the entire mass will actually move forward with us. If we do that we shall in time get an acceleration of this movement such as we cannot dream of now.

The partnership of the proletariat with the peasant masses was one of the key slogans of the new era, hailed as a great Communist accomplishment. Yet making the pace of Soviet development dependent on the peasants' lethargy constituted a tremendous retreat from the original impatience—a "peasant Brest-Litovsk" not easily tolerated by the party stalwarts.

The NEP also brought a considerable relaxation in other respects. The terror came to an end: freedom of self-expression was partially restored; life in Russia returned to a semblance of normalcy, which swept to the surface much of the scum of revolution and civil war but also allowed some quiet mending of the damage. In foreign affairs, the shift coincided with the resumption of peaceful foreign relations. Soviet Russia was forced to coexist with "capitalism." It had to establish diplomatic relations with its neighbors and, if possible, also with the Great Powers. Even if full diplomatic recognition by France, England, and the United States was as yet impossible, efforts were made to resume foreign trade and obtain foreign credit for rebuilding Russia's economy. Capitalist assistance was again solicited, although with greater caution than under Witte. Thus the blockade of Soviet Russia was ended. Soon a trickle of foreign visitors arrived to assess the changes that had occurred and the price that had been paid.

What an incredible test of endurance these years had been for the peoples of Russia! In retrospect, the trials of the war and the year 1917 paled as compared with the agonies of the civil war.

No other people in these years had been so tortured at the outer limits of endurance as the inhabitants of the Russian Empire. Yet amidst the filth, the disease, the hunger, the fear, and the insane slaughter one could also sense a wild exhilaration. There was one boon in anarchy: the freedom to live and die for once by one's deepest convictions, without shame or compromise. And to some of the best minds, the shambles revealed a glimpse of a vital reality which normalcy had always hidden. Pasternak has written of these days in *Dr. Zhivago:*

> Everything established, settled, and everything to do with home and order and the common round has crumbled into dust and been swept away in the general upheaval and reorganization of the whole of society. The whole human way of life has been destroyed and ruined. All that is left is the bare, shivering human soul, stripped to the last shred, the naked force of the human psyche, for which nothing has changed because it was always cold and shivering and reaching out to its nearest neighbor, as cold and lonely as itself.

These were the moments of insight to be remembered through the barren, gray years to come. They have provided the subject matter of the best of Soviet literature ever since.

Thus, after reaching cyclone strength, the great flood tide of spontaneity in Russian life subsided. The survivors, bone tired and chastened by the recent orgy of violence, slowly shuffled back to their traditional routine of making a living, under a regime that despite incredible exertions had lost little of its revolutionary vitality.

IX

THE BASES OF SOVIET STRENGTH, 1921-1924

★

THE EVENTS which had taught Lenin that a socialist economy could be achieved only through a number of transition stages, while slowing down the advance toward that goal, did not touch the core of the Communist myth. The only adjustment required by the tactical retreat concerned the timetable of the dialectic process. The delay, however, was easily justified by the "world historical" magnitude of the Bolshevik Revolution; heaven could not be stormed overnight.* The New Economic Policy, therefore, entailed no relaxation of the inherent drive of communism. Too much was still to be done toward consolidating the dictatorship in the vast territories of the Empire, too many foundations still to be laid before the inevitable resumption of "socialist reconstruction." Despite the exhaustion of Russia, the early years of the NEP were therefore crowded with administrative and political innovation continuing and completing the transformation begun in 1917.

One of the major problems still facing the Soviet regime was the relationship of the non-Russian minorities to the new Soviet power. The elemental tide of revolutionary spontaneity had

---

* Not until the 1960's did the conflict between the Communist myth and reality reach major proportions, presenting the party with a distressing choice between abandoning its myth and finding a substitute (an exceedingly difficult task) or facing increased inefficiency and weakness. At the same time, however, the basic problem of Russian security was solved, *for the first time in history*. Today, under the threat of thermonuclear war, the insecurity of Soviet Russia is that of the United States too, or of any other Great Power that might endanger the Soviet Union.

given new prominence to the ethnic variety within the Empire. Every minority group had felt encouraged to stress its identity and to cultivate its peculiarities. Before the November Revolution, the Bolsheviks, forever in search of revolutionary allies, had boosted this tendency by their slogan of national self-determination. Yet behind this facile phrase lay hidden many mental reservations, the result of a long search for the proper place of nationalism in the Marxist creed. Marx had taught his followers to consider nationalism a bourgeois phenomenon doomed to disappear in the global melting pot which "capitalism" bequeathed to socialism. He and Engels, "Red Prussians" both, had always assumed that the lesser peoples would be duly absorbed by the greater ones, and that, as in business so in government, strict centralization would prevail as the supreme guarantee of rational efficiency; federalism was anathema to them. These assumptions of Marxism did not, however, easily fit the political realities of the Russian Empire, or of many areas in the world where nationalism obviously was still on the rise, often as a revolutionary force. It was Lenin who, after many doctrinal disputes, devised the Bolshevik formula for yoking the revolutionary potential of nationalism to Marxist socialism. He argued that the promise of self-determination would rally the suppressed nationalities to the revolutionary cause and the revolution in turn would hasten the disappearance of nationalism. Having a choice between fragmenting society into many small national units or consolidating it into ever larger supranational blocks, the victorious proletariat of all countries would wisely opt for the latter.

When the Bolsheviks came to power, they formally recognized the importance of the nationality question by creating a People's Commissariat for Nationalities, with Stalin as its chief. Yet as they put Lenin's formula to the test, they met with the most unwelcome results. The advanced non-Russian nationalities along the western border made use of self-determination in order to escape from Bolshevik control, while the many lesser ones, which could not secede because they were surrounded by Russians or incapable of statehood, pressed for federal autonomy as promised in the Social Revolutionary program. Finland, in one of the first Bolshevik decrees, was granted full independence. Yet almost at once Finnish secession was contested by an uprising of Finnish Communists who, under orders from Petrograd, clamored for unification with Soviet Russia. A civil war ensued in which the Finns managed, with German help, to ward off the threat. The Lithuanians, Latvians, and Estonians likewise escaped from Soviet rule, drawing on British as well as German support.* Lacking such allies, the other nationalities had to submit. After many struggles that made a farce of self-determination, the Communists reinforced native Communist elements, which sometimes were minute indeed, with units of the Red Army or Russian settlers, and thus secured adherence to the proletarian cause.

Aware of the strength of nationalism, however, the Communists made two essential concessions which hardly accorded with their Marxist inheritance. They granted cultural autonomy to their subject nationalities and adopted an element of federalism in the formal structure of their state.

Granting cultural autonomy to the non-Russian nationalities under their control implied an acceptance of local custom and language as the medium of social action. Henceforth, each national group conducted its affairs in its own vernacular and in terms of its own national tradition (purged of "feudal" or "capitalist" traits). The Ukrainians, for instance, were allowed to cultivate the Ukrainian language as their official language, which the tsars had never permitted. The most widely hailed products of Soviet nationality policy were the newly devised alphabets for peoples who had never before enjoyed a written language. Yet the new script was also the chief vehicle of Communist propa-

---

* Poland, of course, had been removed from Russian control already, in 1916, by the German advance. It was easy, therefore, (and expedient) for the Provisional Government to grant Poland full independence. The Bolsheviks could do nothing to alter these facts—although it is easy to imagine what they would have done had they captured Warsaw in 1920.

ganda and of the advanced urban-industrial civilization for which Soviet communism stood in the eyes of its underdeveloped subjects. It helped to subvert the native civilization, while ostensibly safeguarding it. Modernization in turn inevitably entailed Russification.

Thus the nationality problem, particularly in the Asian territories of Soviet Russia, became fused with the larger problem of extending modern civilization into backward areas. In central Asia and parts of Siberia, the Communists were creating the same tensions against which they were railing in their relation with the "imperialist" powers. The native nationalism which refused to wither away was often merely an instinctive reaction against the Soviet Russian subversion of the native heritage. The only remedy against such subversion would have been, as a perceptive spokesman of Soviet Moslems, Sultan-Galiev, once wrote, "the dictatorship of the colonies and semi-colonies over the metropoles," which was like asking that water run uphill. The grant of cultural autonomy, in short, did not solve the nationality problem. It did not satisfy the more primitive nationalities, because it did not prevent the gradual dissolution of their native culture. And in the case of the more advanced ones, like the Ukrainians, it was found wanting because it was not accompanied by appropriate political opportunities.

The concession of federalism was designed, to be sure, to meet that objection. Yet federalism remained merely a matter of form.* The nature of Soviet federalism was foreshadowed in the first Soviet constitution of 1918, which organized the ethnic minorities encased in the Russian heartland as autonomous Soviet socialist regions or republics, allowed to conduct their own affairs (under proper supervision). In the aftermath of the civil war, the border nationalities which had meanwhile tasted genuine independence were granted greater privileges, above all

* The Comintern *Theses on the National and Colonial Question* (1920) expressed the Communist ambiguity on this subject: "Federation is a transition form toward the complete union of the working people of all nations. Experience has shown the expediency of federation. . . ."

in the right of secession (a fine case of window dressing). But the essentials of the Communist dictatorship such as armed power, foreign policy, communications, economic planning, and the political police remained under the control of Moscow in form as well as in substance.

Late in 1923, the basic guidelines of Soviet federalism were laid down in the new constitution of the Union of the Soviet Socialist Republics (USSR) then composed of the RSFSR, Byelorussia, the Ukraine, and the Transcaucasian Federation.* Under this constitution, the pattern of Soviet government outlined in 1918 was extended to the entire country, with the difference that the All-Russian Congress of Soviets now became the All-Union Congress of Soviets and its Central Executive Committee (VTsIK) was made a bicameral body constituted of a Council of the Union and a Council of Nationalities. The executive branch of the government, furthermore, was divided horizontally according to the significance of its various functions into (1) exclusively federal agencies (war, foreign policy, communications), (2) mixed agencies with offices both at the center and in the union republics (concerned mostly with economic development), and (3) the republic agencies dealing with justice, education, and internal order for which no central direction was deemed necessary (apart from the common subjection to party control). This threefold stratification proved a fairly satisfactory principle of allocating the functions of government to their proper level in a political framework where no real conflict between the rights of the whole and of the parts was permitted. For in the last analysis, Soviet federalism was but a facade for a rigidly centralized regime controlled by the Communist party. In the ranks of the party, not even a trace of federalism was tolerated. The party remained the same "Russian Communist Party (Bolshevik)" for all the territories of the Soviet Union regardless of the national origin of its members. Thus did the

* Before the decade had ended, these four were joined by the Uzbek and Turkmen republics (in 1924) and the Tajik republic (in 1929).

prerevolutionary heritage of Russian hegemony persist under the new regime. The pre-eminence of the Communist party, incidentally, was not even mentioned in the new constitution.

Whether the non-Russian nationalities improved their lot under Soviet rule is a debatable question. They escaped the worst of Russification, as there lingered in party circles enough suspicion of "Great Russian chauvinism" to curb the former excesses. But like all other Soviet subjects, they fell under the ever stricter political supervision of masters who, like the tsars, spoke Russian and tended to artificially hasten the process of integration. Neither cultural autonomy nor federalism offered any protection against the rising Soviet totalitarianism. In the Communist treatment of the nationality question, one can again trace the paradox of the Bolshevik Revolution. The Communists encouraged spontaneity only to take away its substance in the name of a higher social order which pretended to grant all that had been originally desired (and more). In reality it merely turned out to be a more efficient version of Russian domination (which, under the circumstances, was probably inevitable).*

Another major problem brought under control in these years was the relationship between party and state. As Kerensky had already observed, the soviets were not suited to be organs of government. The Communists proved the point, even though they built an imposing structure of government on them. It was, however, no easy task to reduce to docility the original soviet spontaneity which had helped the Bolsheviks into power. It meant ousting all unruly and hostile elements, eliminating Menshevik and Social Revolutionary competitors, and introducing efficient Communist leadership among the remaining members. The Bolshevik victory in the civil war facilitated the Bolshevization of the soviets by liquidating all organized opposition. It was only in 1921, however, that the last remnants of the Social Revolutionary and Menshevik organizations were outlawed and

* The percentage of the Soviet population officially classified as Russian stands now at about 50 per cent, a considerable increase over 1897.

the Communist party emerged with a clear monopoly of political power. Yet even armed with such exceptional advantages, the Communists could not necessarily rely on their local soviets. Despite the manipulation of elections, the majority of their deputies consisted of nonparty elements, of men and women mostly sympathetic to the regime yet not under party discipline. Their votes had to be won by argument rather than "administrative methods," the Communist euphemism for compulsion. The intermediary soviets of a province or region contained a larger percentage of party members; they were more easily controlled. In the All-Russian (or later All-Union) Congress of Soviets, as in its Central Executive Committee, of course, nearly all deputies were party members.

In the taming of soviet spontaneity, the assertion of central administrative control played a significant part. The Council of People's Commissars issued decrees to all lower soviets which it considered binding upon them, regardless of whether or not they met with local approval. In this respect, too, the years following the civil war completed and regularized the process of uncompromising centralization begun after the seizure of power. In theory, to be sure, a balance was preserved. The local executive committees were bound to two masters, their own electorates and the executive committees of their superior soviet which represented, in the last analysis, the highest organs of state in Moscow. In practice the latter, who occasionally disagreed with each other, handed down their orders at will and usually carried the day if the local soviets dared to disagree. Thus the soviets, instead of expressing the will of the people and guiding the government, became, in Stalin's phrase, mere transmission belts of the party's will from the center of power to the periphery. In return they were expected to transmit essential information on the state of mind among the masses. But the Communist leaders, while sensitive to public opinion in order to mold it effectively, would never defer to it. All other public bodies permitted to the toilers, such as the trade unions or the cooperatives, were likewise considered as transmission belts. In this manner, the executive at the center was closely linked with the masses in a relationship which stunted genuine participation among the population but integrated it into the state. The Soviet peoples, in short, were treated like children still to be educated into a superior Soviet socialist citizenry.

The initiative in this grandiose process of social engineering and its constant supervision in every aspect of Soviet life inevitably rested with the Communist party. The proper relationship between party and state, however, was not easily defined. If the party was to lead, it had to assume administrative responsibility. Yet if it became encumbered with administrative routine, it lost the freedom necessary for effective leadership and became merged with the state. The official rule, laid down in 1919 and subsequently carried into effect as far as possible, stated that the Communist party was to lead the activities of the soviets but not to replace them. But where under any given circumstances did the dividing line between leadership and administration run? In the history of Soviet Russia, the pendulum has swung back and forth several times between administrative involvement by the party and renewed detachment from it. In the highest organs of state, of course, the merger of party and state was complete and, after some debate, accepted as inevitable. Most party leaders were administrators as well, Lenin as Chairman of the Council of People's Commissars (i.e., prime minister), Trotsky as Commissar for War, Stalin as Commissar of Nationalities, and so forth. On the lower rungs of the bureaucracy, party membership rapidly thinned out and the party's role again shrunk to that of a watchdog, at some expense to efficiency and orderliness.

Inevitably the party took precedence over the state. From the start, the important issues of Soviet policy were always considered first in the inner councils of the party; for the party, as the self-appointed vanguard of the proletariat, was the core of the Soviet dictatorship. After the end of the civil war it, too, passed through a process of adjustment and consolidation. With their keen sense for the necessities of power, Lenin and his closest advisers tried to preserve and improve its original character as a militant revolutionary elite. Their success was perhaps the most remarkable feat of Communist rule in this period. The internal cohesion which had always remained imperfect, even while the party was small and persecuted, was still more difficult to accomplish as its membership more than trebled with success, rising from 200,000 to over 700,000 between 1917 and 1921. The Bolshevik triumph, one can imagine, attracted many undesirable and self-seeking elements. In order to guard the party against any weakening of its revolutionary fiber, the top leaders instituted in 1921 a thorough cleansing of the rank and file, a purge directed, as Lenin put it, against all "rascal bureaucrats, dishonest or wavering Communists and . . . Mensheviks who have repainted their facade, but who have remained Mensheviks at heart." In this manner, party membership was again reduced to half a million.

At the same time the party imposed the strictest control over the admission of new cadre. Former members of the privileged classes, of course, need not apply at all. Peasants were likewise distrusted. Workers stood the best chances, but even they had to prove their mettle before being accepted. Only the most energetic and dedicated men and women could live up to the party's stern code of conduct. These were the duties of a Communist (as laid down in 1919). He had:

(a) to observe strict Party discipline, to take an active part in the political life of the Party and of the country, and to carry out in practice the policy of the Party and the decisions of the Party organs;

(b) to work untiringly to raise his ideological equipment, to master the principles of Marxism-Leninism and the important political and organizational decisions of the Party and to explain these to the non-Party masses;

(c) as a member of the ruling Party in the Soviet state, to set an example in the observance of labor and state discipline, to master the techniques of his work and continually raise his production and work qualifications.

Thanks to the party leaders' drive, these duties were never allowed to become a dead letter. A party member must always be a paragon, both as an agitator and as a worker at his job.

The considerable enlargement of party membership called for

a corresponding adjustment in the decision-making process. The Central Committee, which formerly had been the control center of the party, soon proved too large and cumbersome. Its function was taken over by a small committee, the Political Bureau (Politburo), officially sanctioned in March, 1919. It was charged with making "decisions on questions not permitting any delay" and consisted of only five regular members. It sat almost uninterruptedly during the critical days of the civil war and even thereafter; to Communists, politics were as continuous as time itself. At the same time another crucial committee, the Orgburo, was established to take charge of the mounting problems of party organization. In the following year (1920), as party affairs became ever more complex, a standing secretariat was introduced, staffed with three coequal secretaries. Reorganized in 1922 because of inefficiency, it was then entrusted to a Secretary General, Stalin being the man chosen for this position. One of his many tasks was to call to heel the local party cells and their secretaries that had been infected by the prevailing anarchy and thereby to implement the party program of 1919, which echoed Lenin's earlier directives:

> The party finds itself in a situation in which the strictest centralism and the severest discipline are absolute necessities. All decisions of the higher instance are absolutely binding on the lower ones. Every decision must first of all be carried out, and only later can it be appealed to the proper party organ. In this sense the party must possess in the present epoch virtually a military discipline.

Thus the party, like the machinery of state, was welded into a tight apparatus of sociopolitical control. And the ideal party functionary became an *apparatshik*, an unthinking, docile cog in the political machine.

The chief obstacle to party unity, however, did not lie in numbers or the laxity of party discipline in the lower echelons but in the factionalism that rent the party from top to bottom at the most crucial moments. We have already seen how the treaty of

Brest-Litovsk provoked bitter dissension. Later, in the civil war, the question of the proper position of the trade unions in a workers' state aroused another internal tempest. Controversies were inevitable, given the dilemmas of fitting a utopian myth into the harsh realities of Russian conditions. Most frequently the split occurred between idealists who let themselves be carried too far ahead by their lofty visions and realists who were guided by the necessities of the moment. Whatever the merits of each point of view, the party could not afford divisive debates between them, particularly when it was engaged, under the New Economic Policy, in a political retreat. The same party congress which endorsed NEP therefore adopted a resolution designed to end all factional strife. It permitted the Central Committee (which had now become a ratifying rather than decision-making body) to expel, by a two-thirds vote, any factious members from the party. This spelled the end of "party democracy," i.e., of an open debate on current issues within the party ranks. The importance of this decision was not lost upon the more perceptive members. As Karl Radek, an articulate Communist prominent in Comintern affairs, observed, "This [rule] may be turned against us, yet it is less dangerous than any wavering as at present."

In the following year, the party leadership went even one step further. It set the secret police, hitherto only used against the enemies of the regime, to spy on the troublemakers within the party. It is well to remember, however, that these measures were accepted with noticeable unanimity. Like Radek, most Communists realized the seriousness of their party's situation—which showed that the new rules represented an inherent logic of principles to which all Communists were committed. After 1922, in short, the party command had accomplished the seemingly impossible. For the first time in its history, it possessed the disciplinary powers needed to run the party like an army. It was paradoxical that Lenin, whose vision of a monolithic party was becoming reality at last, fell sick in the early summer of 1922 and was forced to withdraw from active leadership. The benefits of these changes accrued only to his successor.

When Lenin died in January, 1924, the Communist party was in a stronger position than ever. The strategic retreat of the New Economic Policy, to be sure, still continued. Just then it seemed particularly precipitous, as the peasants were encouraged to produce more foodstuffs by such arch-capitalist slogans as "get rich." Yet on all the other political fronts a steady advance had taken place. In state and society, the party was the undisputed master.

A Menshevik might still mock, of course, that both the New Economic Policy and the new authoritarian controls proved that Russia was as unfit for socialism as ever. But Lenin, in one of his last and most objective writings, confidently took issue with that reproach:

> If a definite level of culture is required for the building of socialism (although nobody can say just what the definite "level of culture" is, for it differs in every western European country), why cannot we begin by first achieving the prerequisites for that definite level of culture in a revolutionary way and then, with the aid of the workers' and peasants' government and the Soviet system, proceed to catch up with other nations? . . . Why could we not first create such preconditions of civilization in our country as the expulsion of the landlords and the Russian capitalists and then start moving toward socialism?

What Lenin said was that in Russia the proper setting had to be created before industrialization could take effect. This, of course, was the conclusion toward which Witte had already groped. In the essentials of modernization, the Communist party continued where Witte had left off at the beginning of the century. In its first six years in power, it had made considerable progress toward providing that framework. It proved, in short, that it could master the condition of Russia better than the tsars (although in practice it never half lived up to the perfection of its theory).

In the first place, the Communists had introduced a superior form of leadership. Unlike the tsar, who jealously guarded his solitary prerogatives, the Communists possessed a many-headed center of leadership. In the Central Committee (and later the Politburo), Lenin, Trotsky, Stalin, and other leading Bolsheviks —each one a human dynamo in his own right—decided the chief questions of policy conjointly. The Communist party never quite abandoned the ideal of a collegial, cooperative brain center which could concentrate so much more ability and vitality than had been possible under a single autocrat.* The Communist leaders, furthermore, were men of proven leadership. Everyone had earned his position the hard way; everyone of them was passionately committed to the new style of mass politics. In time of crisis they could go into the provinces and rally an army, save a city from the Whites, or solve any other tough political problem that had arisen. They also had at their disposal a reasonably effective machinery of administration, linking them with the population at large through the party, the soviets, the trade unions, and other transmission belts. Never had the tsars been blessed with such a devoted corps of agents. The party members gave zest to government policy at every point of contact with the population. The party, furthermore, was imbued with a keen ambition to rescue Russia from its weakness through a policy of rapid economic development. It was prepared to indoctrinate the entire population with its guiding myth as a necessary precondition of that advance and to battle, if need be, the ingrained popular resistance to drastic change.

The Revolution, moreover, had prepared, at a frightful price, the groundwork for industrialization by drastically simplifying the social structure of Russia. The regime recognized only the toiling masses. The toilers, furthermore, were singularly defenseless against the all-powerful state. Under the New Economic Policy, to be sure, the peasants by the nature of their work still enjoyed a considerable measure of independence; so did the workers under the protection of the trade unions, whose auton-

* Party leadership, to be sure, was not always united; yet as compared with tsarist bureaucracy under Nicholas II its unity of purpose was astounding.

omy had been conceded as a result of embittered controversy within the party. Yet the universal obligation to work was an integral part of the Soviet system. And the conditions of employment for all men and women were determined, in the last analysis, by the state, which thus could draw on the physical energies of its subjects to an unprecedented degree. How much of the social energy released by the Revolution was channeled into the Soviet system and how much was wasted remained, of course, an open question.

Nothing in the past, at any rate, could compare with the Communists' propaganda effort to mobilize that social energy. So geared to propaganda was the entire party that in these early years it never created a separate propaganda agency. All its members and affiliated organs, all the media of mass communications, diffused the Marxist-Leninist creed among the population as the basis of a common Soviet socialist "consciousness." In its endeavor to form the proper attitudes, it took full advantage of Russia's new isolation from western Europe. No longer was "Europe"—now derided as "capitalist" and "decadent"— allowed to influence Russian life at will by the uncontrolled influx of goods and ideas. The party barred, as best it could, all harmful foreign influences and thereby diminished or concealed the traditional subversion from without which had eaten away the authority of previous governments. Not only was true comparison with the conditions of the West made difficult (or downright impossible), but Soviet citizens were actually made to feel superior in the fake comparison undertaken by the party. The following assertion, taken from the introduction to the Constitution of 1923, was typical of this effort:

> There in the camp of capitalism we find national animosities and inequalities, colonial slavery and chauvinism, national oppression and pogroms, imperialist brutality and wars.
> Here in the camp of socialism there is mutual confidence and peace, national freedom and equality, and the fraternal collaboration of nations peacefully dwelling side by side.

[176]

More commonly, Soviet propaganda sounded a much harsher and cruder note. There was hardly a distortion or outright lie to which the regime would not stoop in order to discredit "capitalism." Half a year after his return from New York (where he had lived from January to March, 1917), Trotsky, for instance, spoke to the Petrograd Soviet of food riots in New York "such as we ourselves have never seen here." Such make-belief falsification, partly deliberate, partly—at least in the early years—the result of overenthusiasm and chiliastic expectation, became standard grist in the Soviet publicity mills.

By such desperate—and despicable—means Soviet Russia was now held up as the most advanced society in the world, marching toward socialism, while the "capitalist" world was falling further behind. Increasingly Soviet artists and intellectuals were ordered to create a full-blown autochthonous culture, superior to "capitalist" civilization, on the basis of a Russified Marxism. Thus the Bolsheviks tried to foster the necessary built-in arrogance of superiority which more than any other force cements the loyalty indispensable for modern government. In this new and artificially heightened isolation the Communists could more confidently pursue their social experiment of rapid modernization.*

Yet while the new setting provided many of the conditions necessary for making western technology take root and advance in the Russian environment, it introduced some obstacles of its own. However appropriate as an ideology for the early stages of industrialization, and however superior to the spirit of the tsarist regime, Marxism-Leninism was no suitable creed for the later phases of modernization when Soviet Russia competed with the older industrial countries. It harmonized with modern industrialism as poorly as hammer and sickle with the assembly line (which Henry Ford had perfected even before the Communists came to power). Although easing the transition to industrialism,

* Ideological indoctrination was always an uphill fight. There could be no peaceful "coexistence" in this realm. Standing still meant giving the advantage again to the "capitalist" influences.

the Marxist-Leninist myth, operating with economic concepts suitable to the early nineteenth century, saddled Soviet Russia with antiquated tools of social and economic analysis. The handicap was to tell more strongly as time went by, and particularly when the myth was foisted on the natural sciences.

The greatest—and most tragic—flaw in the Communist dictatorship, however, was the suppression of freedom. At the root of all innovations of the Communist regime, as we have noticed, lay the same paradox: in the name of spontaneity, spontaneity was suppressed. The social energies released by a revolution of liberation and consistently invoked by party propaganda as the mainspring of Soviet life were always in danger of being stifled by the strict controls imposed by the party on every sphere of life. It was spontaneity which accounted for the amazing vitality of western civilization. Yet the free flow of the same creative energy among the Russian people, having proved uncooperative or even anarchic, was increasingly hemmed in and frustrated in the name of the common good. And worse, as the party would never admit this fact, it was forced to cloak its controls in terms of a fake spontaneity. In the process, it tended to pervert by an infusion of crass political expediency every honest, idealist, straightforward human impulse into a rigid, mechanical act of duty. Deceit and falseness thus crept into every nook and cranny of the Soviet system and killed the natural grace and wholesomeness that spring from spontaneity. True creativity was driven back into the furthest recesses of the mind, leading a starved existence in an "inner emigration" deeper than Siberian exile. And yet, what else could the Communists have done so long as spontaneity continued to spell anarchy, and anarchy, weakness? An honest admission of the deceit was impossible, for it would have toppled the elaborate façade of superiority and even scrapped the myth, spreading confusion, disillusionment, and all the ills of renewed subservience to foreign models.

The internal reorganization of Russia was only one part of the Communist design—increasingly the weightier one; the other part was world revolution. Domestic and foreign policy were of the same mold, shaped by the same myth. In foreign affairs the myth carried over into peacetime the brutal absolutes of the war. "Capitalism" (the West) and "socialism" (Soviet Russia), so the myth read, were locked in a mortal combat in which capitalism was ready to go to any lengths of ruthlessness and trickery, and socialism could take no chances. There could be no alliances, no peace, no good faith. At best, there might be temporary ties based on fleeting expediency and at worst the most grueling war, fought by any suitable weapons. In this manner, the myth ruled out Soviet participation in the League of Nations or any other activity of the international community as re-established after the war.* The party stalwarts, too, scrupulously avoided personal contact with the representatives of the western *bourgeoisie,* employing men of lesser standing as go-betweens. In short, Soviet Russia stood apart in deep spiritual isolation.

Thus did the myth infuse the long-festering resentments of the Russian revolutionary intelligentsia into the conduct of international relations. Between the lines of their notes, memoranda, and protests to the western powers one could perceive their sense of inferiority, their vulnerability, their fear of being taken advantage of by the craftier and more experienced western diplomats. In their dealings with them, suspicion alternated with flashes of ambition. How they yearned to turn the tables for once and treat the "capitalists" as they themselves had felt treated for so long! It was indicative of their pride that they never measured themselves but against the most powerful countries, Great Britain at the start and later the United States. The acute uneasiness of their position also produced a heightened craving for independence and self-sufficiency, an air of secretiveness and xenophobia, a self-esteem all too easily offended. They were not, after all, equals in the grand competition of global politics, whatever the pretense of superiority in their myth.

The heightened sensitivity of the Soviet leaders gave Com-

---

* Only in 1934, when circumstances made membership advisable, did the Soviet Union join the League—to be booted out again after its attack on Finland in 1939.

munist doctrine a better appreciation of the varieties of power at work in the global world than could be found in liberal political theory. The Communists knew in their bones that in the relation between states which are not equally matched every form of contact is apt to carry political connotations. It was not only diplomacy, economic pressure, the threat (or force) of arms that constituted effective power. The ubiquitous western cultural influences which had pervaded tsarist Russia and now again knocked at the gates of Soviet Russia contained the ability to change the direction of Russian development. The West, in short, possessed invisible resources of power which Russia signally lacked but which, in the global competition, were crucial. Why should not Russia exude as much of this form of power as the West and become a model in its own right, both for its own protection and for the assertion of its existence in the world, defensively and offensively?

There was another factor of power which the Communists felt more keenly than western statesmen: the stability and cohesion of the body politic. Relatively well-integrated societies like England, France, or the United States, which could afford to grant their citizens full civic freedom without impairing their power in the world, possessed a natural advantage over those which, like Soviet Russia, could enforce the proper social discipline only by compulsion. Invulnerable to invidious comparison, they did not need to channel a significant part of their resources into the maintenance of internal security and control.

Seen from this angle, the inequality between the Soviet Union and the "capitalist" West amounted to much more than Russia's notorious deficiency in the traditional resources of power. In trying to understand Soviet foreign policy, one must keep in mind these invisible forms of power which have shaped so much of recent world history and yet have remained unperceived by those whom they benefited the most. Much of Communist foreign policy was designed to counteract or offset these invisible weapons.

In the first place, the Communists held up their Soviet system as a counter model, which, in the realm of theory at least, was not a particularly difficult achievement. From the start, they had always incorporated the extreme visions of peace and social harmony into their myth as the highest human goals. There still remained the discrepancy between the myth and Soviet realities. But that could be covered up by secrecy or explained away by a variety of clever arguments, all embroidering the contention that the Soviet Union, regardless of its present appearance, had already attained a higher stage of dialectical development than the "capitalist" countries. Given the phenomenal will to believe in utopia so widespread in Europe during the interwar years, the Communists succeeded amazingly well in presenting their counter model as a living reality.

In the second place, they were masters of what one might call "deliberate countersubversion," i.e., of aggravating by the skills of agitation all the cleavages found in "capitalist" society. The freedom of the "capitalist" system indeed provided them with ample opportunity for such attack. They need but cull from the free press of the West or from its literature the evidence of human imperfection in order to furnish themselves with unlimited political ammunition against "capitalism." With such help, the local Communist parties, increasingly under direct orders from the Comintern headquarters in Moscow, cleverly exploited the frustrations of "people living together in one place, without friendship or common understanding, and without capacity, when the test came, to pull together for survival"—a condition, unfortunately, not infrequent in many parts of Europe. Rubbing salt into the social wounds of the "capitalist" countries, sabotaging the process of justice or of government, and tearing at the bonds of community where they were weakest was gain enough for the Soviet leaders even if these activities no longer held out a prospect of genuine revolution. By half-truths and lies they tried to discredit the "capitalist" system and thereby raise the appeal and the power of Soviet Russia. By contrast, the western countries possessed no equal weapons capable of piercing the monolithic crust of the Soviet regime, for, as we have seen, the unchecked subversion by the western model was now ended. Hampered by the fullness of publicity and the complexities of parliamentary procedure, the western democracies found themselves at a disadvantage—much overrated, to be sure—in their day-by-day dealings with the Communist dictatorship. Faint-hearted westerners even began to suspect that the competition between a viable free society and a dictatorship might be won by the latter. Thus did the Bolsheviks win one of their most significant victories.*

Non-Communists, too, were drawn into the service of Soviet Russia. When the chances of revolution subsided, the Communist parties abroad were instructed to cooperate with all men of goodwill, in other socialist parties, in the trade unions, or in "front" organizations especially created for the purpose. Thus the Soviet leaders tapped, for their own carefully disguised aims, the reservoirs of social idealism contained in liberal democracy. In this part of their agitation, they displayed an astounding energy and psychological insight. They enlisted considerable support, collected large funds, and unearthed hidden resentments and weaknesses in individuals that could be turned to good use in building up an underground network for revolutionary action or espionage. They operated at a depth in society and in the individual mind to which liberal-democratic politicians never stooped. Not all such work, however, was successful. Some

---

* In reality, visible beneath the façade of superiority only to the trained eye, the danger of "capitalist" subversion from without continued to haunt the Soviet rulers. Had they been sure of their subjects, they would have had no need of the hermetic isolation and abysmal ignorance of the outside world in which they kept them. Access—and limited access at that—to foreign realities was granted only to the inner circles of the party and in proportion to their political reliability (measured by self-interest, conviction, and rank). Nothing shows better the basic inefficiency of Soviet anti-"capitalist" or anti-American propaganda than the continued demonstrative friendliness of Soviet citizens toward visiting Americans in any setting permitting spontaneity. In the depths of human motivation the subversive appeal of the "capitalist" West (or, at any rate, of some prime ingredients in it) has hitherto outsmarted all Communist propaganda, *and without conscious effort on the part of the West.*

of the leading Communists of western Europe left the cause in militant disillusionment (at some risk to their lives). But they were replaced without too much difficulty by new recruits seeking personal fulfillment in the Communist myth. For a small group of European (and American) intellectuals and workers, Soviet Russia indeed became the model of the good society.*

While experimenting with these new instruments of foreign relations, the Communist regime did not fail to make the most of the traditional tools of diplomacy. Under the condition of "capitalist encirclement," Soviet Russia was one state among others. It had to play its part in the traditional manner, if only to call attention to its accomplishments, draw assistance from naïve profit-seeking capitalists, and exploit the rivalries within the "capitalist" camp. After 1921, Lenin eagerly worked for the diplomatic recognition of the Soviet Union by the "capitalist" governments and for the reestablishment of commercial relations with them, which, as we have seen, accorded well with the principles of the New Economic Policy. It was also natural that, on this level of its foreign relations, Soviet Russia should openly side with Germany, another outcast in the international community, against the western Allies. This it did in the famous Rapallo treaty of 1922, which led even to a secret military liaison with the German army. Yet the following year, the Soviet leaders had no scruples about again inciting the German Communist party to overthrow its government, the ally of the Soviet Union. The duplicity of simultaneously conducting foreign relations on the two mutually exclusive levels of diplomacy and of revolution caused Soviet diplomacy some sharp setbacks. Yet these reverses never annulled the advantages derived from the combination.

Outside Europe, Soviet foreign policy in this period was primarily concerned with the possibilities of revolution in Asia. Here it dealt with simpler societies possessing neither powerful

* Among them one could find even Sidney and Beatrice Webb. For the lure of communism in these years—and the disenchantment—see the essays in *The God that Failed,* edited by R. H. S. Crossman.

capitalists nor a well-organized proletariat. The revolutionary forces were nationalist rather than socialist in outlook. Turkey and Iran, for instance, were ruled after the war by nationalist movements with an antiwestern edge. They fitted, however loosely, into Lenin's grand design. Yet Soviet support for these movements did not rule out a bid for retaining, in the name of anti-imperialism, the privileges which tsarist Russia had once enjoyed. This was true also of Soviet relations with the Chinese government in regard to the Boxer indemnity or the Chinese-Eastern railroad. In the eyes of the Asian masses, however, Soviet Russia posed as liberator and a model for emancipation from colonialism. It even dangled before them the possibility of skipping the capitalist phase altogether and advancing directly into socialism—with Soviet help. In order to spread this gospel, the Communists spent considerable sums in drawing young Asians to Moscow for study and indoctrination.

The Soviet example found its most ardent response among young Chinese intellectuals at the University of Peking, the promoters of the Fourth of May Movement, who were deeply aroused by the Japanese expansion into their country. In 1921 they founded the Chinese Communist party (at a girls' school in Shanghai) and, amidst the usual disputes and with direct Soviet prompting, slowly made it into a minor political force in the seaboard cities. From Moscow's perspective, however, the Chinese nationalist movement, the Kuomintang, was of still greater significance. In the mid-1920's its leaders, Sun Yat-sen and, after his death, Chiang Kai-shek, were advised by a famous Russian agent, Michael Borodin. Soon, however, it became apparent that Soviet encouragement of antiwestern national movements in Asia did not add up to world revolution. The nationalists resented being used as Soviet tools and before long made their peace with the West. Even where the local Communists survived such a debacle, as in China, they were reduced to impotence for many years. In the long run, too, they found it difficult (or impossible) to carry the Soviet prototype into their almost exclusively agrarian societies—a fact which sooner or later impaired their usefulness or reliability as Soviet agents. Mao Tse-tung, for instance, pioneered his peasant-oriented communism independently of Moscow, and against Soviet advice.

Whether in Europe or Asia, the Soviet regime was, in short, far less successful than at home. Lenin's expectations of world revolution had not been fulfilled. Yet despite this failure—and despite the appalling lack of the hard assets of power—Soviet foreign policy had achieved a remarkable feat. It had succeeded in keeping an exceedingly weak Soviet Russia in the global forefront. The specter of world revolution was stalking the globe. As long as communism did not have to meet the test of war, its potency was roughly equal to what it was thought to be. Indeed, the greater the fear of communism the greater was its power. That was no mean triumph.

Yet the effectiveness of global communism, in the last analysis, depended on the strength of the revolutionary movement and on the acuteness of social and political disintegration in Europe and Asia. In a period of "capitalist consolidation," when the wounds of the war were healing and the basic cohesion of the western democracies was reasserting itself; when vigorous anti-Communist dictatorships appeared where—according to their theory—the Communists should have prevailed; when, furthermore, the national liberation movements in Asia turned pro-western and conservative, the potency of the novel instruments of foreign policy waned. Against the threat of war, Soviet Russia needed the traditional tools of war, a strong, well-armed home base and an industrial society to support it. This, in 1924, was still a distant goal. At the time of Lenin's death, Soviet Russia had not much advanced, in terms of military and industrial power, beyond the point where tsarist Russia had ignominiously left off. But the day of the decisive attack on the trammels of weakness was rapidly approaching.

X

CULMINATION: THE STALIN REVOLUTION, 1924–1930

✪

Two TRAITS stood out in the history of Russian communism as shaped by Lenin. The first was the boundless will to advance the country (not as an accidental base of world revolution but as Russia—Holy Russia) to a position of global pre-eminence, particularly in terms of industrial strength, the basis of modern civilization. Soviet socialism was the guarantee that this goal could be reached. The other trait was a fanatical reliance on organization, "our fighting method," as Lenin had called it in 1918. There were times, of course, when dire necessity, such as the ruin of Russia in 1921, set a limit to what organization could do. Yet the very retreat of NEP led to a reaffirmation of this principle, as the tightening of party and state apparatus indicated. He, then, who could give vigor to these Leninist traits and advance them with the same monstrous impatience which Lenin had shown almost to the end of his career would be his true heir. In these essentials, Stalin was indeed the perfect Leninist by more than his own, all too brazenly proclaimed judgment. His rise to power did not mark, therefore, a Thermidorian reaction, but rather Fructidor, the high summer of fruition for the most dynamic and emotion-charged element of Bolshevism. If there entered with Stalin an element of retrogression, it came, inevitably, as the result of Russian backwardness.

Joseph Vissarionovich Djugashvili, known in the revolutionary underground as the Man of Steel or Stalin, did not possess the residual sensitivity of the Russian intelligentsia, the ear for the music of humaneness which Lenin had retained, however unwillingly. He came from the toughest ethnic stock in the Empire, the Georgian mountaineers, who had feuded for centuries with each other and their neighbors. He was further hardened by his rise from a lowly station and by his subsequent career as a professional revolutionary. While Lenin had lived abroad in relative ease, Stalin had worked and suffered for the cause inside Russia. The exiles' mastery of Marxist theory and their cultural refinement were out of his reach. But he possessed an advantage over them by representing the agitators and organizers without whom they were impotent. To all appearances, he was a humble man who put the party before personality and honored Lenin with a steadfast loyalty; he was always calm and dependable. At the time of the Bolshevik Revolution, he did not match Trotsky's brilliance but he was an indispensable member of the Bolshevik high command. As such, he received an important assignment in the new Soviet government as People's Commissar for Nationalities. Subsequently he also headed the Workers' and Peasants' Inspection, an agency which was to realize Lenin's dream of checking the abuses of bureaucracy by letting the toilers, even the housewives, take turns at public administration.

Yet his chief service always lay within the inner circles of the party. Here he proved without peers. He was appointed to the Politburo and the Orgburo when they were first constituted; he continued to serve on them even after he was named Secretary General. Thus he combined more vital functions in his own person than any other party official, including Lenin himself. He was a model chairman, tending to keep himself in the background and getting things done with a monumental capacity for work. Although Stalin quarreled bitterly with Trotsky during the civil war, his appointment to so many posts caused no controversy within the party; no one else seemed so well suited to perform the unwanted drudgery of party administration. It was he, then, who made the party into the model monolith by supervising the entire membership, appointing reliable men to key positions in the lower echelons, and keeping them alert and docile. And it was he who laid down the basic rules of power adjustment within this ever-growing leviathan which Kremlinologists have ever since watched as the key to Soviet policies.

What he lacked were the very qualities in which the former exiles excelled. He was not much of a writer or speaker. His style was stodgy, repetitious, interspersed with simple rhetorical questions to which, catechismlike, he gave simple answers, only occasionally lighted up by trivial jokes or a touch of folklore. Yet while devoid of flair, it was not ineffectual; like all the trappings of the Stalin regime as they evolved over the years, it catered to an audience of naïve, slow-witted, overworked, and bewildered people who retained a fairy-tale wonder for the demigods who shaped their destinies.

His style as an administrator was also several degrees too rough, even for Lenin. But it was not Lenin who had to cope with the stubborn realities of the new Soviet Empire. A monolithic party composed of former revolutionaries who, like most Russians, lacked the capacity of spontaneous mutual accommodation, was indeed no "girls' dormitory"; it required drastic methods of compulsion. And what was true of the party was even more true of the country as a whole. All the devils of disunity and division in the Empire that had plagued the tsars also beset the Soviet regime. Stalin had no respect for mass participation in public administration. What counted in his eyes was masterminding the minute and unending details of control, observing the drift of power at the articulation points of organization, and being willing to go to any lengths of ruthlessness for the sake of success. Against the Whites or the Georgian Mensheviks (as, later, against his opponents within the party and potential enemies throughout the body politic), Stalin showed the extremes to which he might go. His harshness in imposing Bolshevik rule on his native Georgia shocked even Lenin, who during the last months of his life became rather critical of the Secretary General's crudities. Yet were ruthlessness and terror not part of the Leninist tradition, the price which the Russian revolutionaries had always been willing to pay for their ideals?

It was proof of Stalin's ability as an administrator that his hold over the party was discovered only when it could no longer be effectively challenged. In order to secure the succession, he merely needed to prove that he possessed the required support among the membership (which he largely controlled) and then invoke party discipline against all dissenters. In this contest he drew on all the advantages of his cold-blooded endurance and superior craftiness in a game where everybody played for the highest stakes. Politics for Stalin was a round-the-clock, year-in, year-out watch on the quarter-deck. Those who could not stand the strain counted themselves out.

There is no need here to relate the sordid tale of deceit, lies, defamation, threats, punishment, recantation, surrender, self-doubt, self-torture, and police torture which sum up the struggle for Lenin's succession. Suffice it to ask: Who among Stalin's rivals possessed the qualities necessary for carrying the Leninist heritage to its logical conclusion in a Soviet Russia? Trotsky, who possessed the strongest claim, was no statesman capable of sustaining the continuous burden of supreme responsibility. He did not even seem to comprehend the fact that effective leadership called for meticulous, large-scale, and unrelenting organization. Besides, he showed an amazing lack of nerve at the time of Lenin's death. Instead of brushing aside Stalin's objections and rushing at once to Moscow, he idled away his time at a southern spa where he had gone in order to cure an "indisposition." The other contenders counted even less. Zinoviev was a coward, Bukharin too soft. The rest did not really possess the proper format. And since there was no settled machinery of succession, every one of these men, had *he* risen to the top, would have had to eliminate his rivals by some form of wolfishness. A militant Communist party required a single head. No collegium could maintain in the long run the dynamic drive of the Communist myth. Thus Stalin emerged as the first complete heir of the Imperial autocrat. Under the prevailing conditions, Russian society did not manage to produce a more civilized dictator. The blame, if blame there must be, falls on the country and on circumstances rather than on the man.

Stalin completed the fatal progress toward dictatorship inherent in Lenin's concept of the Bolshevik party. Before the Revolution, the organization of the party had already taken the place of the party itself. Afterward the Central Committee—and later the Politburo—took the place of the organization, and finally, under Stalin, the dictator took the place of the Central Committee and even the Politburo. At the same time, Stalin became the charismatic "leader" and the all-wise "father" of the Soviet peoples, providing in these comforting symbols a better emotional resting place for his subjects' worries than the tsars had ever furnished.

No other man in the twentieth century has wielded such unlimited power over so many subjects during so long and critical a time. Needless to say, that incredible power corrupted him. It brought out the weaknesses in his character, his desire to revenge the condescension with which the intellectuals in the party had always treated him, his suspicion of rivals, and his penchant for brutal and primitive solutions. Yet for a mortal in that rare category of self-made Caesars, he bore his burden comparatively well, certainly better than Mussolini, Hitler, or even Napoleon. His deified public image always remained a propaganda façade. Having come to his high station relatively late in life (he turned fifty in 1929), he remained free of flamboyant megalomania or idle showmanship and retained the outward simplicity—and at least a shred of the inward humility—prescribed for a true Communist leader. Only in old age, after a life of superhuman perils, did the controls of common sense break down and his rule decay into crass tyranny.*

* It is too early for a balanced historical judgment of this gigantic, many-faceted tyrant. Part of the difficulty stems from insufficient documentation; we are poorly informed about his life and his work. The greater part lies in the absence of applicable standards for measurement. The criteria for statecraft that have grown out of the confined and relatively well-ordered societies of Western Europe and the United States are patently out of place in the chaotic and cataclysmic conditions that confronted Russia in Stalin's time. New standards of crisis-dimension and global scope must be developed for the great men of the twentieth century in 'na enlarged framework we catch a glimpse of a man very human, morally frail, hardened to inhumanity by the hardness of the times to which he was more exposed than others, yet still linked to a vision of social perfection and national greatness.

At the time of Lenin's death, there had been need for a strong man. However completely the party now controlled the country, its future course was shrouded in doubts. Lenin had faded from leadership without indicating a successor or even leaving a clear-cut legacy. On the one hand, his followers remembered the Bolshevik militancy of his prime; on the other, they were bound by the hesitation and caution of his last years. His directives for NEP were unprecedently tame. They emphasized the need to appease the peasants and to make Soviet progress dependent on their willingness to change. He had also left open the basic question of whether Soviet Russia could, within the foreseeable future, move into full socialism. It had been generally assumed that a predominantly agrarian society like Russia's could be propelled into socialism only with the help of a socialist West (or at least a socialist Germany). Now that revolution in Europe was ruled out, was the Soviet regime merely to mark time?

Against these undercurrents of doubt and amidst the din of the struggle for the succession, Stalin sponsored, in an uncertain and fumbling way, a note of optimism which resumed the earlier buoyancy of Bolshevism. At the fourteenth party congress in December, 1925, a historic resolution was passed which again set the sights far ahead. The party pledged itself to carry on economic construction with the intention of "transforming the USSR from a country importing machines and equipment into one producing machines and equipment, so that the USSR under the conditions of capitalist encirclement cannot be made into an economic adjunct of world capitalism, but will represent an independent economic unit built in the socialist manner and capable . . . of serving as a powerful means of revolutionizing the workers of all countries and the suppressed peoples of the colonies and semi-colonies."

Subsequently the resolution stated the theoretical premise for the projected advance, saying that "Russia possesses all that is necessary for the construction of a socialist society." This was Stalin's famous doctrine of "Socialism in One Country," which taught that Soviet Russia could confidently go ahead by itself on the road to socialism.

WHY LENIN? WHY STALIN?

In the following year (1926), another party gathering pointed even more emphatically toward industrialization as the fulfillment of Soviet ambition:

> The biggest historical task set before the dictatorship of the proletariat, the creation of socialist society, demands the concentration of all forces of the party, the government, and the working class on the problems of economic policy.

The goals of that policy were now set sky high. Nothing less would do than "overtaking and surpassing the level of industrial production in the leading capitalist countries in a relatively short span of time."

Yet how were these ambitions to be put into practice? Party economists were sharply divided over the proper course of Soviet economic development. One group, led by N. Bukharin, proceeded from Lenin's directives for NEP. It wanted to give the peasants, particularly the kulaks, still more freedom. It resumed, as it were, Stolypin's policy. Only when a strong and prosperous rural base had been established, so ran the argument, could—and should—industry grow. Yet this approach, echoing the criticism levied against the Witte system, endangered the monolithic nature of the Soviet dictatorship. A house divided between a free peasantry and a regimented urban working class could not long survive; granting freedom to the peasants would push the regime back toward liberal democracy. And what, meanwhile, would become of Soviet Russia's security in a hostile, "capitalist" world?

The other group, led by Trotsky and E. Preobrazhensky, started like Witte from the need for rapid industrial growth. If agriculture was to produce more, it had to be supplied with more and better industrial goods. Yet this was bound to become more difficult as the existing industrial equipment, inherited from tsarist days, began to wear out. Under these conditions, even maintaining the current level of industrial production (which had steadily risen after 1921 without, however, regaining prewar levels) would be impossible, let alone advancing to socialist plenty. The escape from this difficulty, so this group argued, lay in deliberate industrial expansion. Unfortunately, this policy cost the country dearly. In the absence of foreign capital, the huge capital outlays could be obtained only by further lowering the standard of living, by "primitive socialist accumulation," as Preobrazhensky indiscreetly put it. That, from a political point of view, seemed suicidal. Had not the Soviet regime promised a higher income to the toilers of Russia? This school of thought thus ran into the same predicament that had forced Witte's dismissal from the Ministry of Finance. The Russian people would not tolerate any further sacrifices. In short, whichever direction economic analysis took, it ended in a cul-de-sac.

By 1928, when Stalin's power over the party was at last firmly entrenched, the problem of Soviet economic development could no longer be disregarded. While his own authority was limited and the experts had disagreed, he had straddled the fence, urging rapid industrialization yet also inclining toward Bukharin's side, not wishing to antagonize the peasantry. By 1928, however, Bukharin's policy had proved a fiasco. Under the freedom which the party allowed the peasants, they did not increase their production to the limit; on the contrary, they curtailed it. Were they thus to slow down the economic advance to which the party had repeatedly pledged itself ever since 1925, and was the entire regime to bog down in the peasant sloth? Furthermore, the loss of political momentum which accompanied the struggle over the succession was already spreading corruption in party circles.

At this point, as grave a crisis as faced Soviet Russia after the civil war, Stalin returned to the full fury of Leninism. Not possessing Lenin's ability to dramatize the new phase of Soviet policy with subtle theoretical premises, he changed course clumsily and crudely, relying more on will and brute force than on technical finesse. Yet the change contained all the ingredients of a major turning point. The first thing Stalin did was to paint the international scene, just then brightened by the "spirit of Locarno" and the Kellogg-Briand pact, in dark and ominous colors. He wanted to conjure up again (on dubious evidence) the wartime phobia about "capitalist" invasion and the fighting mood of the early Comintern in order to prepare the peoples of Russia for the sacrifices to come.

Unjustified as this doctrinaire interpretation of "capitalist" policy appeared in 1928, its pessimism was more realistic than the optimism of the West. After the outbreak of the Great Depression in the next year, the international scene changed for the worse. In the wake of the depression, the flimsy precautions of collective security crumbled and most of the new democratic regimes established after the war perished, if they had not already done so. The trend toward dictatorship was running strong in the twenties, as events in Italy, Spain, Portugal, Poland, and Lithuania had shown; now it accelerated. The entire western tradition of promoting public welfare by private initiative seemed wrecked, as unemployment and poverty suddenly descended upon millions of unsuspecting peoples.

Out of these unprecedented calamities emerged the aggressive forces responsible for the second World War. In Germany, they brought to power a totalitarian movement not without parallels to Soviet communism, despite its diametrically opposed ideology. National socialism, too, was the product of the imperialist age. It though in terms of global power—not of a class, to be sure, but of nationality and its supposed essence, race—and it throbbed with a national pride made fanatical by the recent defeat of Germany. It, too, was geared to the age of psycho-politics, with techniques of appeal and agitation often copied from Marxist experience. At the same time it aroused more spontaneous mass support than communism enjoyed even in Russia.

It might be argued that the Great Depression offered Stalin unrivaled opportunities for revolutionary agitation abroad. The final crisis of "capitalism" seemed imminent; communism gained new disciples everywhere. Yet weighing the solid advantages of a strong Soviet base against the uncertainties of world revolution, Stalin had long decided that the strength of Soviet Russia must have precedence. Like Witte he dreaded the weakness of Russia, and like him he realized that concentration on industrial development at home ruled out costly foreign adventures. Indeed, the immediate effect of Stalin's first Five Year Plan was a distinct weakening of Soviet strength. Thus, despite the new fierceness of Soviet revolutionary propaganda—foreign Communists were ordered to turn against the moderate socialists (now branded as "social fascists"), which signally aided Hitler's rise to power*—Soviet foreign policy on all levels bore an essentially defensive character. (There is even evidence to suggest that Stalin welcomed Hitler's victory as a guarantee of sharpened division within the capitalist camp.) Lenin's vision of a revolutionary counter power to the "imperialist" West was not forgotten, but it was giving way to the Stalinist conviction that world revolution stood a better chance if it possessed an impregnable base in the Soviet Union. Thus Soviet Russia's self-interest moved steadily into the foreground as the drive for industrialization got into high gear and the age-old ambitions of Russian pride were mobilized to support it.

In 1928, Stalin pledged the Communist party "to be responsible for the escape from backwardness." In the following year, digging even deeper into the recesses of Russian ambition, he boasted:

> We are going full steam ahead toward socialism through industrialization, leaving our century-old "racial" background behind. We are becoming a land of metals, a land of automobiles, a land of tractors, and when we set the USSR on an automobile and the *muzhik* on a tractor, let the noble capitalists, so proud of their "civilization," attempt to catch up. We shall see then which countries can be labeled as backward and which as advanced.

Finally, in 1931, when the Stalinist revolution was at its height, he summed up the humiliations of centuries in a famous speech which by its odd mixture of Russian nationalism and Leninist socialism revealed the true nature of Soviet communism:

> One feature of the history of old Russia was the continual beatings she suffered for falling behind, for her backwardness. She was beaten by the Mongol Khans. She was beaten by the Turkish beys. She was beaten by the Swedish feudal lords. She was beaten by the Polish and Lithuanian gentry. She was beaten by the French and British capitalists. She was beaten

* During the last years of the Weimar regime, the German Communists often joined the Nazis in their attack on parliamentary democracy.

by the Japanese barons. All beat her—for backwardness, for military backwardness, for cultural backwardness, for political backwardness, for industrial backwardness, for agricultural backwardness. She was beaten because to beat her was profitable and went unpunished. . . . In the past we had no fatherland and could have none. Now, however, that we have overthrown capitalism and the workers wield power in our country, we have a fatherland and shall defend its independence. Do you want our Socialist fatherland to be beaten and to lose its independence? If you do not want that, then you must abolish its backwardness and develop a really Bolshevik pace in the establishment of its Socialist economy. . . . We are fifty or a hundred years behind the advanced countries. We must make good this lag in ten years. Either we accomplish this or we will be crushed.*

The dire choice between advance or extinction, familiar in imperialist rhetoric from Disraeli to Hitler, now hounded the Soviet citizens as they tried to fulfill their production quotas under the preposterous, inhuman experiment of rapid industrialization known as the first Five Year Plan. The plan set forth, in the Marxist terms of rational economic control which the party had already proclaimed as its ideal in 1919, the goals of industrial production to be reached within a five-year period (starting in 1928). As the official text stated:

It is a plan for the radical reconstruction of the productive foundations of our country. . . . Our country makes the unprecedented experiment of tremendous capital construction carried out at the expense of current consumption, at the price of a harsh regime of economy and by sacrificing the satisfactions of today's needs in the name of great historical aims.

The plan was no beggar's gamble to patch his economic garment from the insufficient scraps of cloth available but a dicta-

---

* It is true that in recounting Russia's defeats Stalin forgot the many victories that had led to the phenomenal expansion of Russia in the past six centuries. Yet in one respect he was right. Against the Great Powers of the West, Russia had never won an unqualified victory (luckily for western civilization as we know it).

tor's command that a gala uniform be provided at any cost and on the double. The goals were exceedingly specific. From 1928-1933, gross industrial output was to increase 235.9 percent, that of the heavy industries alone by 279.2 percent. Production costs were decreed to fall by 35 percent, prices by 24 percent, and labor productivity to rise by 110 percent, thus allowing internal savings to finance part of the expansion.

The decimal-point precision of the plan was, to be sure, mere show. Its directives were shot through with a thousand inconsistencies, bottlenecks, and other flaws. Underneath the impressive façade it was never more than a loosely meshed set of goals which bore scant relation to economic reality. One grave miscalculation, for instance, was made in regard to foreign trade, through which vital industrial equipment was to be procured. Despite the Communist claim to understand the laws of history, the Great Depression had not been foreseen. As it ran its course, it knocked out the carefully planned export-import schedules and upset everything geared to them. Before the five years were out, the plan had to be terminated, to be followed by further and somewhat more refined Five Year Plans. Yet whatever the appalling waste and human sacrifice that accompanied the first Five Year Plan, a determined start toward the distant goals had been made.

The industrial plan, however, was only half of the economic offensive. The other half was the compulsory collectivization of agriculture. If the industrial drive was to succeed, agricultural production could not be left to the discretion of recalcitrant peasants. They too had to be subjugated to state control. This, of course, had been the Communists' ambition from the start. In 1917, they had let the land pass into peasant hands only because the Revolution needed peasant support. Yet in their minds they had always subscribed to the Marxist conviction that effective agriculture was possible only in large, mechanized units resembling factories. For that reason, the Communists had tried to save the latifundia and the model farms of tsarist Russia from the peasants' land hunger and transform them into state farms. They had also experimented with various forms of collective farming, without arousing much interest in the countryside. Under the NEP, these experiments subsided as peasant agriculture reverted to the prewar pattern of small-scale farming. Unfortunately, because of the absence of large estates producing for the market, less grain was delivered to the urban consumers than before the war, a fact which neatly confirmed the Marxist analysis. Considering the peasants' limited resources and their innate conservatism (their "petty-bourgeois natures," as the Communists put it), there could be little hope of any basic improvement. Obviously, peasant spontaneity was bound to leave Russian agriculture backward, a drag on economic progress.

Economic and political necessity thus drove Stalin to seek a better method of controlling Soviet agriculture. The instrument chosen for this purpose was the collective farm, a compromise between private farming and the farm-factory. It consolidated many small household plots into large units suitable for mechanized equipment, combined the herds and draft animals, and pooled the equipment needed to operate the new holding. Machinery, however, was handled separately by the Machine Tractor Stations, which served a number of collective farms. The peasant, now raised to the dignity of a "collective farmer," merely retained his hut, a small plot of land to go with it, and a few animals for his private needs.

In theory the collective farm was run democratically, through an elected leadership. In reality the chairman was appointed by the local party secretary, and the guiding decisions on production were determined by the national plan. The collective farmers could do as they pleased with their private plots—from them they have provisioned much of the urban population to the present day—but the collective had to deliver to the state its planned products according to schedule, regardless of the vagaries of the harvest. While the collective farm was not quite as effectively controlled as a factory, a long stride toward that goal had been made.

The transition from private to collective farming was pushed forward with utter recklessness in 1929 and early 1930. For the countryside, it meant a far more brutal upheaval than any previous agrarian measure since the imposition of serfdom. Word went out that the kuklaks, i.e., the most successful peasants under the NEP and all other recalcitrant peasants who sided with them, were to be "liquidated as a class." What household did not feel resentful at having to surrender its land, livestock, and costly implements! The more it possessed, the more it fought against collectivization. Thus millions of families who resisted it were uprooted and separated: the men were sent to forced labor in the new industrial centers and the wastelands; the women and children were left behind to shift for themselves. Thousands of peasants were killed on the spot in pitched battles that recalled the atrocities of the civil war. Famine broke out in the wake of collectivization, and millions of valuable animals were slaughtered. The loss of livestock and draft animals was so severe as to offset for decades the gains of control achieved by collectivization.

The years of the first Five Year Plan and of collectivization were indeed bleak ones, a new Iron Age visiting untold hardship and sacrifice on a population that had barely recovered from the civil war. Yet the suffering which had been dreaded by both Bukharinites and Trotskyites in the controversy over Soviet economic development produced no insurrection, no revolution. How, one cannot help wondering, did Stalin produce such a political miracle? The answer points to the heart of the Stalin revolution. While the economic transformation was underway, Stalin developed to their fullest potential the controls which the Bolshevik Revolution had prepared. For the first time, the political and social framework was ready to permit the concentration upon economic development which the party for so long had had to postpone. And it was ready also to absorb the shock of the sudden, enforced transition into an industrial society without visible damage to the regime.

Political leadership, as we have seen, was now centralized as never before. It was agreed, furthermore, on the need for hurried industrialization. The will of the party also permeated the machinery of the state, and the state controlled the energies of its subjects to an unprecedented degree Private initiative, for all practical purposes, was eliminated. The party, through the state, took charge of all public affairs. The state was the only employer; all independent sources of income were wiped out. Even the peasants (except for their garden plots) were now subject to state supervision. There could arise no tensions between different social groups, no class struggle in the traditional sense. The relations between the various categories of state employees were regulated according to state necessity, not by their independent social bargaining power.

The Stalinist revolution also transformed the role of the trade unions, which had hitherto still enjoyed a measure of autonomy as spokesmen for the industrial workers. They were now made into agencies of production, transmission belts of the economic plan, on the theory that the workers in a workers' state needed no protection against themselves. Even social security and housing, administered by the trade unions, were used to enforce labor discipline and to increase production. The change, however, was not without some gains to the workers. The trade unions took charge of all the problems facing a new labor force all too suddenly shifted from fields to factory. The newcomers no longer had to cope with the harassment of adjustment unaided, as under the tsars.

Another radical change was the abandonment of the original Bolshevik egalitarianism. Wages were now graded according to a man's output and his contribution to the plan's success: "from each according to his ability, to each according to his deserts," as the new slogan, derived from Marx himself, proclaimed. Thus originated a differentiation in income levels that approached—and at times exceeded—the divergence between rich and poor in the "capitalist" countries. In the awards of nonmonetary incentives, medals, titles, and other insignia of honor, it even surpassed them, reverting again to the carefully graded hierarchy of tsarist officialdom. These incentives were part of "socialist competition," a device designed to offset the lethargy resulting from the replacement of private initiative by state directives.

Now that the individual's energies were enlisted in state activity as never before, the individual's conduct also came under close state scrutiny. Stalin carried to an extreme Lenin's earlier call for proletarian self-control for the sake of greater productivity. Social discipline, still lax after the Revolution, was greatly tightened. Mme. Kollontai's libertinism was outlawed, the legal bonds of marriage were again strengthened, divorce made difficult, abortion prohibited. Sex was banished from sight and mind to a degree incomprehensible in the West. Parents' authority over their children was likewise reinstated, as was the teachers' power over their pupils. Students were now drilled in their subjects as in the old days. And the old days of Russia, denigrated as "capitalist" or "feudal" in the first exuberance of the Revolution, were reincorporated into the Soviet tradition as part of a great national heritage. The official new Soviet patriotism indeed drew heavily on Russian national pride, at times boosting it by claiming many great inventions of modern technology as Russian discoveries. Stalin even arranged a truce with the church. While fitfully promoting antireligious propaganda, the party now permitted at least a bare minimum of religious worship, provided that it did not compete with the party's claim over its subjects' "consciousness."

The Stalinist revolution indeed paid the closest possible attention to the "consciousness" of the Soviet peoples. It wanted to form "the whole man," knowing that this could be done only through the control of his mind. Everything shaping that vital center was scrupulously controlled—art, literature, music, journalism, aesthetics, philosophy, historical writing, even scientific research. The poets were bidden by Stalin to become "engineers of the soul." In all these fields, the party closely prescribed the canons of proletarian rectitude. In the arts, the guiding formula was "socialist realism," a style presumably set by Maxim Gorky, yet in its righteous and roseate simplicity more expressive of petty-bourgeois Philistinism. In all these efforts, the chief responsibility for developing the proper consciousness was laid on the individual himself. He could be punished if he continued to harbor "capitalist" or "anti-Soviet" views. This was no laughable pretension. The party was astonishingly resourceful in devising a great variety of pressures on the individual to mend his consciousness.

The avowed purpose of these efforts was the creation of a "new Soviet man," the type of citizen required for successful industrialization. Scrutiny of his attributes reveals him as essentially a blend of Bolshevik militancy and Victorian respectability, a disciplined, clean-living, neat, cooperative, patriotic citizen, thinking as much of the public good as his own advancement, and an intransigent Leninist. Unfortunately, he was never a man of flesh and blood but an abstraction foisted on an unresponsive people and therefore basically hollow. A man had to strive exceedingly hard—too hard for happiness—to live up to that ideal.

There is no question that Stalin succeeded in arousing a measure of popular idealism, particularly among Soviet youth. Incredible feats of heroism were performed during these years on the battlefronts of industrial construction. Yet Stalin himself did not trust the strength of that enthusiasm. He used compulsion as well, in order to enforce conformity of thought and action among the Soviet masses and to spur them to the utmost exertions. From the start of the industrial drive, he staged impressive trials for public show designed to prod the hesitant and to silence the critics. As time went by, his terror purges sank a black fear deep into his subjects' souls, drying up the mainsprings of spontaneity and rooting out its twin, Russian anarchism. Industrial society, after all, requires an incredible docility at the base of its freedoms. Yet, at the same time, he inhibited the dynamic and many-sided creativity also necessary for successful industrialism, depriving the country of the ultimate successes that he craved. Was the flaw the result of his personal rule or of the damnable conditions of Russia which he wanted to overcome?

Thus a raw, fanatical Stalinist Russia emerged, decked out ever more deceitfully as the highway to socialist utopia and the embodiment of the will of the toilers, yet making a mockery of what most socialists had expected of the Communist ideal.* In-

---

* It will have become obvious by now that Soviet socialism (or communism) proves nothing about the nature of socialism (or communism)

evitably the disillusionment was turned against Stalin who, as a man of action, was not given to elaborate theoretical justifications which might have absolved him. Yet was the disillusionment not also the fault of those who, as in the old days, wanted the benefits of a modern industrial society without being willing to pay the price under the dishearteningly adverse conditions of Russia? The incredible social discipline of the advanced countries, trained over centuries of none-too-gentle coaxing (one need only think of the court of Star Chamber in England or the suppression of the *Fronde* in France), could not be easily matched by the peoples of Russia, not even under the most drastic Stalinist compulsions.

There is no need here to trace the course of the Stalinist revolution into the 1930's. This essay must conclude with the fact that by 1930 the process of revolution begun around the turn of the century had come to an end. By the letter as well as the spirit of their political system (though not by the bonds of spontaneity) the government and the people were now in alignment, the people integrated into the state, and both government and people set to work with breath-taking singlemindedness on the tasks of economic modernization. On this harsh foundation Soviet Russia has continued, with minor adjustments and many flaws that belied the monolithic nature of Soviet rule, to the present day. On this basis it has established itself as a super power.

---

as a sociopolitical doctrine. Soviet practice merely testifies to the conditions of Russia.

CONCLUSION

★

LET US ADMIT that, even after the Stalinist revolution, the revolution in Russian life has not ended. The former revolution from without and below has merely been replaced by another one—the revolution from above. That revolution, inherent in the nature of autocratic government and vastly accelerated after 1917, will be unfinished as long as Soviet Russia retains its ambition to surpass and overtake the leading "capitalist" countries which, despite all denials, still serve as its model. From the start in 1917 it has been a controlled revolution, conducted under native guidance in a manner confirming rather than destroying native leadership. It has permitted the concentration of all resources of state and society on the single task of preserving and increasing Russia's competitive strength in the global age.

One might argue, then, that Lenin and Stalin have done no more for their country than to arrange the pattern of backwardness in a more modern form. Russia has gained in industrial strength and efficient leadership, in the two respects crucial for meeting the competition of power politics. And it has stood the supreme test. Ten years after Stalin's famous speech in 1931, Hitler invaded Soviet Russia. In 1943, during the battle of Stalingrad, Soviet Russia did show that, despite several blunders on Stalin's part, it was able to defend itself by its own resources. Massive American aid arrived only subsequently, permitting the quick rebound of the Soviet armies. It has also risen into the ranks of the global models, claiming to offer a prescription of a

[204]

successful escape from backwardness for other developing countries.

At the same time, however, the Soviet peoples have lost much. They are still poor, exposed to great physical and moral hardships, and subject to a ruinous falsification of their deepest values and ideals in the name of "Soviet spontaneity." They have sacrificed their art and literature, their heartiness, their exuberance. Their lives and actions lack grace and harmony. They suffer bitterly from the loss of true creativity, of wholesomeness, of the gentle forces that quietly and unobtrusively have made the West into the universal model. The black sores in Russian society and Russian minds, though carefully concealed, are not healing; the system itself perpetuates them. Reality and ideality are still eternities apart.

By this count the totalitarian revolution from above defeats its purpose. It will never enable Soviet Russia to overtake its "capitalist" rivals, for it deprives its subjects of the essence of cultural creativity, of freedom. Only underneath, in the hidden depths of Russian life, do these forces persist. And whenever they are allowed to rise to the surface, as they have occasionally since the death of Stalin, they at once show their loathing for the Soviet goad. The tap roots of backwardness are not easily severed. They lie embedded in the elusive, innermost promptings of human volition. They can be torn out only by a spontaneous eagerness to adopt a new and more severe self-discipline, not by a command to change.

Yet our indictment of Soviet rule cannot stop at this point. We must still ask whether these undercurrents of true creativity and wholesomeness would have been better served had the country remained weak and, as a result, been overrun by foreign armies. It may be difficult for Americans to feel in their bones the tensions of international relations shaping the ambitions of Witte, Lenin, or Stalin. Yet on the ground of our own immeasurable past security, we have no right to condemn their frantic effort to advance their country to strength and glory. Even at present, when the madness of imperialism has given way to a somewhat soberer mood, we must still ask the same question. Is it necessarily in the interest of the Soviet peoples to relax the Soviet controls and to allow them to lapse back into the old anarchic spontaneity which lurks underneath the Soviet harness? Should they forfeit their ambition to match the hegemony of the western model and settle down to a second-rate existence? As long as we in the United States and the West set the standards of global pre-eminence, both in terms of political strength and cultural leadership, it seems hypocritical on our part to deny similar pretensions to our Soviet rivals. The decision, at any rate, is not in our hands.

By our standards (and the best of theirs), the hard political necessities that shaped and still shape the Soviet regime stand condemned; they kill the indispensable poetry of life. Yet true poetry in Soviet Russia, as expressed by the Pasternaks or the young writers of the present generation, also stands condemned because it has no comprehension of that pervasive political necessity and strict social discipline under which all advanced societies operate. In terms of a power-conscious urban-industrial society, it is destructive. The tragedy of modern Russian history lies in the fatal incompatibility of spontaneity and political discipline, the inseparable partners of successful statehood. And there is no end in sight, unfortunately, for this tragedy as long as the harsh global competition for power continues.

The Soviet leadership, however, will derive no small comfort from the fact that the West—especially the United States—is approaching a historic crisis of its own. After more than five decades of premature prophecy of a "capitalist" collapse, the social, political, and above all spiritual forces that have given western society its past buoyancy are approaching a stage of disintegration; the old single-mindedness of purpose is vanishing. In the age of the global confluence the happy combination of a sense of individual freedom with a collective social and political self-discipline sufficient for leadership in the world is falling apart. Among college-bred Americans, especially, a deep sense of alienation and unfreedom is spreading. Among the proofs of global leadership the boons of freedom certainly stand foremost. If the consciousness, and hence the legal and political practice, of freedom in the United States should disappear (or at least be seriously weakened), the Soviet Union will have scored a tremendous relative advance. Its position in the world will then have approached true equality with its chief rival. Yet even then, we might speculate, the Soviet Union will hardly enjoy tranquility. The power conflicts of the global age will continue. And any advance in Soviet Russia's external security will more than ever call into question among the Soviet peoples the harsh means employed to achieve it.

This essay, however, is not concerned with the future but with the rise of Soviet Russia in a past age, under conditions (still hardly understood) now receding into the background. While the West was forging ahead at a rapid clip, no backward country, caught in the coils of its imperfection, could match the enormous creativity of self-disciplined free initiative. Then the West's weaknesses lay on the surface, to be worked on and mended, as a challenge to human ingenuity. When they had been overcome, they passed out of sight and joined the invisible foundations of strength. In Soviet Russia, on the other hand, the reverse was apt to be true. Soviet strength lay on the surface; the weaknesses were carefully hidden or are invisible even to Communist eyes. Under these circumstances the culmination of western achievement, the secure combination of spontaneity for the individual with global power for the state, of civic freedom with the ability of society to set a universal norm, forever eluded the Soviet regime.

It may seem—to round off these pages with a few reflections on the fundamentals of Soviet-Western relations—that this essay has pressed the course of recent Russian history into an unduly determinist cast. Like the unseen cunning stagehands of Reason in Hegelian dialectics, the two underlying necessities, the need for identification between rulers and ruled and the need for industralization, have been made to shift the historical scenery from Nicholas II to Stalin according to a preordained design. Yet denying the validity of such prearrangement means overlooking the most crucial aspect of the Russian Revolution.

As compared with the drift of events in the western nations, above all in the United States, Great Britain, France, and even, from the Russian perspective, Germany, the direction of Russian development was indeed predetermined. The model countries were free to grope ahead in the unpredictable manner resulting from the coincidental interplay of their internal forces, visible and invisible, known and unknown, rather than from external pressures.* If they sometimes followed a similar trend, it was not because they deliberately copied each other, but because they were sufficiently alike in basic respects. Russia, on the other hand, found itself in an altogether different position. It could meet the common challenge of the global power competition only by a special effort of imitation. Under the face-saving guise of a superior norm it had to copy the ability of the models to mobilize the energies of their citizens to the full, lest it fall behind and be dissolved as a Great Power. Russia's defeats from the Crimean war to Brest-Litovsk compelled imitation, and imitation in turn predetermined the course of Russia's development.†

This dependence also put the Russian Revolution into a different category from the French Revolution. The Russian Revolution, as we have seen, was a double, or mixed, revolution. Up to the summer of 1917 it resembled, one might say, the European prototype, for it aimed at the overthrow of all inequalities and restrictions on popular participation in politics. It was a revolution of liberation and a revolution from below. Unlike the liberal revolution, however, the March Revolution released no novel resources of social discipline suited to an industrial age. From the summer of 1917, therefore, a new pattern came to prevail,

* This is not to deny that external affairs, such as two World Wars and the Cold War, have had their effect on recent American history. No one will argue, however, that the change has been imitative of an external model (even where, in certain aspects of our security measures, we have moved closer to Soviet practices).

† There are constant factors of great potency and long durability in the history of every country, as for instance insularity and external security in the case of Great Britain. Recognizing their importance does not make a historian a philosophical determinist, although it may, perhaps, make him somewhat humbler than his contemporaries when assessing man's control over his destiny.

that of the revolt against backwardness, already foreshadowed in the character of Leninism. Although still employing the terminology of a revolution of liberation, and thus forever forestalling a clear analysis of their accomplishments, the Bolsheviks carried out a revolution from above, imposing a new and extraneous discipline on a population leveled and rendered defenseless by the liberation that preceded and accompanied their seizure of power.

This second revolution was a peculiarly Russian phenomenon, in the tradition of Peter the Great, relevant only to countries on the fringes of European civilization. The Bolsheviks still claimed the traditional universality for their revolution, but, as events have shown, their self-proclaimed universality carried little appeal to countries higher on the cultural slope. And since the 1960s its relevance to countries lower on the slope, like China, is also open to doubt. The Chinese Communists did not manage, even by the application of extreme Stalinist principles, to "leap forward" into rapid industrialization. These limitations rob Soviet communism of the global potency of the western model, which applies to all.

This indeed was—and will remain for a while—the most terrifying aspect of the power of the western countries: they set the direction of the internal evolution of all the others. To this day the Communist's implicit determination "to overtake and surpass" the "advanced capitalist" countries gives proof of their fealty to the "capitalist" model. Year after year, decade after decade, Soviet promises and development schemes are adjusted in order to follow the latest shifts in western technology, style of clothing, or way of life. And when Khrushchev wanted to "bury" the United States, he made it abundantly clear that he would give us a state burial. If communism finally arrives, so we are assured, it will contain all the boons of "capitalism" (and more).* In the sober present meanwhile, Soviet Russia,

---

* The Soviet ambition to surpass and overtake the United States has been much muted under Brezhnev and Kosygin. The extravagant expectations raised by Khrushchev obviously proved a continuous embarrassment to his successors.

like all developing countries, must still pursue the same basic pattern of development which the western countries have pioneered, with one major exception.

The divisive difference lies in the fact (likely to remain true as long as the imitation of an alien model remains a necessity of state) that the imitators, particularly when pressed for time, have to eliminate the free play of spontaneity. If they permitted that basic freedom, they would surely remain where they were; their subjects, left to their own devices, obviously have not managed to do what is needed in order to modernize the country (otherwise they would already have done it!). Under these circumstances the task of their rulers, as these pages have tried to show, is not only to introduce modern technology but to provide the total framework of socio-political organization and of the proper human motivation as well, the nutrient solution as it were, in which industry in the West has grown to its modern significance. This is a gigantic, if not impossible, undertaking. Soviet totalitarianism, for that reason, was ever more comprehensive than, say, Nazi totalitarianism. Whereas Hitler aimed at creating a "new man" in a political sense (already finding superb resources of labor discipline and industrial production readily at his disposal), Stalin had to penetrate into much deeper layers of human motivation.

It is exactly in the sphere of motivation control, the essence of Soviet totalitarianism, that the Russian Communists have made their greatest and most original contribution. In the unending imitation implicit in "catching up," the experiments of total control seemed the only creative outlet of political action possible. From the western point of view these were sad, infamous experiments. Yet the Communists deserve some admiration for their pioneering ingenuity in coping with problems that did not exist in the West and for which the West, for once, offered no remedy.

This fact can hardly be overstressed. In the essentials of socio-political organization and inward human motivation, the model countries have nothing to teach the underdeveloped peoples who must graft the western way of life—or the western sources of political power (which amounts to the same thing)—on their native traditions. We cannot penetrate to the core of native feeling. We do not know—and, as outsiders, will hardly ever know—the original fabric into which we are weaving our own civilization. And how little even the native leaders, their analytic insights derived from the western model, know themselves! If western civilization has played havoc with native tradition, the Communists too have dealt cruelly with their Russian heritage. There exists as yet no pattern for peaceful fusion, at least not when the security of the state is involved and time is of the essence—and where, sooner or later, is this not the case?

As the West can give no valid advice on the absorption of its way of life into an alien environment, so this essay does not pretend to any relevance for Soviet readers. Its efforts to explain the peculiarities of Russian development out of Russian and global conditions, its emphasis on the insuperable difficulties, its destructive analysis of the Communist myth, and its denial of the superiority of Soviet socialism, all destroy what this essay itself has shown to be indispensable bases for self-confidence and self-preservation. From the Soviet point of view, "bourgeois objectivity" (the Communist term for the impartiality of western scholarship) is a ruthless, hostile force. It is one of the invisible weapons of the West that weakens the determination of Soviet Russia and undermines its power, like western political morality in general. Applying our own high standards of scholarly integrity and political morality to Soviet Russia constitutes a power thrust at the heart of the Soviet system. If these standards took hold in the Soviet Union, the present regime would surely melt away and Russian politics, for an indefinite period, be reduced to travail if not chaos. This, in turn, would alter the global balance of power in the "capitalists'" favor and revive the ancient dangers to the security of the Soviet peoples, even of those who, like the Ukrainians, might be tempted to secede from the Union. Is it surprising then that the Communists have built elaborate ideological defenses and an Iron Curtain to guard them?

Thus the global power struggle permeates every phase of life.

In the twentieth century, international relations, particularly be · tween the model countries and the developing peoples, are indeed "total." Every form of contact, whether of individuals, goods, or ideals, carries potent political connotations; it creates a battlefield of its own. Small wonder that those who lack the invisible forms of power will strike back with whatever weapons they command—vituperation, deliberate subversion, trickery, and every conceivable kind of hostility.

This reaction has confronted western attitudes toward the Soviet Union with an almost insoluble dilemma. Any attitude of kindness and tolerance is bound to be exploited by the Soviet rulers as a sign of weakness until the Soviet Union itself enjoys the attributes of a superior global model. There was never a chance that the bitterness forged over centuries of humiliation could suddenly be dissolved by any feeble show of sympathy or even a wartime coalition against a common enemy. A "liberal" foreign policy toward Soviet Russia under these circumstances would easily lead to a strengthening of Soviet power without a corresponding relaxation of its innate psychological insecurity and consequent drive for revenge. And even western liberals, no matter how eager to reduce international tension, have never been prepared to surrender the traditional western ascendancy. A "hard" policy, on the other hand, would be sure to deepen still further the Russian resentment and perpetuate (and even refine) the burden of totalitarianism for the Soviet peoples. Nothing positive could be gained from this alternative either. Even a policy of "containment," occupying a middle ground between these extremes, could offer no escape from the dilemma, for it too aims at thwarting Soviet ambition. As with any other Great Power, nothing short of total defeat would extirpate that basic will for self-assertion. And the total defeat of Soviet Russia has always been clearly out of the question.

In short, no version of western diplomacy was (or still is) likely to alter the uncompromising Soviet stance toward the "capitalist" West (even if there should ever be a Soviet socialist West, the old resentments would prevail). If there is to be a transformation in the Soviet attitude, it must proceed from the very source. It must start where Soviet attitudes were created in the first place, in the West itself. If the analysis set forth in this essay is correct, it was the West which, by the model of its superior power, has largely shaped the Soviet dictatorship. Soviet totalitarianism has basically no more than the caricature echo of western state and society, the best copy feasible under Russian conditions. Only when the model itself has undergone a metamorphosis will the Soviet version follow suit.

This fact imposes upon all Western society, in its present indecision, a serious moral challenge (alas, every interpretation of Soviet Russia culminates in a moral). If the West is to make much progress in its relations with Soviet communism, it must rearrange all facets of its foreign impact, visible and invisible. It must eschew deliberate domination and reorient its political values so as to be of service to the global community which it has created in its own image; it must do so largely on the latter's own terms. It must make an effort to understand the thousand-fold problems with which it has saddled all pre-industrial societies and lend them its own resources and skills as they themselves wish to use them. It must show a new humility and solicitude for all native traditions which it has undermined and uprooted. It must spread a novel appreciation of the human responsibilities of paramount global power.

We should be aware, however, that such outgoing empathy creates serious consequences for the single-mindedness of American purpose and, more broadly, for the American presence in the world. As we begin to understand others on their own terms, what becomes of the validity of traditional American (or western) values? The cultural and political relativism of the analysis here set forth undermines the universality of the specific Americanisms that have hitherto cemented American society and produced the miraculous coincidence of freedom with power. In the age of the global confluence the impact of the non-Western, nonliberal, nonurban industrial world on our own society is as subversive as the Western impact on the non-Western world. The philosophies of alienation are the revenge which the victims of westernization inflict upon their masters; alienation is creeping into the very heart of American motivation. American youths, more susceptible to the values of the non-American world than their elders, are growing apart from their society at a rapid clip.

There are some, therefore, who will deplore the cultural and political relativism of this essay as a factor weakening the American resolve and thereby adversely affecting the overall balance of power between the United States and the Soviet Union. There is no denying the validity of that charge. On the other hand, it is clear that all efforts to stem that tide are condemned to failure. Traditionally Americans have favored commerce and a sympathetic openness toward all the world. The very wars that try to stop the subversion of Americanism actually promote it; they cannot help but intensify the interaction. As Vietnam proved, military or cultural service abroad no longer guarantees loyalty to American ideals. Thus, we are faced with extraordinarily difficult questions in extraordinarily difficult times.

For our guidance we might sketch a few obvious attitudes regarding the Soviet experience. The West, we should say, must never counter Soviet arrogance with its own adamance (except, of course, to prevent Soviet military aggression). It must stop its all-too-common haughty moralizing on Soviet affairs, the tawdry editorial gloating over Communist misfortunes and failures, over the low standard of living, the lack of freedom, the flagrant discrepancy between pretention and reality, or the vain efforts to end basic flaws by constant organizational patching. There may indeed come a time when the misery of our own affairs knocks out all ground from underneath our past moral superiority. It will be wiser, therefore, to give due credit for what the Soviet rulers and their subjects have accomplished despite frightful and disheartening difficulties (while, of course, never accepting every Soviet boast at face value). It must find a place for them in the world, an opportunity for equality not in terms of domination but of service. Having pioneered the techniques of social control for the adopting of western technology, the Russian Communists can justly proffer the gist of their experience to other peoples who find themselves in similar straits. As a model of limited scope, they have not been unsuccessful. Among the countries risen to statehood after the end of World War II, we find hardly one which, while shying away from Soviet totalitarianism, has not deliberately copied some feature of the Soviet system.

Once these basic changes of attitude are accomplished, one may look forward to an appropriate foreign policy toward the Soviet Union that in the long run may count on a civil response. Evidence of a significant advance in this direction has already emerged in the past decade. The tone of American official relations with the Soviet government, for instance, is no longer as stridently self-righteous as it once was, even under provocation. Moreover, American policy of giving aid to the developing countries has evoked a similar policy on the part of the Soviet Union. In bidding for the sympathy and support of the new countries of Asia and Africa, Soviet policy has adopted, to a large extent, the American pattern. In India, indeed, American and Soviet service compete on almost equal terms. So sharp has been the turn in Soviet policy that the Chinese critics have had good cause for accusing it of betraying its Leninist heritage. Needless to say, the atomic bomb has also had a sobering effect, accentuating the danger attendant on the use of brute force or even of brutal language.

At the twentieth century, we are faced with large issues that may easily take a fatal turn. Let us not be deceived, therefore, in the recurring crises, by the shallow surface of global politics, but search for the hidden depths of power and for the growing chances for cooperation. Let us aim at an ever better understanding of the political realities in other states and societies and in their relations with us. Our position in the world has been (and still is) much stronger than we realize. We owe the world and the peoples of Russia as well as their masters the generosity that befits our past natural advantages.

Beyond that, let us prepare for the reconciliations that loom behind the still growing chaos created by the cultural and political relativism of the global confluence. The dissolution of traditional values and forms of social life has become inevitable all over the world. All past responses to the challenge of human existence, including the American way of life, are now being tested against each other. In that competition it may be that the Russian quality of endurance under adversity shows a greater resilience than American sensibility, or Japanese group loyalty greater persistence than American individualism. Who knows? Who knows, moreover, what violence and destruction will precede the intermingling of peoples, races, and cultures that give rise to more inclusive truths, more expansive life styles, and larger polities at peace within themselves? All we know at this moment is that this generation of Americans has suddenly been expelled from the innocence of its traditions, its peace and security, and that it is forced, very much against its will, to reexamine its substance in the vastnesses of the global perspective and of the basic questions of life and death now stretched to cover all of mankind as well.

Into that hollow and dark glass of the future this account of the Russian revolution has cast, I hope, a faint glimmer of hope, confidence, and compassion.

Suggestions for Further Reading

★

Books marked with an asterisk are available in paperback.

In case this volume should tempt a reader into further study, I should like to recommend some additional reading. Having concluded the final chapter on an apocalyptic note, I am listing first three books that may serve as a framework for an assessment of our times. They are: A. J. Toynbee's *Civilization on Trial,* G. Barraclough's *An Introduction to Contemporary History,* and my own *The Global City.* Next, I suggest a few narrative works through which the reader might start with A. Moorehead, *The Russian Revolution,** follow it up by L. Trotsky's brilliant though obviously biased *The History of the Russian Revolution,** or consult W. H. Chamberlin, *The Russian Revolution.* Adam B. Ulam, *The Bolsheviks,* is the most up-to-date and complete history of the Bolshevik victory, starting with Lenin's childhood. R. V. Daniels, *Red October,* concentrates on the Bolshevik seizure of power.

If next an eager reader should take an interest in the background of the revolution, he can choose from several excellent works, such as B. Pares, *The Fall of the Russian Monarchy;** D. M. Wallace, *Russia on the Eve of the War and Revolution;** P. Miliukov's penetrating *Russia and Its Crisis;** R. D. Charques, *The Twilight of Imperial Russia;* H. Troyat, *Daily Life in Russia under the Last Tsar;* or finally H. Seton-Watson, *The Decline of Imperial Russia.** He might even sample Witte's autobiography, *The Memoirs of Count Witte.* T. G. Stavrou, *Russia under the Last Tsar,* sums up the controversies that have arisen over the viability of the tsarist regime in the age of industrialism and mass politics.

If it is the careers and characters of the revolutionaries that entice this eager reader, he might reach for A. Yarmolinsky, *Road to Revolution;** D. Footman, *Red Prelude;* L. Trotsky, *My Life;** A. Balabanova, *My Life as a Rebel;* B. Nikolaevsky, *Azeff the Spy;* I. Deutscher's biographies of Stalin and Trotsky; or several lives of Lenin (D. Shub's or N. Gourfinkel's*). B. D. Wolfe, *Three Who Made a Revolution,** treats in one volume the entire trinity, Lenin, Trotsky, and Stalin. Lenin's own writings are published in any number of English editions; A. G. Meyer has written a good analysis entitled *Leninism.** Stalin's works are likewise readily available. As for the views of other revolutionaries, Rosa Luxemburg's critical comments on Leninism, published under the title *The Russian Revolution,** are worth looking at.

Much has been written about Russia during the first World War My choice would be M. T. Florinsky, *The End of the Russian Empire,** *An Ambassador's Memoirs* by M. Paléologue (three breath-takingly brilliant volumes of first-hand observation *after* the events), and the memoirs of his British colleague, Sir George Buchanan, *My Mission to Russia.* Speaking of diplomats, everyone interested in the Russian revolution and its relation to American policy will read with pleasure George Kennan's two volumes, *Russia Leaves the War** and *the Decision to Intervene.** A third volume, *Russia and the West under Lenin and Stalin,** deals with Soviet foreign policy during the revolutionary period (and later years) in a more summary but hardly less expert manner.

The events of 1917, too, have been extensively discussed. The following books are among the most interesting: G. Katkov, *Russia 1917, The February Revolution;* A. M. Kerensky, *Russia and History's Turning Point;* V. M. Chernov; *The Great Russian Revolution;* and N. N. Sukhanov, *The Russian Revolution 1917** (a diary of a keen observer from among the revolutionaries themselves, but anti-Bolshevik).† John Reed's *Ten Days That Shook the World**

† For an analysis of the soviets in 1917 see the monograph by O. Anweiler, *Die Rätebewegung in Russland.*

is a classic on the Bolshevik seizure of power, pro-Bolshevik, yet suppressed during the Stalinist period. The course and results of the civil war may be studied in D. Footman's *Civil War in Russia;* the harrowing novel *Between White and Red* by E. E. Dwinger, a German prisoner of war who lived through some of the worst of it; in the Russian novels listed at the end; and several books already listed. As for the rise of international communism, F. Borkenau, *World Communism;* H. Seton-Watson, *From Lenin to Khruschev,** or the original documents edited by J. Degras, *The Communist International, 1919-1943,* avoid the sensationalism which so often mars the subject.

The writings on the early Soviet regime are numberless. The reader can hardly go wrong by studying M. Fainsod, *How Russia Is Ruled;* E. H. Carr's detailed analysis of Soviet policy, *The Bolshevik Revolution,* and the subsequent volumes of his *History of Soviet Russia* leading up to the Stalin period; G. von Rauch's *A History of Soviet Russia,** or B. Moore, *Soviet Politics—The Dilemma of Power.* D. Jarowsky has written a fascinating account of the impact of Marxism-Leninism upon Soviet science, *Soviet Marxism and Natural Science, 1917-1932.* An amusing—even hilarious—Soviet effort to popularize the first Five Year Plan is M. Ilin's *New Russia's Primer.* It should be compared with E. Lyon's account of life in Russia during those years, *Assignment in Utopia,* and with J. Scott's *Behind the Urals.* And for a strong sniff of Stalinism the reader might sample the once-official *History of the Communist Party (Bolshevik), Short Course.*

Nobody, however, can penetrate to the depths of the Russian revolution without having been moved by the Russian novelists' sagas of those years. I have in mind particularly A. Tolstoy's *Road to Calvary,* M. Sholokhov's *Quietly Flows the Don** and *The Don Flows to the Sea** and above all B. Pasternak's *Dr. Zhivago.**

If all these books should still leave the heroic reader unsatisfied, he may open up storehouse after storehouse of knowledge by consulting D. Shapiro, *Select Bibliography of Works in English on Russian History, 1801-1917* (1962), P. Grierson, *Books on Soviet Russia 1917-1943* (1943), and R. N. Carew Hunt, *Books on Com-*

munism (1959). More recent and complete is **P. L.** Herecky, ed., *Russia and the Soviet Union, A Bibliographical Guide to Western-Language Publications* (1965). The *Slavic Review*, published quarterly, will direct any student to more recent publications. Those who like to sample the Soviet press in translation, will turn to the admirably edited weekly *Current Digest of the Soviet Press.* Indeed, every American student of Soviet affairs should avail himself of the direct access to the Soviet press which this periodical affords.

If, finally, this paragon of readers should wish to search further into current speculation on the relationship between the Soviet regime and its predecessors, he should consult three recent volumes of essays and papers, all concerned with the theme set by the opening three words in the title of the first: *Continuity and Change in Russian and Soviet Thought* (E. J. Simmons, ed., 1955); *The Transformation of Russian Society* (C. E. Black, ed., 1960); *Russian Foreign Policy* (I. J. Lederer, ed., 1962).

INDEX